7.1 *Involve the Users* 149

7.2 *Build Confidence* 151

7.3 *Migrate Systems Incrementally* 153

7.4 *Prototype the Target Solution* 155

7.5 *Always Have a Running Version* 157

7.6 *Regression Test after Every Change* 159

7.7 *Make a Bridge to the New Town* 160

7.8 *Present the Right Interface* 163

7.9 *Distinguish Public from Published Interfaces* 164

7.10 *Deprecate Obsolete Interfaces* 166

7.11 *Conserve Familiarity* 168

7.12 *Use Profiler before Optimizing* 169

8.1 *Compare Code Mechanically* 175

8.2 *Visualize Code as Dotplots* 180

9.1 *Move Behavior Close to Data* 190

9.2 *Eliminate Navigation Code* 199

9.3 *Split Up God Class* 208

10.1 *Transform Self Type Checks* 217

10.2 *Transform Client Type Checks* 225

10.3 *Factor Out State* 234

10.4 *Factor Out Strategy* 237

10.5 *Introduce Null Object* 240

10.6 *Transform Conditionals into Registration* 243

Praise for Object-Oriented Reengineering Patterns

"How" to refactor is already well covered in the literature. However, "When" and "Why" can only be learned by experience. This book will give you a head start in learning when to start redesigning a system, when to stop for now, and what effects you can expect to see from your efforts.

—Kent Beck, Director, Three Rivers Institute

This book is full of practical, hands-on reengineering knowledge and expertise presented in a form that makes it easy to understand and use. The patterns in this book thus help everyone who is concerned with using reengineering to guide their work. I wished I had had this book in my library earlier.

—Frank Buschmann, Senior Principal Engineer, Siemens AG

This book is more than its title advertises. Effective reengineering is really about purposeful and efficient *reading* of someone else's code in order to produce predictable change. The same processes the authors highlight as patterns of skillful reengineering behavior can easily be cast as the skills you need to create readable, maintainable software systems.

—Adele Goldberg, Neometron, Inc.

If a guy named Dave brought a large box to my office that contained a lot of documentation and two CDs—installation disks for software that my company wanted to reengineer—I'd be happy to have the authors of this book by my side. Barring that, having their book is the next best thing. No silver bullets, no hype, no promises that this will be easy—just a down-to-earth, easy-to-read, extremely useful book of helpful guidelines to tackle the project. Buy this book and browse it before Dave arrives in your office! It just might save you and your company a lot of grief.

—Linda Rising, Independent Consultant

Object-Oriented Reengineering Patterns

About the Authors

Serge Demeyer is a professor in the Department of Mathematics and Computer Science at the University of Antwerp in Belgium. He leads a research group investigating the theme of software reengineering, particularly reengineering in an object-oriented context. He is an active member of the corresponding international research communities, serving in various conference organizations and program committees.

Stéphane Ducasse is an assistant professor in the Software Composition Group at the University of Bern where he serves as co-technical leader of the FAMOOS esprit project—a project whose goal is to come up with a set of reengineering techniques and tools to support the development of object-oriented frameworks. He has been involved in the organization of several workshops (at ECOOP and ESEC) and one tutorial concerning object-oriented reengineering.

Oscar Nierstrasz is a professor of computer science at the University of Bern where he leads the Software Composition Group. He has been active in the object-oriented research community for many years, serving on program committees of ECOOP, OOPSLA, ESEC, and others. He has given several tutorials and invited talks on object-oriented technology at various international conferences and workshops.

Object-Oriented Reengineering Patterns

Serge Demeyer
Stéphane Ducasse
Oscar Nierstrasz

MORGAN KAUFMANN PUBLISHERS

AN IMPRINT OF ELSEVIER SCIENCE

AMSTERDAM   BOSTON   LONDON   NEW YORK
OXFORD   PARIS   SAN DIEGO   SAN FRANCISCO
SINGAPORE   SYDNEY   TOKYO

Acquisitions Editor   Tim Cox
Assistant Publishing Services Manager   Edward Wade
Production Editor   Howard Severson
Editorial Coordinator   Stacie Pierce
Cover Design   Yvo Riezebos
Text Design and Composition   Rebecca Evans & Associates
Illustration   Dartmouth Publishing Industries
Copyeditor   Ken DellaPenta
Proofreader   Carol Leyba
Indexer   Ty Koontz
Printer   Maple-Vail Book Manufacturing Group

Cover credit: Rene Magritte, L'Univers demarque. 1932.
© Herscovici/Art Resource, NY

Designations used by companies to distinguish their products are often claimed as trademarks or registered trademarks. In all instances in which Morgan Kaufmann Publishers is aware of a claim, the product names appear in initial capital or all capital letters. Readers, however, should contact the appropriate companies for more complete information regarding trademarks and registration.

Morgan Kaufmann Publishers
An Imprint of Elsevier Science
340 Pine Street, Sixth Floor
San Francisco, CA 94104-3205, USA
www.mkp.com

Library of Congress Control Number: 2002104269
ISBN: 1-55860-639-4

This book is printed on acid-free paper.

For Ann, Sara, Niels, and the expected baby.
For Florence, Quentin, and Thibaut.
For Angela and Frida.

Foreword

Martin Fowler
ThoughtWorks, Inc.

For a long time it's puzzled me that most books on software development processes talk about what to do when you are starting from a blank sheet of editor screen. It's puzzled me because that's not the most common situation that people are in when they are writing code. Most people have to make changes to an existing code base, even if it's their own. In an ideal world this code base is well designed and well factored, but we all know how often the ideal world appears in our careers.

This book is important because it's written from the perspective of what to do with an imperfect yet valuable code base. I also like the fact that it's based on an effective mix of academic and industrial work. I visited the FAMOOS group in their early days during a chill early winter in Bern. I liked the way that they cycled between the field and the lab, trying out ideas on real projects, then coming back to the lab to reflect.

This resulting book speaks with that experience. It gives you the building blocks for a plan to tackle a difficult code base, and it gives you context for techniques like refactoring. It is a sad fact that there are too few of these kinds of books out there, when reengineering is still a common event. But I'm at least glad to see that while there aren't many books in this vein, this book is an example of how good they are.

Foreword

Ralph E. Johnson
University of Illinois at Urbana-Champaign

One of the signs of a good pattern is when experts who read it are likely to say, "Of course, everybody knows that" but beginners are likely to say, "Interesting, but will it work?" Patterns should be easy to follow, but the most valuable patterns are those that are not obvious. Experts have learned from experience that patterns work, but beginners have to take patterns on faith until they use them and develop their own experience.

Over the last couple of years, I've had the chance to give the patterns in this book to a wide variety of people and discuss them. My pattern discussion group has a few members who have decades of consulting experience, and they can quickly regale the group with stories of using these patterns. The younger members love the stories, as they are convinced of the value of the patterns.

I made students in my software engineering class read some of the patterns as part of a section on reengineering. The section went well even though none of the students were excited about the patterns. They didn't have the experience to evaluate them. However, one of the students came back to me after his summer job and said that of everything in the course, the content that was the most useful was the patterns on reverse engineering. Before that experience, the patterns seemed believable. Afterwards, they were believed!

If you have a lot of experience with software reengineering then you probably won't learn much from this book. You should read it anyway, because you will want to give copies to people you work with, and you will want to use the vocabulary of the book when you talk with them. If you are new to reengineering, you should read the book, learn the patterns, and try them. You will learn a lot that will be valuable. Don't expect to understand the patterns completely before you try them because patterns are practical, and practical knowledge has to be experienced to be fully understood. Nevertheless, the book will give you a big advantage. It is much easier to learn when you have a path to follow, and this book provides a reliable guide.

Contents

Preface   **xvii**

Chapter 1   **Reengineering Patterns**   **1**

Why Do We Reengineer?   1
What's Special about Objects?   4
The Reengineering Life Cycle   5
Reengineering Patterns   9
The Form of a Reengineering Pattern   11
A Map of Reengineering Patterns   11

P   A   R   T
I   **Reverse Engineering**   **15**

Chapter 2   **Setting Direction**   **17**

Forces   17
Overview   18
Pattern 2.1   *Agree on Maxims*   18
Pattern 2.2   *Appoint a Navigator*   19
Pattern 2.3   *Speak to the Round Table*   20
Pattern 2.4   *Most Valuable First*   20
Pattern 2.5   *Fix Problems, Not Symptoms*   23
Pattern 2.6   *If It Ain't Broke, Don't Fix It*   24
Pattern 2.7   *Keep It Simple*   24

Chapter 3 **First Contact** **27**

Forces 27
Overview 29
What Next 30
Pattern 3.1 *Chat with the Maintainers* 31
Pattern 3.2 *Read All the Code in One Hour* 38
Pattern 3.3 *Skim the Documentation* 44
Pattern 3.4 *Interview during Demo* 50
Pattern 3.5 *Do a Mock Installation* 58

Chapter 4 **Initial Understanding** **65**

Forces 65
Overview 67
What Next 67
Pattern 4.1 *Analyze the Persistent Data* 68
Pattern 4.2 *Speculate about Design* 76
Pattern 4.3 *Study the Exceptional Entities* 84

Chapter 5 **Detailed Model Capture** **95**

Forces 95
Overview 96
What Next 97
Pattern 5.1 *Tie Code and Questions* 98
Pattern 5.2 *Refactor to Understand* 103
Pattern 5.3 *Step through the Execution* 107
Pattern 5.4 *Look for the Contracts* 109
Pattern 5.5 *Learn from the Past* 113

PART

II **Reengineering** **119**

Chapter 6 **Tests: Your Life Insurance!** **121**

Forces 121
Overview 122
Pattern 6.1 *Write Tests to Enable Evolution* 123
Pattern 6.2 *Grow Your Test Base Incrementally* 128

Pattern 6.3   *Use a Testing Framework*   130
Pattern 6.4   *Test the Interface, Not the Implementation*   136
Pattern 6.5   *Record Business Rules as Tests*   139
Pattern 6.6   *Write Tests to Understand*   142

Chapter 7   **Migration Strategies**   **147**

Forces   147
Overview   147
Pattern 7.1   *Involve the Users*   149
Pattern 7.2   *Build Confidence*   151
Pattern 7.3   *Migrate Systems Incrementally*   153
Pattern 7.4   *Prototype the Target Solution*   155
Pattern 7.5   *Always Have a Running Version*   157
Pattern 7.6   *Regression Test after Every Change*   159
Pattern 7.7   *Make a Bridge to the New Town*   160
Pattern 7.8   *Present the Right Interface*   163
Pattern 7.9   *Distinguish Public from Published Interface*   164
Pattern 7.10   *Deprecate Obsolete Interfaces*   166
Pattern 7.11   *Conserve Familiarity*   168
Pattern 7.12   *Use Profiler before Optimizing*   169

Chapter 8   **Detecting Duplicated Code**   **173**

Forces   173
Overview   174
Pattern 8.1   *Compare Code Mechanically*   175
Pattern 8.2   *Visualize Code as Dotplots*   180

Chapter 9   **Redistribute Responsibilities**   **187**

Forces   187
Overview   188
Pattern 9.1   *Move Behavior Close to Data*   190
Pattern 9.2   *Eliminate Navigation Code*   199
Pattern 9.3   *Split Up God Class*   208

Chapter 10   **Transform Conditionals to Polymorphism**   **215**

Forces   215
Overview   216
Pattern 10.1   *Transform Self Type Checks*   217

Pattern 10.2 *Transform Client Type Checks*   225
Pattern 10.3 *Factor Out State*   234
Pattern 10.4 *Factor Out Strategy*   237
Pattern 10.5 *Introduce Null Object*   240
Pattern 10.6 *Transform Conditionals into Registration*   243

Appendix   **Thumbnail patterns**   **253**

Testing Patterns   **253**
A.1   *Retest Persistent Problems*   253
A.2   *Test Fuzzy Features*   254
A.3   *Test Old Bugs*   254
Refactorings   **254**
A.4   *Encapsulate Field*   254
A.5   *Extract Method*   255
A.6   *Move Method*   255
A.7   *Rename Attribute*   255
A.8   *Rename Method*   255
A.9   *Replace Conditional with Polymorphism*   255
Design Patterns   **256**
A.10 *Abstract Factory*   256
A.11 *Adapter*   256
A.12 *Facade*   256
A.13 *Factory Method*   256
A.14 *Flyweight*   256
A.15 *Null Object*   257
A.16 *Quantity*   257
A.17 *Singleton*   257
A.18 *State*   257
A.19 *State Patterns*   257
A.20 *Strategy*   258
A.21 *Template Method*   258
A.22 *Visitor*   258

References   **259**

Index   **267**

Preface

A Fairy Tale

Once upon a time there was a Good Software Engineer whose customers knew exactly what they wanted. The Good Software Engineer worked very hard to design the Perfect System that would solve all the Customers' problems now and for decades. When the Perfect System was designed, implemented, and finally deployed, the Customers were very happy indeed. The Maintainer of the System had very little to do to keep the Perfect System up and running, and the Customers and the Maintainer lived happily every after.

Why isn't real life more like this fairy tale?

Could it be because there are no Good Software Engineers? Could it be because the Customers don't really know what they want? Or is it because the Perfect System doesn't exist?

Maybe there is a bit of truth in all of these observations, but the real reasons probably have more to do with certain fundamental laws of software evolution identified several years ago by Manny Lehman and Les Belady [Lehm85]. The two most striking of these laws are

- *The law of continuing change:* A program that is used in a real-world environment *must* change, or become progressively less useful in that environment.

- *The law of increasing complexity:* As a program evolves, it becomes more *complex,* and extra resources are needed to preserve and simplify its structure.

In other words, we are kidding ourselves if we think that we can know all the requirements and build the perfect system. The best we can hope for is to build a useful system that will survive long enough for it to be asked to do something new.

What Is This Book?

This book came into being as a consequence of the realization that the most interesting and challenging side of software engineering may not be building brand-new software systems, but rejuvenating existing ones.

From November 1996 to December 1999, we participated in a European industrial research project called FAMOOS (ESPRIT Project 21975—Framework-based Approach for Mastering Object-Oriented Software Evolution). The partners were Nokia (Finland), Daimler-Benz (Germany), Sema Group (Spain), Forschungszentrum Informatik Karlsruhe (Germany), and the University of Berne (Switzerland). Nokia and Daimler-Benz were both early adopters of object-oriented technology and had expected to reap significant benefits from this tactic. Now, however, they were experiencing many of the typical problems of legacy systems: they had very large, very valuable object-oriented software systems that were very difficult to adapt to changing requirements. The goal of the FAMOOS project was to develop tools and techniques to rejuvenate these object-oriented legacy systems so they would continue to be useful and would be more amenable to future changes in requirements.

Our idea at the start of the project was to convert these big, object-oriented applications into *frameworks*—generic applications that can be easily reconfigured using a variety of different programming techniques. We quickly discovered, however, that this was easier said than done. Although the basic idea was sound, it is not so easy to determine which parts of the legacy system *should* be converted, and exactly how to convert them. In fact, it is a nontrivial problem just to *understand* the legacy system in the first place, let alone figuring out what (if anything) is wrong with it.

We learned many things from this project. We learned that, for the most part, the legacy code was not bad at all. The only reason that there were problems with the legacy code was that the requirements had changed since the original system was designed and deployed. Systems that had been adapted many times to changing requirements suffered from *design drift*—the original architecture and design was almost impossible to recognize—and that made it almost impossible to make further adaptations, exactly as predicted by Lehman and Belady's laws of software evolution.

Most surprising to us, however, was the fact that, although each of the case studies we looked at needed to be reengineered for very different reasons—such as unbundling, scaling up requirements, porting to new environments, and so on—the actual technical problems with these systems were oddly similar. This suggested to us that perhaps a few simple techniques could go a long way to fixing some of the more common problems.

We discovered that pretty well all reengineering activity must start with some *reverse* engineering, since you will not be able to trust the documentation (if you are lucky enough to have some). Basically you can analyze the source code, run the system, and interview users and developers to build a model of the legacy system. Then you must determine what are the obstacles to further progress and fix them. This is the essence of *reengineering*, which seeks to transform a legacy system into the system you would have built if you had the luxury of hindsight and could have known all the new requirements that you know today. But since you can't afford to rebuild everything, you must cut corners and just reengineer the most critical parts.

Since FAMOOS, we have been involved in many other reengineering projects and have been able to further validate and refine the results of FAMOOS.

In this book we summarize what we learned in the hope that it will help others who need to reengineer object-oriented systems. We do not pretend to have all the answers, but we have identified a series of simple techniques that will take you a long way.

Why Patterns?

A pattern is a recurring motif, an event or structure that occurs over and over again. *Design patterns* are generic solutions to recurring design problems [Gamm95]. It is because these design problems are never exactly alike, but only very similar, that the solutions are not pieces of software, but *documents that communicate best practice.*

Patterns have emerged in recent years as a literary form that can be used to document best practice in solving many different kinds of problems. Although many kinds of problems and solutions can be cast as patterns, they can be overkill when applied to the simplest kinds of problems. Patterns as a form of documentation are most useful and interesting when the problem being considered entails a number of conflicting *forces,* and the solution described entails a number of *trade-offs.* Many well-known design patterns, for example, introduce run-time flexibility at the cost of increased design complexity.

This book documents a catalogue of patterns for reverse engineering and reengineering legacy systems. None of these patterns should be applied blindly. Each patterns resolves some forces and involves some trade-offs. Understanding these trade-offs is essential to successfully applying the patterns. As a consequence the pattern form seems to be the most natural way to document the best practices we identified in the course of our reengineering projects.

A *pattern language* is a set of related patterns that can be used in combination to solve a set of complex problems. We found that clusters of patterns seemed to function well in combination with each other, so we have organized this book into chapters that each presents such a cluster as a small pattern language.

We do not pretend that these clusters are "complete" in any sense, and we do not even pretend to have patterns that cover all aspects of reengineering. We certainly do not pretend that this book represents a systematic method for object-oriented reengineering. What we do claim is simply to have encountered and identified a number of best practices that exhibit interesting synergies. Not only is there strong synergy within a cluster of patterns, but the clusters are also interrelated in important ways. Each chapter therefore contains not only a pattern map that suggests how the patterns may function as a "language," but each pattern also lists and explains how it may be combined or composed with other patterns, whether in the same cluster or a different one.

Who Should Read This Book?

This book is addressed mainly to practitioners who need to reengineer object-oriented systems. If you take an extreme viewpoint, you could say that *every* software project is a reengineering project, so the scope of this book is quite broad.

We believe that most of the patterns in this book will be familiar to anyone with a bit of experience in object-oriented software development. The purpose of the book is to document the details.

Acknowledgments

We would like to thank first and foremost our FAMOOS partners at Nokia, Daimler, FZI, and Sema who provided the context for discovering these patterns. People like Juha (Julho) Tuominen, Roland Trauter, Eduardo Casais, and Theo Dirk Meijler played a crucial role while starting the project. We would especially like to thank our coauthors of the prototype for this book, *The FAMOOS Object-Oriented Reengineering Handbook:* Holger Bär, Markus Bauer, Oliver Ciupke, Michele Lanza, Radu Marinescu, Robb Nebbe, Michael Przybilski, Tamar Richner, Matthias Rieger, Claudio Riva, Anne-Marie Sassen, Benedikt Schulz, Patrick Steyaert, Sander Tichelaar, and Joachim Weisbrod. Special thanks go to Perdita Stevens for the first discussions on reengineering patterns.

We gratefully acknowledge the financial support of the European Union toward ESPRIT Project 21975 (FAMOOS) as well as that of the Swiss government toward projects NFS-2000-46947.96 and BBW-96.0015. The University of Antwerp provided financial support in the form of a grant entitled "Object Oriented Reengineering," while the Fund for Scientific Research in Flanders sponsored a research network named "Foundations of Software Evolution."

Some of the material in this book was presented in the graduate course "Object-Oriented Software Reengineering," held at the University of Bern in the winter semesters of 1998 and 1999, and at several tutorials at OOPSLA and ECOOP. We would like to thank the participants of the courses and tutorials for their feedback and input. We also would like to thank members of the Software Composition Group at the University of Bern for participating in several pattern workshops and giving valuable feedback on many of the patterns in this book: Michele Lanza, Pietro Malorgio, Robbe Nebbe, Tamar Richner, Matthias Rieger, and Sander Tichelaar.

Several of the patterns in this book have been presented elsewhere. We would like to thank our EuroPLoP shepherds Kent Beck (1998), Kyle Brown (1999), Neil Harrison (2000), Mary Lynn Manns (2000), Don Roberts (1998), and Charles Weir (1998), and all participants of the writers' workshops where these patterns have been discussed. Special thanks go to Jens Coldewey for helping us out with pattern forms and forces.

We would like to thank the members and friends of Ralph Johnson's Software Architecture Group who workshopped several chapters of this book: John Brant, Brian Foote, Alejandra Garrido, Peter Hatch, Ralph Johnson, Brian Marick, Andrew Rosenfeld, Weerasak Witthawaskul, and Joe Yoder. Downloading and playing voluminous megabytes of workshop recordings in mp3 format truly made each of us feel like a "fly on the wall"!

We would like to thank Tim Cox, our editor, Stacie Pierce, his assistant, and the team at Morgan Kaufmann for following our project with such dedication. Also, thanks to Christa Preisendanz at DPunkt Verlag for putting us in touch with Tim in the first place! We especially appreciated the two very thorough rounds of reviews that this book underwent, and we only regret that the final draft of this book is nothing like the definitive work some of the reviewers clearly hoped it would be! We thank our reviewers for reading between the lines and helping to explain many of these patterns to us: Kyle Brown, Thierry Cattel, Oliver Ciupke, Koen De Hondt, Jim Coplien, Gert Florijn, Neil Harrison, Mary Lynn Manns, Alan O'Callaghan, Don Roberts, and Benedikt Schulz.

## CHAPTER 1

Reengineering Patterns

Why Do We Reengineer?

A *legacy* is something valuable that you have inherited. Similarly, *legacy software* is valuable software that you have inherited. The fact you have inherited it may mean that it is somewhat old-fashioned. It may have been developed using an outdated programming language or an obsolete development method. Most likely it has changed hands several times and shows signs of many modifications and adaptations.

Perhaps your legacy software is not even that old. With rapid development tools *and* rapid turnover in personnel, software systems can turn into legacies more quickly than you might imagine. The fact that the software is *valuable*, however, means that you do not want to just throw it away.

A piece of legacy software is critical to your business, and that is precisely the source of all the problems: in order for you to be successful at your business, you must constantly be prepared to adapt to a changing business environment. The software that you use to keep your business running must therefore also be adaptable. Fortunately a lot of software can be upgraded, or simply thrown away and replaced when it no longer serves its purpose. But a legacy system can neither be replaced nor upgraded except at a high cost. The goal of reengineering is to reduce the complexity of a legacy system sufficiently that it can continue to be used and adapted at an acceptable cost.

The specific reasons that you might want to reengineer a software system can vary significantly. For example:

- You might want to *unbundle* a monolithic system so that the individual parts can be more easily marketed separately or combined in different ways.

- You might want to improve *performance*. (Experience shows that the right sequence is "first do it, then do it right, then do it fast," so you might want to reengineer in order to clean up the code before thinking about performance.)

- You might want to *port the system to a new platform*. Before you do that, you may need to rework the architecture to clearly separate the platform-dependent code.

- You might want to *extract the design* as a first step to a new implementation.

- You might want to *exploit new technology*, such as emerging standards or libraries, as a step toward cutting maintenance costs.

- You might want to *reduce human dependencies* by documenting knowledge about the system and making it easier to maintain.

Although there may be many different reasons for reengineering a system, as we shall see, the actual technical problems with legacy software are often very similar. It is this fact that allows us to use some very general techniques to do at least part of the job of reengineering.

Recognizing the Need to Reengineer

How do you know when you have a legacy problem?

Common wisdom says, "If it ain't broke, don't fix it." This attitude is often taken as an excuse not to touch any piece of software that is performing an important function and seems to be doing it well. The problem with this approach is that it fails to recognize that there are many ways in which something may be "broken." From a functional point of view, something is broken only if it no longer delivers the function it is designed to perform. From a maintenance point of view, however, a piece of software is broken *if it can no longer be maintained.*

So how can you tell that your software is going to break very soon? Fortunately there are many warning signs that tell you that you are headed toward trouble. The following symptoms usually do not occur in isolation but several at a time.

- *Obsolete or no documentation.* Obsolete documentation is a clear sign of a legacy system that has undergone many changes. Absence of documentation is a warning sign that problems are on the horizon, as soon as the original developers leave the project.

- *Missing tests.* Even more important than up-to-date documentation is the presence of thorough unit tests for all system components, and system tests that cover all significant use cases and scenarios. The absence of such tests is a sign that the system will not be able to evolve without high risk or cost.

- *Departure of the original developers or users.* Unless you have a clean, well-documented system with good test coverage, it will rapidly deteriorate into an even less clean, more poorly documented system.

- *Disappearance of inside knowledge about the system.* This is a bad sign. The documentation is out of sync with the existing code base. Nobody really knows how it works.

- *Limited understanding of the entire system.* Not only does nobody understand the fine print, but hardly anyone has a good overview of the whole system.

- *Too long to turn things over to production.* Somewhere along the line the process is not working. Perhaps it takes too long to approve changes. Perhaps automatic regression tests are missing. Or perhaps it is difficult to deploy changes. Unless you understand and deal with the difficulties it will only get worse.

- *Too much time to make simple changes.* This is a clear sign that Lehman and Belady's law of increasing complexity has kicked in: the system is now so complex that even simple changes are hard to implement. If it takes too long to make simple changes to your system, it will certainly be out of the question to make complex changes. If there is a backlog of simple changes waiting to get done, then you will never get to the difficult problems.

- *Need for constant bug fixes.* Bugs never seem to go away. Every time you fix a bug, a new one pops up next to it. This tells you that parts of your application have become so complex that you can no longer accurately assess the impact of small changes. Furthermore, the architecture of the application no longer matches the needs, so even small changes will have unexpected consequences.

- *Maintenance dependencies.* When you fix a bug in one place, another bug pops up *somewhere else.* This is often a sign that the architecture has deteriorated to the point where logically separate components of the system are no longer independent.

- *Big build times.* Long recompilation times slow down your ability to make changes. Long build times may also be telling you that the organization of your system is too complex for your compiler tools to do their job efficiently.

- *Difficulties separating products.* If there are many clients for your product, and you have difficulty tailoring releases for each customer, then your architecture is no longer right for the job.

- *Duplicated code.* Duplicated code arises naturally as a system evolves, as a shortcut to implementing nearly identical code, or merging different versions of a software system. If the duplicated code is not eliminated by refactoring the common parts into suitable abstractions, maintenance quickly becomes a nightmare as the same code has to be fixed in many places.

- *Code smells.* Duplicated code is an example of code that "smells bad" and should be changed. Long methods, big classes, long parameter lists, switch statements, and data classes are a few more examples that have been documented by Kent Beck and others [Fowl99]. Code smells are often a sign that a system has been repeatedly expanded and adapted without having been reengineered.

What's Special about Objects?

Although many of the techniques discussed in this book will apply to any software system, we have chosen to focus on *object-oriented legacy systems*. There are many reasons for this choice, but mainly we feel that this is a critical point in time at which many early adopters of object-oriented technology are discovering that the benefits they expected to achieve by switching to objects have been very difficult to realize.

There are now significant legacy systems even in Java. It is not *age* that turns a piece of software into a legacy system, but the *rate* at which it has been developed and adapted without having been reengineered.

The wrong conclusion to draw from these experiences is that "objects are bad, and we need something else." Already we are seeing a rush toward many new trends that are expected to save the day: patterns, components, UML, XMI, and so on. Any one of these developments may be a Good Thing, but in a sense they are all missing the point.

One of the conclusions you should draw from this book is that, well, objects are pretty good, but *you must take good care of them.* To understand this point, consider why legacy problems arise at all with object-oriented systems, if they are supposed to be so good for flexibility, maintainability, and reuse.

First of all, anyone who has had to work with a nontrivial, existing object-oriented code base will have noticed that *it is hard to find the objects.* In a very real sense, the architecture of an object-oriented application is usually hidden. What you see is a bunch of classes and an inheritance hierarchy. But that doesn't tell you which objects exist at run time and how they collaborate to provide the desired behavior. Understanding an object-oriented system is a process of reverse engineering, and the techniques described in this book help to tackle this problem. Furthermore, by reengineering the code, you can arrive at a system whose architecture is more transparent and easier to understand.

Second, anyone who has tried to extend an existing object-oriented application will have realized that *reuse does not come for free.* It is actually very hard to reuse any piece of code unless a fair bit of effort was put into designing it so that it could be reused. Furthermore, it is essential that investment in reuse *requires management commitment* to put the right organizational infrastructure in place and should only be undertaken with clear, measurable goals in mind [Gold95].

We are still not very good at managing object-oriented software projects in such a way that reuse is properly taken into account. Typically reuse comes too late. We use object-oriented modeling techniques to develop very rich and complex object models, and hope that when we implement the software we will be able to reuse something. But by then there is little chance that these rich models will map to any kind of standard library of components except with great effort. Several of the reengineering techniques we present address how to uncover these components after the fact.

The key insight, however, is that the "right" design and organization of your objects is not something that is or can be evident from the initial requirements alone, but rather *as a consequence of understanding how these requirements evolve.* The fact that the world is constantly changing should not be seen purely as a problem, but as the key to the solution.

Any successful software system will suffer from the symptoms of legacy systems. Object-oriented legacy systems are just successful object-oriented systems whose architecture and design no longer respond to changing requirements. A *culture of continuous reengineering* is a prerequisite for achieving flexible and maintainable object-oriented systems.

The Reengineering Life Cycle

Reengineering and reverse engineering are often mentioned in the same context, and the terms are sometimes confused, so it is worthwhile to be clear about what we mean by them. Chikofsky and Cross [Chik92] define the two terms as follows:

> *Reverse Engineering* is the process of analyzing a subject system to identify the system's components and their interrelationships and create representations of the system in another form or at a higher level of abstraction.

That is to say, reverse engineering is essentially concerned with trying to *understand* a system and how it ticks.

> *Reengineering* . . . is the examination and *alteration of a subject system* to reconstitute it in a new form and the subsequent implementation of the new form.

Reengineering, on the other hand, is concerned with *restructuring* a system, generally to fix some real or perceived problems, but more specifically in preparation for further development and extension.

The introduction of the term "reverse engineering" was clearly an invitation to define "forward engineering," so we have the following as well:

> Forward Engineering is the traditional process of moving from high-level abstractions and logical, implementation-independent designs to the physical implementation of a system.

How exactly this process of forward engineering can or should work is a matter of great debate, although most people accept that the process is iterative and conforms to Barry Boehm's so-called *spiral model* of software development [Boeh88]. In this model, successive versions of a software system are developed by repeatedly collecting requirements, assessing risks, engineering the new version, and evaluating the results. This general framework can accommodate many different kinds of more specific process models that are used in practice.

If forward engineering is about moving from high-level views of requirements and models toward concrete realizations, then reverse engineering is about going backward from some concrete realization to more abstract models, and reengineering is about transforming concrete implementations to other concrete implementations.

Figure 1.1 illustrates this idea. Forward engineering can be understood as being a process that moves from high-level and abstract models and artifacts to increasingly concrete ones. Reverse engineering reconstructs higher-level models and artifacts from code. Reengineering is a process that transforms one low-level representation to another, while recreating the higher-level artifacts along the way.

The key point to observe is that reengineering is not simply a matter of transforming source code, but of transforming a system *at all its levels.* For this reason it makes sense to talk about reverse engineering and reengineering in the same breath. In a typical legacy system, you will find that not only the source code, but all the documentation and specifications are out of sync. Reverse engineering is therefore a *prerequisite* to reengineering since you cannot transform what you do not understand.

Reverse Engineering

You carry out reverse engineering whenever you are trying to understand how something really works. Normally you only need to reverse engineer a piece of software if you want to fix, extend, or replace it. (Sometimes you need to reverse engineer software just in order to understand how to use it. This may also be a sign that some reengineering is called for.)

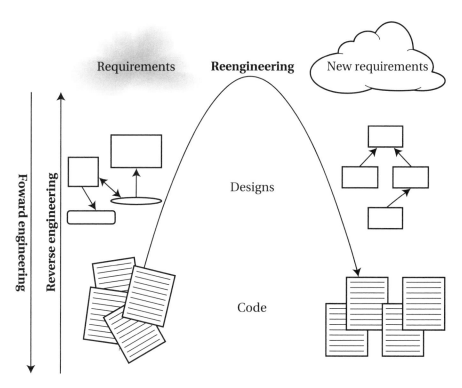

FIGURE **1.1**   Forward, reverse, and reengineering.

As a consequence, reverse engineering efforts typically focus on *redocumenting* software and *identifying potential problems,* in preparation for reengineering.

You can make use of a lot of different sources of information while reverse engineering. For example, you can

- read the existing documentation
- read the source code
- run the software
- interview users and developers
- code and execute test cases
- generate and analyze traces
- use various tools to generate high-level views of the source code and the traces
- analyze the version history

As you carry out these activities, you will be building progressively refined models of the software, keeping track of various questions and answers, and cleaning up the technical documentation. You will also be keeping an eye out for problems to fix.

Reengineering

Although the reasons for reengineering a system may vary, the actual technical problems are typically very similar. There is usually a mix of coarse-grained architectural problems and fine-grained design problems. Typical coarse-grained problems include the following:

- *Insufficient documentation:* Documentation either does not exist or is inconsistent with reality.
- *Improper layering:* Missing or improper layering hampers portability and adaptability.
- *Lack of modularity:* Strong coupling between modules hampers evolution.
- *Duplicated code:* "Copy, paste, and edit" is quick and easy, but leads to maintenance nightmares.
- *Duplicated functionality:* Similar functionality is reimplemented by separate teams, leading to code bloat.

The most common fine-grained problems occurring in object-oriented software include the following:

- *Misuse of inheritance:* for composition and code reuse rather than polymorphism
- *Missing inheritance:* duplicated code and case statements to select behavior
- *Misplaced operations:* unexploited cohesion—operations outside instead of inside classes
- *Violation of encapsulation:* explicit type-casting, C++ "friends"
- *Class abuse:* lack of cohesion—classes as namespaces

Finally, you will be preparing the code base for the reengineering activity by developing exhaustive test cases for all the parts of the system that you plan to change or replace.

Reengineering similarly entails a number of interrelated activities. Of course, one of the most important is to evaluate which parts of the system should be repaired and which should be replaced.

The actual code transformations that are performed fall into a number of categories. According to Chikofsky and Cross:

> *Restructuring* is the transformation from one representation form to another at the same relative abstraction level, while preserving the system's external behavior.

Restructuring generally refers to source code translation (such as the automatic conversion from unstructured "spaghetti" code to structured, or "goto-less," code), but it may also entail transformations at the design level.

Refactoring is restructuring within an object-oriented context. Martin Fowler defines it this way [Fowl99]:

> *Refactoring* is the process of changing a software system in such a way that it does not alter the external behavior of the code yet improves its internal structure.

It may be hard to tell the difference between software "reengineering" and software "maintenance." IEEE has made several attempts to define software maintenance, including this one:

> . . . the modification of a software product after delivery to correct faults, to improve performance or other attributes, or to adapt the product to a changed environment.

Most people would probably consider that "maintenance" is routine whereas "reengineering" is a drastic, major effort to recast a system, as suggested by Figure 1.1. Others, however, might argue that reengineering is just a way of life. You develop a little, reengineer a little, develop a little more, and so on [Beck00]. In fact, there is good evidence to support the notion that a culture of *continuous* reengineering is necessary to obtain healthy, maintainable software systems.

Continuous reengineering, however, is not yet common practice, and for this reason we present the patterns in this book in the context of a major reengineering effort. Nevertheless, keep in mind that most of the techniques we present will apply just as well when you reengineer in small iterations.

Reengineering Patterns

Patterns as a literary form were introduced by the architect Christopher Alexander in his landmark 1977 book, *A Pattern Language*. In this book, Alexander and his colleagues presented a systematic method for architecting a range of different kinds of physical structures, from rooms to buildings and towns. Each issue was presented as a recurring *pattern,* a general solution that resolves a number of forces, but must be applied in a unique way to each problem according to the specific circumstances. The actual solution presented in each pattern was not necessarily so interesting, but rather the discussion of the *forces* and *trade-offs* consisted of the real substance they communicated.

Patterns were first adopted by the software community as a way of documenting recurring solutions to design problems. As with Alexander's patterns, each design pattern entailed a number of forces to be resolved, and a number of trade-offs to consider when applying the pattern. Patterns turn out to be a compact way to communicate *best practice:* not just the actual techniques used by experts, but the motivation and rationale behind them. Patterns have since been applied to many aspects of software development other than design, and particularly to the *process* of designing and developing software.

The process of reengineering is, like any other process, one in which many standard techniques have emerged, each of which resolves various forces and may entail many trade-offs. Patterns as a way of communicating best practice are particularly well suited to presenting and discussing these techniques.

Reengineering patterns codify and record knowledge about modifying legacy software: they help in diagnosing problems and identifying weaknesses that may hinder further development of the system, and they aid in finding solutions that are more appropriate to the new requirements. We see reengineering patterns as stable units of expertise that can be consulted in any reengineering effort: they describe a process without proposing a complete methodology, and they suggest appropriate tools without "selling" a specific one.

Many of the reverse engineering and reengineering patterns have some superficial resemblance to design patterns, in the sense that they have something to do with the design of software. But there is an important difference in that design patterns have to do with choosing a particular solution to a design problem, whereas reengineering patterns have to do with *discovering an existing design,* determining what *problems* it has, and *repairing* these problems. As a consequence, reengineering patterns have more to do with the *process of discovery and transformation* than purely with a given design structure. For this reason the names of most of the patterns in this book are process-oriented, like Always Have a Running Version (Pattern 7.5), rather than being structure-oriented, like Adapter (Pattern A.11) or Facade (Pattern A.12).

Whereas a design pattern presents a solution for a recurring *design* problem, a reengineering pattern presents a solution for a recurring *reengineering* problem. The artifacts produced by reengineering patterns are not necessarily designs. They may be as concrete as refactored code, or in the case of reverse engineering patterns, they may be as abstract as insights into how the system functions.

The marks of a good reengineering pattern are (1) the clarity with which it exposes the advantages, the cost, and the consequences of the target artifacts with respect to the existing system state, and *not* how elegant the result is, and (2) the description of the reengineering *process*: how to get from one state of the system to another.

Reengineering patterns entail more than code refactorings. A reengineering pattern may describe a process that starts with the detection of the symptoms and ends with the refactoring of the code to arrive at the new solution. Refactoring is only the last stage of this process and addresses the technical issue of automatically or semiautomatically modifying the code to implement the new solution. Reengineering patterns also include other elements that are not part of refactorings: they emphasize the context of the symptoms, by taking into account the constraints that reengineers are facing, and include a discussion of the impact of the changes that the refactored solution may introduce.

The Form of a Reengineering Pattern

In Figure 1.2 we see an example of a simple pattern that illustrates the format we use in this book. The actual format used may vary slightly from pattern to pattern, since they deal with different kinds of issues, but generally we will see the same kinds of headings.

The name of a pattern, if well chosen, should make it easy to remember the pattern and to discuss it with colleagues. ("I think we should Refactor to Understand or we will never figure out what's going on here.") The intent should communicate very compactly the essence of a pattern and tell you whether it applies to your current situation.

Many of the reengineering patterns are concerned with code transformation, in which case a diagram may be used to illustrate the kind of transformation that takes place. Typically such patterns will additionally include steps to detect the problem to be resolved, as well as code fragments illustrating the situation before and after the transformation.

A Map of Reengineering Patterns

The patterns in this book are organized according to the reengineering life cycle presented earlier. In Figure 1.3 we can see the chapters in this book represented as clusters of patterns along the life cycle. The diagram suggests that the patterns may be applied in sequence. Although this may well be the case, in practice you are more likely to iterate between reverse engineering and reengineering tasks. The diagram is simplistic in the same

PATTERN
2.6   If It Ain't Broke, Don't Fix It

> The name is usually an action phrase.

Intent: Save your reengineering effort for the parts of the system that will make a difference.

> The intent should capture the essence of the pattern.

Problem   Which parts of a legacy system should you reengineer?

> The problem is phrased as a simple question. Sometimes the context is explicitly described.

This problem is difficult because

- Legacy software systems can be large and complex.
- Rewriting everything is expensive and risky.

Yet, solving this problem is feasible because

- Reengineering is always driven by some concrete goals.

> Next we discuss the forces! They tell us why the problem is difficult and interesting. We also pinpoint the key to solving the problem.

Solution   Only fix the parts that are "broken"—those that can no longer be adapted to planned changes.

> The solution sometimes includes a recipe of steps to apply the pattern.

Trade-offs   Pros

You don't waste your time fixing things that are not on your critical path.

Cons

Delaying repairs that do not seem critical may cost you more in the long run.

> Each pattern entails some positive and negative trade-offs.

Difficulties

It can be hard to determine what is "broken."

Rationale   There may well be parts of the legacy system that are ugly but work well and that do not pose any significant maintenance effort. If these components can be isolated and wrapped, it may never be necessary to replace them.

> We explain why the solution makes sense.

Known Uses   Alan M. Davis discusses this in his book, *201 Principles of Software Development.*

> We list some well-documented instances of the pattern.

Related Patterns   Be sure to Fix Problems, Not Symptoms (Pattern 2.5).

What Next   Consider starting with the Most Valuable First (Pattern 2.4).

> Related patterns may suggest alternative actions. Other patterns may suggest logical follow-up action.

FIGURE **1.2**   The format of a typical reengineering pattern.

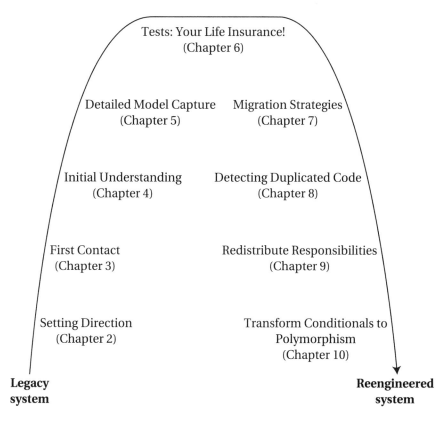

FIGURE **1.3**   A map of reengineering pattern clusters.

sense that the "waterfall" life cycle is simplistic: it may be a useful way to keep track of the different software engineering activities and their relationships, even though we know that they are not carried out sequentially but iteratively.

Each cluster of patterns is presented as a simple "pattern language"—a set of related patterns that may be combined to address a common set of problems. As such, each chapter will typically start with an overview and a map of the patterns in that chapter, suggesting how they may be related.

"Setting Direction" (Chapter 2) contains several patterns to help you determine where to focus your reengineering efforts and make sure you stay on track. "First Contact" (Chapter 3) consists of a set of patterns that may be useful when you encounter a legacy system for the first time. "Initial Understanding" (Chapter 4) helps you to develop a first simple model of a legacy system, mainly in the form of class diagrams. "Detailed Model Capture" (Chapter 5) helps you to develop a more detailed model of a particular component of the system.

"Tests: Your Life Insurance!" (Chapter 6) focuses on the use of testing not only to help you understand a legacy system, but also to prepare it for a reengineering effort. "Migration Strategies" (Chapter 7) helps you keep a system running while it is being reengineered and increases the chances that the new system will be accepted by its users. "Detecting Duplicated Code" (Chapter 8) can help you identify locations where code may have been copied and pasted, or merged from different versions of the software. "Redistribute Responsibilities" (Chapter 9) helps you discover and reengineer classes with too many responsibilities. "Transform Conditionals to Polymorphism" (Chapter 10) will help you to redistribute responsibilities when an object-oriented design has been compromised over time.

PART 1

Reverse Engineering

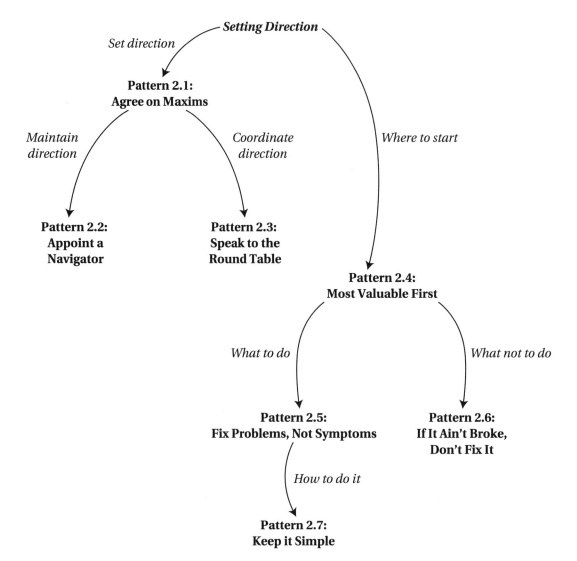

FIGURE **2.1**   Principles and guidelines to set and maintain direction in a reengineering project.

## CHAPTER 2

Setting Direction

When you start a reengineering project, you will be pulled in many different directions, by management, by the users, by your own team. It is easy to be tempted to focus on the parts that are technically the most interesting, or the parts that seem like they will be easiest to fix. But what is the best strategy? How do you set the direction of the reengineering effort, and how do you maintain direction once you have started?

Forces

The following is a list of forces you should be aware of during the course of a reengineering project.

- A typical reengineering project will be burdened with a lot of interests that pull in different directions. Technical, ergonomic, economic, and political considerations will make it difficult for you and your team to establish and maintain focus.

- Communication in a reengineering project can be complicated by either the presence or absence of the original development team.

- The legacy system will pull you toward a certain architecture that may not be the best for the future of the system.

- You will detect many problems with the legacy software, and it will be hard to set priorities.

- It is easy to get seduced by focusing on the technical problems that interest you the most, rather than what is best for the project.

- It can be difficult to decide whether to wrap, refactor, or rewrite a problematic component of a legacy system. Each of these options will address different risks and will have different consequences for the effort required, the speed with which results can be evaluated, and the kinds of changes that can be accommodated in the future.

- When you are reengineering the system, you may be tempted to over-engineer the new solution to deal with every possible eventuality.

Overview

Setting Direction is a cluster of patterns that can apply to any development project, but also has special relevance to a reengineering effort (see Figure 2.1 on page 16). As such, we have chosen a streamlined pattern format to describe them (Problem, Solution, and Discussion).

You should Agree on Maxims (Pattern 2.1) in order to establish a common understanding within the reengineering team of what is at stake and how to achieve it. You should Appoint a Navigator (Pattern 2.2) to maintain the architectural vision. Everyone should Speak to the Round Table (Pattern 2.3) to maintain team awareness of the state of the project.

To help you focus on the right problems and the critical decisions, it is wise to tackle the Most Valuable First (Pattern 2.4). Note that this will help you to Involve the Users (Pattern 7.1) and Build Confidence (Pattern 7.2). In order to decide whether to wrap, refactor, or rewrite, you should Fix Problems, Not Symptoms (Pattern 2.5). Change for change's sake is not productive, so If It Ain't Broke, Don't Fix It (Pattern 2.6). Although you may be tempted to make the new system very flexible and generic, it is almost always better to Keep It Simple (Pattern 2.7).

PATTERN

| 2.1 | **Agree on Maxims** |

Problem How do you establish a common sense of purpose in a team?

Solution Establish the key priorities for the project and identify guiding principles that will help the team to stay on track.

Discussion Any reengineering project must cope with a large number of conflicting interests. Management wants to protect its legacy by improving competitiveness of its product and reducing maintenance costs. Users want improved functionality without disrupting their established work patterns. Developers and maintainers would like their jobs to become simpler without being made obsolete. Your team members may each have their own ideas about what a new system should look like.

Unless there is a clear understanding about certain fundamental questions, such as *What is our business model?* or *Who is responsible for what?* you risk that the team will be pulled apart by conflicting interests, and you will not achieve your goal. Maxims are rules of conduct that can help steer a project that is pulled in many directions. Goldberg and Rubin [Gold95] give numerous examples of maxims, such as "Everyone is responsible for testing and debugging" and "You cannot do it right the first time."

All of the patterns in this chapter can be read as maxims (rather than as patterns), since they are intended to guide a team and keep it on track. A maxim like Most Valuable First (Pattern 2.4), for example, is intended to prevent a team from squandering reengineering effort on technically interesting but marginal aspects that neither protect nor add value to the legacy system. Agree on Maxims is itself a maxim that can help a team detect when it is rudderless.

A key point to remember is that any maxim may only have a limited lifetime. It is important to periodically reevaluate the validity of any maxims that have been adopted. A project can get completely off track if you agree on the wrong maxims, or the right ones but at the wrong time.

PATTERN

2.2   Appoint a Navigator

Problem   How do you maintain architectural vision during the course of a complex project?

Solution   Appoint a specific person whose responsibility in the role of Navigator is to ensure that the architectural vision is maintained.

Discussion   The architecture of any system tends to degrade with time as it becomes less relevant to new, emerging requirements. The challenge of a reengineering project is to develop a new architectural vision that will allow the legacy system to continue to live and evolve for several more years. Without a Navigator, the design and architecture of the old system will tend to creep into and take over the new one.

You should tackle the Most Valuable First (Pattern 2.4) so you can determine what are the most critical issues that the new architecture should address, and test those aspects early in the reengineering project.

A sound architecture will help you to Fix Problems, Not Symptoms (Pattern 2.5).

Alan O'Callaghan also refers to the Navigator as the "Keeper of the Flame" [Ocal99].

PATTERN

2.3   Speak to the Round Table

Problem   How do you keep your team synchronized?

Solution   Hold brief, regular round table meetings.

Discussion   Knowledge and understanding of a legacy system is always distributed and usually hidden. A reengineering team is also performing archeology. The information that is extracted from a legacy system is a valuable asset that must be shared for it to be exploited.

Nobody has time for meetings, but without meetings, communication is ad hoc and random. Regular, focused round table meetings can achieve the goal of keeping team members synchronized with the current state of affairs. Round table meetings should be brief, but everyone must be required to contribute. A simple approach is to have everyone say *what they have done* since the last meeting, *what they have learned* or perhaps *what problems they have encountered,* and *what they plan to do* until the next meeting.

Round table meetings should be held at least once a week, but perhaps as often as daily.

Minutes of a meeting are important to maintain a log of progress, but keeping minutes can be an unpleasant task. To keep it simple, record only *decisions* taken and *actions* to be performed by a certain deadline.

Beck and Fowler recommend "Stand Up Meetings" (meetings without chairs) as a way to keep round table meetings short [Beck01].

PATTERN

2.4   Most Valuable First

Problem   Which problems should you focus on first?

Solution   Start working on the aspects that are most valuable to your customer.

Discussion   A legacy system may suffer from a great number of problems, some of which are important, and others of which may not be at all critical for the customer's business. By focusing on the most valuable parts first, you increase the chances that you will identify the right issues at stake and that you will be able to test early in the project the most important decisions, such as which architecture to migrate to or what kind of flexibility to build into the new system.

By concentrating first on a part of the system that is valuable to the client, you also maximize the commitment that you, your team members, and your customers will have in the project. You furthermore increase your chances of having early positive results that demonstrate that the reengineering effort is worthwhile and necessary.

Nevertheless there are a number of difficulties in applying this pattern. First, who is your customer?

- There are many stakeholders in any legacy system, but only one of these is your customer. You can only set priorities if you have a clear understanding of who should be calling the shots.

Second, how do you tell what is valuable?

- It can be difficult to assess exactly what is the most valuable aspect for a customer. Once a company asked us to assess if a system could be modularized because they wanted to switch their architecture. After long discussions with them, however, it turned out that in fact they really wanted to have a system where business rules could be more explicit, a system that new programmers could understand more easily, to reduce the risk that only one programmer understands it.

- Try to understand the customer's business model. This will tell you how to assess the value of the various aspects of the system. Everything that does not relate directly to the business model is likely to be a purely technical side issue.

- Try to determine what *measurable goal* the customer wants to obtain. This must be an external manifestation of some aspect of the system or its evolution, for example, better response time, faster time to market of new features, or easier tailoring to individual clients needs.

- Try to understand whether the primary goal is mainly to *protect an existing asset,* or rather to *add value* in terms of new features or capabilities.

- Examine the change logs and determine where the most activity has historically been in the system. The most valuable artifact is often the one that receives the most change requests (see Learn from the Past, Pattern 5.5).

- If the customer is unwilling or unable to set priorities, then play the *Planning Game* [Beck01]: collect requirements from all the stakeholders, and make a ballpark estimate of the effort required for each identifiable task. Given an initial budget of effort for an early first milestone, ask the customer to select tasks that will fit in the budget. Repeat this exercise at each iteration.

- Beware of *changing perceptions.* Initially the customer may draw your attention to certain symptoms of problems with the legacy system, rather than the problems themselves (see Fix Problems, Not Symptoms, Pattern 2.5).

Third, isn't there a risk of raising expectations too high?

- If you fail to deliver good initial results, you will learn a lot, but you risk losing credibility. It is therefore critical to choose carefully initial tasks that not only demonstrate value for the customer, but also have a high chance of success. Therefore, take great care in estimating the effort of the initial tasks.

- The key to success is to plan for small, frequent iterations. If the initial task identified by the customer is too large to demonstrate initial results in a short time frame (such as two weeks), then insist on breaking it down into smaller subtasks that can be tackled in shorter iterations. If you are successful in your first steps, you will certainly raise expectations, but this is not bad if the steps stay small.

Finally, what if the most valuable part is a rat's nest?

- Unfortunately, reengineering a legacy system is often an act of desperation, rather than a normal, periodic process of renovation. It may well be that the most valuable part of the system is also the part that is the most complex, impenetrable, and difficult to modify and debug.

- High change rates may also be a sign of large numbers of software defects. Typically 80% of software defects occur in 5% of the code, thus the strategy to "Renovate the Worst First" [Davi95] can pay off big by eliminating the most serious source of problems in the system. There are nevertheless considerable risks: (1) it may be hard to demonstrate early, positive results, (2) you are tackling the most complicated part of the system with little information, and (3) the chances are higher that you will fall flat on your face.

- Determine whether to wrap, refactor, or rewrite the problematic component by making sure you Fix Problems, Not Symptoms (Pattern 2.5).

Once you have decided what is the most valuable part of the system to work on, you should Involve the Users (Pattern 7.1) in the reengineering effort so you can Build Confidence (Pattern 7.2). If you Migrate Systems Incrementally (Pattern 7.3), the users will be able to use the system as it is reengineered and provide continuous feedback.

PATTERN

| 2.5 | **Fix Problems, Not Symptoms** |

Problem How can you possibly tackle all the reported problems?

Solution Address the source of a problem, rather than particular requests of your stakeholders.

Discussion Although this is a very general principle, it has a particular relevance for reengineering. Each stakeholder has a different viewpoint of the system and may only see part of it. The problems they want you to fix may be just manifestations of deeper problems in the system. For example, the fact that you do not get immediate feedback for certain user actions may be a consequence of a dataflow architecture. Implementing a workaround may just aggravate the problem and lead to more workarounds. If this is a real problem, you should migrate to a proper architecture.

A common difficulty during a reengineering effort is to decide whether to wrap, refactor, or rewrite a legacy component. Most Valuable First (Pattern 2.4) will help you determine what priority to give to problems in the system and will tell you which problems are on your critical path. Fix Problems, Not Symptoms tells you to focus on the source of a problem, and not its manifestation. For example:

- If the code of a legacy component is basically stable, and problems mainly occur with changes to clients, then the problem is likely to be with the interface to the legacy component, rather than its implementation, no matter how nasty the code is. In such a case, you should consider applying Present the Right Interface (Pattern 7.8) to just fix the interface.

- If the legacy component is largely defect free, but is a major bottleneck for changes to the system, then it should probably be refactored to limit the effect of future changes. You might consider applying Split Up God Class (Pattern 9.3) to migrate toward a cleaner design.

- If the legacy component suffers from large numbers of defects, consider applying Make a Bridge to the New Town (Pattern 7.7) as a strategy for migrating legacy data to the new implementation.

This pattern may seem to conflict with If It Ain't Broke, Don't Fix It (Pattern 2.5), but it doesn't really. Something that is not really "broken" cannot really be the source of a problem. Wrapping, for example, may seem to be a workaround, but it may be the right solution if the real problem is just with the interface to a legacy component.

PATTERN

| 2.6 | **If It Ain't Broke, Don't Fix It** |

Problem   Which parts of a legacy system should you reengineer and which should you leave as they are?

Solution   Only fix the parts that are "broken"—those that can no longer be adapted to planned changes.

Discussion   Change for change's sake is not necessarily a good thing. There may well be parts of the legacy system that may be ugly, but work well and do not pose any significant maintenance effort. If these components can be isolated and wrapped, it may never be necessary to replace them.

Anytime you "fix" something, you also risk breaking something else in the system. You also risk wasting precious time and effort on marginal issues.

In a reengineering project, the parts that are "broken" are the ones that are putting the legacy at risk:

- Components that need to be frequently adapted to meet new requirements, but are difficult to modify due to high complexity and design drift

- Components that are valuable, but traditionally contain a large number of defects

Software artifacts that are stable and do not threaten the future of the legacy system are not "broken" and do not need to be reengineered, no matter what state the code is in.

PATTERN

| 2.7 | **Keep It Simple** |

Problem   How much flexibility should you try to build into the new system?

Solution   Prefer an adequate but simple solution to a potentially more general but complex solution.

Discussion   This is another general principle with special significance for reengineering. We are bad at guessing how much generality and flexibility we really need. Many software systems become bloated as every conceivable feature is added to them.

Flexibility is a double-edged sword. An important reengineering goal is to accommodate future change. But too much flexibility will make the new system so complex that you may actually impede future change.

Some people argue that it is necessary to "plan for reuse," hence to make an extra effort to make sure that every software entity that might conceivably be useful to somebody else is programmed in the most general way possible, with as many knobs and buttons as possible. This rarely works, since it is pretty well impossible to anticipate who will want to use something for what purpose. The same holds for end user software.

"Do the simplest thing that will work" is a maxim of extreme programming [Beck00] that applies to any reengineering effort. This strategy reinforces Involve the Users (Pattern 7.1) and Build Confidence (Pattern 7.2) since it encourages you to quickly introduce simple changes that users can evaluate and respond to.

When you do the complex thing, you will probably guess wrong (in terms of what you really need) and it will be harder to fix. If you keep things simple, you will be done faster, get feedback faster, and recover from errors more easily. Then you can make the next step.

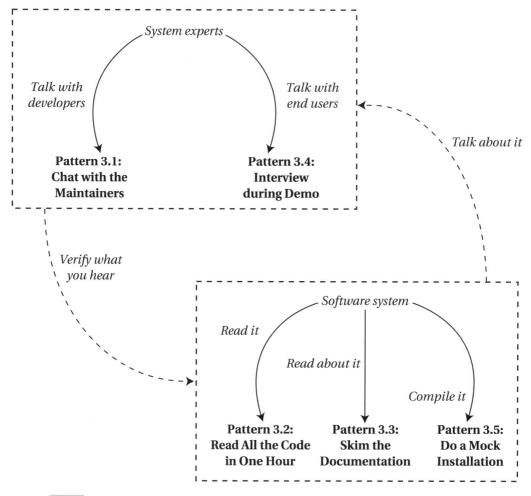

FIGURE **3.1** Assess the *feasibility* of the project during your "First Contact" with the system.

## CHAPTER 3

First Contact

You are part of a Swiss team developing a software system named proDoc that supports doctors in their day-to-day operations. The main functional requirements concern (1) maintaining patient files and (2) keeping track of the money to be paid by patients and health insurance companies. The health care legislation in Switzerland is quite complicated and changes regularly, hence there are few competitors to worry about. Nevertheless, a fresh start-up company has recently acquired considerable market share with a competing product named XDoctor. The selling features of XDoctor are its platform independence and its integration with the Internet. The system offers a built-in email client and Web browser. XDoctor also exploits the Internet for the transaction processing with the health insurance companies.

To ensure its position in the market, your company has purchased XDoctor and now wants to recover as much as possible from the deal. In particular, they want to lift the Internet functionality out of XDoctor to reuse it in proDoc. You are asked to make a first evaluation and develop a plan on how to merge the two products into one. At the outset, there is very little known about the technical details of the competing product. From the original development team of four people, only one has joined your company. His name is Dave and he has brought a large box to your office containing lots of paper (the documentation?) and two CDs. The first is the XDoctor installation disk containing an installer for Windows, MacOS, and Linux. The other contains about 50,000 lines of Java code and another 10,000 lines of C code. Looking kind of desperately at this box sitting on your desk, you're wondering, "Where on earth do I start?"

Forces

It is surprising how often reengineering projects get started. Not only does it happen after a fusion of two companies, but we also encountered projects in which code libraries were obtained from companies that later went bankrupt, or in which complete maintenance teams quit their project, leaving behind a very valuable but incomprehensible piece of code. Of course, the obvious question to ask is "Where do I start?" It turns out that this is one of the crucial questions to answer during a reengineering project, which is why we devote an entire chapter to its answer.

All the patterns in this cluster can be applied to the very early stages of a reengineering project: you're facing a system that is completely new to you, and within a few days you must determine whether something can be done with it and present a plan on how to proceed. Making such an initial assessment is difficult, however, because you quickly need accurate results while considering the long-term effects of your decisions. To deal with the inherent conflict between quick, accurate, and longer-term effects, the patterns in this cluster must resolve the following forces:

- *Legacy systems are large and complex.* Scale is always an issue when dealing with legacy systems.[1] However, there is only so much a single reengineering team can do, and when the legacy system is too big or too complex, you can't do the job in one shot. *Consequently, split the system into manageable pieces, where a manageable piece is one you can handle with a single reengineering team.*

  How much a single team can manage varies with the goal of the reengineering project, the state of the original system, the experience and skills in your team, and the culture in your organization. Our teams consisted of three to five people, and they could handle between 500,000 and a million lines of code. However, these figures will certainly have to be adapted for the reengineering project you are facing. As a rule of thumb, assume that a single team can reengineer as much code as they can write from scratch. Improve your estimates during the reengineering project by keeping logs of how much your team actually reengineered.

  If you need to split the code up, stay as close as possible to current system structure and the organization of the maintenance team. Once you have a good understanding of the system structure, consider alternatives that are better suited for the project goal.

- *Time is scarce.* Wasting time early in a project has severe consequences later on. This is especially relevant during reverse engineering because there you feel uncertain and then it is tempting to start an activity that will keep you busy for a while instead of addressing the root of the problem. *Consequently, consider time as your most precious resource.* Therefore, defer all time-consuming activities until later and use the first days of the project to assess the feasibility of the project's goals. All pat-

---

1. During the FAMOOS project we faced systems ranging between 500,000 lines of C++ and 2.5 million lines of Ada.

terns in this cluster are meant to quickly identify the opportunities and risks for your project and as such will help you set the overall direction of the project.

- *First impressions are dangerous.* Making important decisions based on incomplete knowledge implies that there is a chance you will make the wrong decision. There is no way to avoid that risk during your first contact with a system; however, you can minimize its impact if you *always double-check your sources.*

- *People have different agendas.* Normally, you will join a group of people where several members will have lots of experience with the system to be reengineered. Perhaps members of the original development team are still available or maybe the reengineering team includes people who have been maintaining the system for some time. At least there will be end users and managers who believe enough in this system to request a reengineering project. You are supposed to complement the team with your reengineering skills and expertise; hence you should know whom you are dealing with.

  Typically, your new colleagues will fall into three categories. The first category comprises the *faithful,* the people who believe that reengineering is necessary and who trust that you are able to (help them) do it. The second is the category of the *skeptical,* who believe this whole reengineering business is just a waste of time, either because they want to protect their jobs or because they think the whole project should start again from scratch. The third category is the category of the *fence sitters,* who do not have a strong opinion on whether this reengineering will pay off, so they just wait and see what happens. *Consequently, in order to make the project a success, you must keep convincing the faithful, gain credit with the fence sitters, and be wary of the skeptics.*

Overview

Wasting time is the largest risk when you have your first contact with a system; therefore these patterns should be applied during a short time span, say, one week. After this week you should grasp the main issues and based on that knowledge plan further activities, or—when necessary—cancel the project.

The patterns Chat with the Maintainers (Pattern 3.1) and Interview during Demo (Pattern 3.4) will help you get acquainted with the people involved (see Figure 3.1 on page 26). As a rule of thumb, spend four days to gather information and use the last day of the week to compile all this information into a first project plan. There is no strict order in which to apply the patterns, although the order suggested by the sequence in this book is typical. Nevertheless, we have often found ourselves combining fragments of these patterns because of the necessity to double-check. For instance, during a second meeting with the maintainers we usually start with an Interview during Demo (Pattern 3.4) but ask questions about what we have learned from Read All the Code in One Hour (Pattern 3.2) and Skim the Documentation (Pattern 3.3). Also, after an interview we quickly check the source code and documentation to confirm what has been said.

In certain situations we have experienced that some patterns are not applicable due to a lack of resources. For instance, if all the maintainers have left the company, you cannot Chat with the Maintainers (Pattern 3.1). Also, certain systems lack an external user interface, and then it is pointless to try an Interview during Demo (Pattern 3.4) with an end user. This isn't necessarily a problem because some of these patterns may be irrelevant for your project goal anyway. However, the absence of resources is an extra risk to the project, and it should be recorded as such in the first project plan.

What Next

Once you have the necessary information, it is time to compile the first project plan. Such a plan is very similar to the plans you normally use when launching a project, and the standard document templates used in your company should therefore be used. When necessary, bend the rules to include at least the following items:

- *Project scope.* Prepare a short (half a page) description of the project, including its context, its goals, and the criteria that will be used to verify whether you reached those goals. Involve the Users (Pattern 7.1) and Agree on Maxims (Pattern 2.1) to write this part of the plan.

- *Opportunities.* Identify those factors you expect will contribute to achieve the project goals. List the items that you have discovered during the first contact, such as the availability of skilled maintainers and power users, the readability of the source code, or the presence of up-to-date documentation.

- *Risks.* Consider elements that may cause problems during the course of the project. List those items that you did not find or where the quality was inferior, such as missing code libraries or the absence of test suites. If possible, include an assessment of the likelihood (unlikely, possible, likely) and the impact (high, moderate, low) for each risk. Special attention must be paid to the critical risks, that is, the ones that are possible/likely and have a moderate/high impact or the ones that are likely but have a low impact.

- *Go/no-go decision.* At some point you will have to decide whether the project should be continued or canceled. Use the opportunities and risks you have identified to argue that decision.

- *Activities.* In the case of a "go" decision, prepare a fish-eye view of the upcoming period, explaining how you intend to reach the project goal. In a fish-eye view, the short-term activities are explained in considerable detail, while for the later activities a rough outline is sufficient. Most likely, the short-term activities will correspond to the patterns described in "Initial Understanding" (Chapter 4). For the later activities check the subsequent chapters.

  The list of activities should exploit the opportunities and reduce the (critical) risks. For instance, if you list the presence of up-to date documentation as an opportunity and the absence of a test suite as a critical risk, then you should plan an activity that will build a test suite based on the documentation.

Chat with the Maintainers

Intent: Learn about the historical and political context of your project through discussions with the people maintaining the system.

Problem   How do you get a good perspective on the historical and political context of the legacy system you are reengineering?

This problem is difficult because

- Documentation, if present, typically records decisions about the solution, not about the factors that have influenced that solution. Consequently, the important events in the history of the system (i.e., its historical context) are rarely documented.

- The system is valuable (otherwise they wouldn't bother to reengineer it), yet management has lost control (otherwise they wouldn't need to reengineer the system). At least some of the people-related issues concerning the software system are messed up; thus the political context of a legacy system is problematic by nature.

- People working with the system might mislead you. Sometimes people will deliberately deceive you, especially when they are responsible for the problematic parts of the system or when they want to protect their jobs. Most of the time they will mislead you out of ignorance, especially when chief developers are now working on other projects and the junior staff are the only ones left for system maintenance.

Yet, solving this problem is feasible because

- You are able to talk to the maintenance team. While they might not know everything about the original system context, they most likely know a great deal about how the system got to its current state.

Solution   Discuss the problem with the system maintainers. As technical people who have been intimately involved with the legacy system, they are well aware of the system's history and the people-related issues that influenced that history.

To avoid misleading information, treat the maintainers as "brothers in arms." Try to strike a kind of bargain where you will make their job easier (more rewarding, more appreciated, . . . whatever is most likely to convince them) if they will just take some time to explain to you about what they are doing. This has the extra benefit that it will gain you the respect you need for the later phases of your reengineering project.

Hints

Here are some questions that may help in your discussion with the maintainers. It is best to ask these questions during an informal meeting (no official minutes, no official agenda), although you should be prepared to make notes after the meeting to record your main conclusions, assumptions, and concerns.

- What was the easiest bug you had to fix during the last month? And what was the most difficult one? How long did it take you to fix each of them? Why was it so easy or so difficult to fix that particular bug?

  These kinds of questions are good starters because they show that you are interested in the maintenance work. Answering the questions also gives the maintainers the opportunity to show what they excel at, which will make them less protective of their jobs. Finally, the answers will provide you with some concrete examples of maintenance problems you might use in later, more high-level discussions.

- How does the maintenance team collect bug reports and feature requests? Who decides which request gets handled first? Who decides to assign a bug report or feature request to a maintainer? Are these events logged in some kind of database? Is there a version or configuration management system in place?

These questions help to understand the organization of the maintenance process and the internal working habits of the maintenance team. As far as the political context concerns, it helps to assess the relationship within the team (task assignment) and with the end users (collection of bug reports).

- Who was part of the development/maintenance team during the course of years? How did they join/leave the project? How did this affect the release history of the system?

These are questions that directly address the history of the legacy system. It is a good idea to ask about personnel because people generally have a good recollection of former colleagues. By asking how they joined or left the project, you get a sense for the political context as well.

- How good is the code? How trustworthy is the documentation?

These questions are especially relevant to see how well the maintenance team itself can assess the state of the system. Of course you will have to verify their claims yourself afterward (see Read All the Code in One Hour (Pattern 3.2) and Skim the Documentation (Pattern 3.3).

- Why was this reengineering project started? What do you expect from this project? What will you gain from the results?

It is crucial to ask what the maintainers will gain from the reengineering project, as it is something to keep in mind during the later phases. Listen for differences—sometimes subtle—in what management told you they expect from the project and what the maintainers expect from it. Identifying the differences will help you get a sense of the political context.

Trade-offs   Pros

- *Obtain information effectively.* Most of the significant events in the lifetime of a software system are passed on orally. Discussing these with the maintainers is the most effective way to tap into this rich information source.

- *Get acquainted with your colleagues.* By discussing the situation with the maintainers, you have a first chance to appraise your colleagues. As such, you're likely to gain the necessary credibility that will help you in the later phases of the reengineering project.

PATTERN 3.1 *continued*

Cons

- *Obtain anecdotal evidence only.* The information you obtain is anecdotal at best. The human brain is necessarily selective regarding which facts it remembers; thus the recollection of the maintainers may be insufficient. Worse, the information may be incomplete to start with, since the maintainers are often not the original developers of the system. Consequently, you will have to complement the information you obtained by other means (see, for instance, Skim the Documentation, Pattern 3.3; Interview during Demo, Pattern 3.4; Read All the Code in One Hour, Pattern 3.2; and Do a Mock Installation, Pattern 3.5).

Difficulties

- *People protect their jobs.* Some maintainers may not be willing to provide you with the information you need because they are afraid of losing their jobs. It's up to you to convince them that the reengineering project is there to make their job easier, more rewarding, more appreciated. Consequently, you should ask the maintainers what they expect from the reengineering project themselves.

- *Teams may be unstable.* Software maintenance is generally considered a second-class job, often left to junior programmers and often leading to a maintenance team that changes frequently. In such a situation, the maintainers cannot tell you about the historical evolution of a software system, yet it tells you a great deal about its political context. Indeed, you must be aware of such instability in the team, as it will increase the risk of your project and reduce the reliability of the information you obtain. Consequently, you should ask who has been part of the development/maintenance team over the course of the years.

Example   While taking over XDoctor, your company has been trying to persuade the original development team to stay on and merge the two software systems into one. Unfortunately, only one member—Dave—has agreed to stay, and the three others have left for another company. As it is your job to develop a plan for how to merge the two products, you invite Dave to lunch to have an informal chat about the system.

During this chat you learn a great deal. The good news is that Dave was responsible for implementing the Internet communication protocols handling the transactions with the health insurance companies. As this was one of the key features lacking in your product, you're happy to have this experience added to your team. More good news is that Dave tells you his former colleagues were quite experienced in object-oriented technology, so you suspect a reasonable design and readable source code. Finally, you hear that few bug reports were submitted and that most of them have been handled fast. Likewise, a list of pending product enhancements exists and is reasonably small. So you conclude that the customers are quite happy with the product and that your project will be strategically important.

The not-so-good news is that Dave is a hard-core C programmer who was mainly ignored by his colleagues and left out of the design activity for the rest of the system. When you ask about his motives to stay in the project, he tells you that he originally joined because he was interested in experimenting with Internet technology but that he is kind of bored with the low-level protocol stuff he has been doing and wants to do more interesting work. You ask him what he means by "more interesting," and he replies that he wants to program with objects.

After the discussion, you make a mental note to check the source code to assess the quality of the code Dave has written. You also want to have a look at the list of pending bugs and requests for enhancements to compare the functionality of the two products you are supposed to merge. Finally, you consider contacting the training department to see whether they have courses on object-oriented programming as this may be a way to motivate your new team member.

Rationale

The major problems of our work are not so much technological as sociological in nature.

[DeMa99]

Accepting the premise that the sociological issues concerning a software project are far more important than the technological ones, any reengineering project must at least know the political context of the system under study.

Organizations which design systems are constrained to produce designs which are copies of the communications structure of these organizations.

[Conw68]

(Conway's law—often paraphrased as "If you have 4 groups working on a compiler, you'll get a 4-pass compiler.")

One particular reason why it is important to know about the way the development team was organized is because it is likely that this structure will somehow reflect the structure of the source code.

PATTERN 3.1 *continued*

A second reason is that before formulating a plan for a reengineering project, you must know the capabilities of your team members as well as the peculiarities of the software system to be reverse engineered. Holding discussions with the maintainers is one of the ways—and given the "time is scarce" principle, a very efficient one—to obtain that knowledge.

> Maintenance fact #1. In the late '60s and throughout the '70s, production system support and maintenance were clearly treated as second-class work.
>
> Maintenance fact #2. In 1998, support and maintenance of production systems continues to be treated as second-class work.
>
> [Thom98]

While talking with the maintainers, you should be aware that software maintenance is often considered second-class work. If that's the case for the maintenance team you are talking with, it may seriously disturb the discussion, either because the maintenance team has changed frequently, in which case the maintainers themselves are unaware of the historical evolution, or because the people you talk with are very protective about their jobs, in which case they will not tell you what you need to know.

Known Uses   During our experience with reengineering projects we made it a habit to kick off the project during a meeting with the maintenance team. Only in retrospect did we understand how crucial such a meeting is to build up the trust required for the rest of the project. We learned the hard way that maintainers are very proud of their job and very sensitive to criticism. Therefore, we emphasize that such a kick-off meeting must be "maintainer oriented," that is, aimed to let the maintainers show what they do well and what they want to do better. Coming in with the attitude that you—the newcomer—will teach these stupid maintainers how to do a proper job will almost certainly lead to disaster.

> The RT-100 . . . was developed by a third-party software vendor in the late 1980s and acquired by Nortel in 1990. For the next three years Nortel enhanced and maintained it before outsourcing it to another vendor to be systematically rewritten. This effort failed and the system was returned to Nortel in mid 1994. By this time, the original design team had been disbanded and scattered, and the product's six customers' organizations were quite unhappy.
>
> RT-100 was assigned to Nortel's Atlanta Technology Park laboratory. No staff members there had any experience with ACD software, and, due to another project's cancellation, staff morale was quite low.
>
> [Ruga98]

The above quote is from a paper that describes the story of a reengineering project and depicts very well the typical desperation a reengineering project has to start with. Yet—as described in the paper itself—this early assessment of the historical and political context made it possible for the project to succeed because they knew very well which factors would make the stakeholders happy and consequently could motivate the new reengineering team.

In one of the case studies of the DESEL (Designing for Ease of System Evolution) project, Stephen Cook reports that it is crucial to talk to the maintainers because they know best which aspects of the domain are likely to change and which ones are likely to remain stable [Cook01]. As such, the maintainers have submerged knowledge about how the system could have been built—knowledge that is seldom documented. Yet, during this discussion one must emphasize a "design for evolution" mind set, to force the maintainers to detach themselves from the latest problems they have been solving.

Related Patterns

There are several pattern languages that explicitly deal with the way a software development team is organized [Copl95] [Harri96] [Tayl00] [Beed00]. Although they were developed for forward engineering situations, it is good to be aware of them while talking with the maintainers because it may help you assess the situation more quickly.

What Next

During the discussion, you should avoid jumping to conclusions. Therefore, make sure that whatever you learn from the discussion is verified against other sources. Typically these sources are the people working with the system (Interview during Demo, Pattern 3.4), the documentation (Skim the Documentation, Pattern 3.3), and the system itself (i.e., Read All the Code in One Hour, Pattern 3.2, and Do a Mock Installation, Pattern 3.5).

With this verification, you have a solid basis to write down an initial plan for tackling the legacy system, including the possibility to cancel the project altogether. The discussion with the maintainers will influence this plan in various ways. First of all, you have a sense of the willingness of the maintenance team to cooperate, which will affect the work plan considerably. Second, you know the history of the system, including those parts that make it valuable and those events that caused most of the maintenance problems. Your plan will aim to resurrect the valuable parts and tackle those maintenance problems. Third, you have a sense of how the maintenance team communicates with the other stakeholders, which is important to get the plan accepted.

PATTERN

| 3.2 | **Read All the Code in One Hour** |

Intent: Assess the state of a software system by means of a brief but intensive code review.

Problem   How can you get a first impression of the quality of the source code?

This problem is difficult because

- The quality of the source code will vary quite a lot, depending on the people that have been involved in the development and maintenance of the system.
- The system is large, so there is too much data to inspect for an accurate assessment.
- You're unfamiliar with the software system, so you do not know how to filter out what's relevant.

Yet, solving this problem is feasible because

- You have reasonable *expertise* with the implementation language being used; thus you can recognize programming idioms and code smells.
- Your reengineering project has a *clear goal,* so you can assess the kind of code quality required to obtain that goal.

Solution   Grant yourself a reasonably short amount of study time (e.g., approximately one hour) to read the source code. Make sure that you will not be disturbed (unplug the telephone and disconnect your email) and take notes sparingly to maximize the contact with the code.

After this reading session, produce a short report about your findings, including

- a general assessment of whether reengineering seems feasible and why (not)
- entities that seem important (e.g., classes, packages, and so on)
- suspicious coding styles discovered (i.e., "code smells" [Fowl99])
- parts that must be investigated further (e.g., tests)

Keep this report short, and name the entities as they are mentioned in the source code.

Hints

The "time is scarce" principle demands some preparation. A checklist might help you focus your effort during the reading session. Such a checklist may be compiled from various sources:

- The development team may have employed *code reviews* as part of their quality assurance. If they did, make sure you incorporate the checklists used during the reviews. If they didn't, try some generic checklists used to review the kind of code you are dealing with.

- Some development teams may have applied *coding styles,* and if they did, it is good to be aware of them. Naming conventions are especially crucial to scan code quickly.

- The programmers might have used *coding idioms* (e.g., C++ [Copl92] [Meye98] [Meye96]; Smalltalk [Beck97]) that help you recognize typical language constructs.

- You probably have some *questions* that you would like answers to.

Here are some other items you might add to your checklist because they provide good entry points for further examination:

- *Functional tests and unit tests* convey important information about the functionality of a software system. They can help to verify whether the system is functioning as expected, which is very important during reengineering (see "Tests: Your Life Insurance," Chapter 6).

- *Abstract classes and methods* reveal design intentions.

- *Classes high in the hierarchy* often define domain abstractions; their subclasses introduce variations on a theme.

- Occurrences of the Singleton pattern (Pattern A.17) may represent information that is constant for the entire execution of a system.

- Surprisingly *large structures* often specify important chunks of functionality.

- *Comments* reveal a lot about the design intentions behind a particular piece of code, yet may often be misleading.

Tradeoffs Pros

- *Start efficiently.* Reading the code in a short amount of time is very efficient as a starter. Indeed, by limiting the time and yet forcing yourself to look at all the code, you mainly use your brain and coding expertise to ferret out what seems important.

P A T T E R N 3 . 2 *continued*

- *Judge sincerely.* By reading the code directly, you get an unbiased view of the software system, including a sense of the details and a glimpse of the kind of problems you are facing. Because the source code describes the functionality of the system—no more, no less—it is the only accurate source of information.

- *Learn the developers' vocabulary.* Acquiring the vocabulary used inside the software system is essential to understanding it and communicating about it with other developers. This pattern helps to acquire such a vocabulary.

Cons

- *Obtain low abstraction.* Via this pattern, you will get some insight into the solution domain, but only very little about how these map onto problem domain concepts. Consequently, you will have to complement the information you obtained with other, more abstract representations (for instance, Skim the Documentation, Pattern 3.3, and Interview during Demo, Pattern 3.4).

Difficulties

- *Does not scale.* Reading *all* the code does not scale very well; from our experience a rate of 10,000 lines of code per hour is reasonable. When facing large or complex code, don't try to spend more time to read more code because intensive reading is most effective when done in short bursts of time (no more than two hours). Instead, if you have a clear criterion to split the source code, try to pass a series of sessions. Otherwise, just go through all of the code and mark those parts that seem more important than others (based on Chat with the Maintainers, Pattern 3.1) and then read in different sessions.

  However, given the "time is scarce" principle, you should force yourself to be brief. Consequently, when dealing with large or complex code, don't bother too much with the details, but remind yourself of the goal of reading the code, which is an initial assessment of the suitability for reengineering.

- *Comments may mislead you.* Be careful with comments in the code. Comments can help you in understanding what a piece of software is supposed to do. However, just like other kinds of documentation, comments can be outdated, obsolete, or simply wrong. Consequently, when you find a comment, mark on your checklist whether it seems helpful or whether it seems outdated.

Example From the discussion with Dave (the sole person left from the original development team and the one responsible for the low-level C code), you recall that their system was mainly written in Java, with some low-level parts written in C and the database queries in SQL. You have experience with all these languages, so you are able to read the code.

You start by preparing a checklist, and besides the normal items (coding styles, tests, abstract classes and methods, classes high in the hierarchy), you add a few items concerning some questions you want resolved. One of them is "readability of the C code" because you want to verify the coding style of Dave, your new team member. A second is the "quality of the database schema" because you know that the data of the two systems sooner or later will have to be integrated. A third is the "handling of currencies" because Switzerland will join the Euro region and within six months all financial data must be converted to this new currency.

From reading the C code, you learn that this part is quite cryptic (short identifiers with mysterious abbreviations, long multiexit loops). Nevertheless, the modules handling the Internet protocols have unit tests, which makes you feel more confident about the possibility of incorporating them into your system.

The Java code presents a problem of scale: you can't read 50,000 lines of code in a single hour. Therefore, you pick some files at random and you immediately discover that most class names have a two-character prefix, which is either UI or DB. You suspect a naming convention marking a two-tiered architecture (database layer and user interface layer), and you make a note to investigate this further. Also, you recognize various class and attribute names as being meaningful for the health care domain (such as class DBPatient with attributes name, address, health insurance, . . .). You even perceive a class DBCurrency, so you suppose that switching to the Euro won't cause a lot of problems, since the developers took the necessary precautions. Most of the classes and methods have comments following the javadoc conventions, so you suspect that at least some of the documentation will be up to date. Finally, you identified a large singleton object that contains various strings that are displayed on the screen, which leads you to conclude that it will even be possible to localize the system.

All this looks rather promising; however, there are also a number of discouraging observations. What makes you most pessimistic is the presence of numerous long methods with large parameter lists and complex conditionals. Many of them seem to mix UI logic (enabling/disabling of buttons and menu items) with business logic (updating database records). One thing (the calculation of prices) seems especially complicated, and you make a note to investigate this further.

Concerning the database, you again recognize various table names and column names that are meaningful in the context of the health care domain. At first glance, the schema looks normalized, which for reverse engineering

PATTERN 3.2 *continued*

seems promising. The database also employs some stored procedures, which warrants further investigation.

After the reading session, you summarize your conclusions in the following notes:

- Incorporating the Internet protocols is feasible: unit tests and responsible programmer available.
- Suspect a two-tiered architecture based on naming convention. What about the business logic—mixed in with UI? (Further verification!)
- Readable code with meaningful identifiers; reverse engineering looks promising.
- Currency object is present; Euro conversion looks feasible. (Further investigation!)
- javadoc conventions used; verify documentation.
- Calculation of prices seems complicated. Why?
- Database schema looks promising. Stored procedures require further investigation.

Rationale   Code reviews are widely acknowledged as being a very effective means to find problems in programs written by peers [Gilb93] [Glass97]. Two important prerequisites have to be met in order to make such reviews cost-effective: (1) a *checklist* must be prepared to help the reviewer focus on the relevant questions, and (2) a review session must be kept *short* because reviewers cannot concentrate for a very long time (two hours at maximum).

> I took a course in speed reading and read "War and Peace" in twenty minutes. It's about Russia.
>
> —Woody Allen

There is an important difference between traditional code reviews and the ones you perform during your first contact with a software system. The former is typically meant to detect errors, while the latter is meant to get a first impression. This difference implies that you need to care less about details so that you can read more code. Typical guidelines for code reviews state that about 150 statements per hour can be reviewed [Barn94]. However, during your first contact you don't need such a detailed analysis and thus can increase the volume of code to be reviewed. We didn't perform any serious empirical investigation, but from our experience 10,000 lines of code per hour seems reasonable.

Known Uses The original pattern was suggested by Kent Beck, who stated that it is one of the techniques he always applies when starting a consulting job on an existing system. Robson [Robs91] reports code reading as "the crudest method of gaining knowledge about a system" and acknowledges that it is the method most commonly used to understand an existing program. Some case study reports also mention that reading the source code is one of the ways to start a reengineering project [Bray95] [Jack00].

While writing this pattern, one of our team members applied it to reverse engineer the Refactoring Browser [Robe97]. The person was not familiar with Smalltalk, yet was able to get a feel for the system structure by a mere inspection of class interfaces. Also, a special hierarchy browser did help to identify some of the main classes, and the comments provided some useful hints about what parts of the code were supposed to do. Applying the pattern took a bit more than an hour, which seemed enough for a relatively small system; the slow progress was due to the unfamiliarity with Smalltalk.

One particularly interesting occurrence of this pattern took place toward the end of the FAMOOS project. During the course of one week, a heterogeneous team of reverse engineers went for an on-site visit to participate in a kind of reverse engineering contest. The assignment was to invest four days and use the available reverse engineering tools to learn as much as possible about a particular C++ system. The fifth day was then used to report the findings to the original developers for verification. One of the team members finished his assignment too early and took the opportunity to Read All the Code in One Hour. It turned out that this one person had a much better overview of the system: he could participate in all discussions and could even explain some of the comments of the developers.

What Next After you Read All the Code in One Hour you should Do a Mock Installation (Pattern 3.5) to evaluate the suitability for reengineering. You may complement your findings if you Skim the Documentation (Pattern 3.3) and carry out an Interview during Demo (Pattern 3.4) to maximize your chances of getting a coherent view of the system. Before actually making a decision on how to proceed with the reengineering project, it is probably worthwhile to Chat with the Maintainers (Pattern 3.1) once more.

At the end of your first contact with the system, you should decide on how to proceed with (or cancel) the project. Reading the code will influence this decision in various ways. First of all, you have assessed the quality of the code (i.e., the presence of coding idioms and suspicious coding styles) and thus of the feasibility of the reengineering project. Second, you have identified some important entities, which are good starting points for further exploration.

PATTERN 3.2 *continued*

The list of the important entities (e.g., classes, packages, and so on) resulting from Read All the Code in One Hour can be used to start to Analyze the Persistent Data (Pattern 4.1) and Study the Exceptional Entities (Pattern 4.3). This way you can refine your understanding of the source code, especially the way it represents the problem domain.

PATTERN

3.3 Skim the Documentation

Intent: Assess the relevance of the documentation by reading it in a limited amount of time.

Problem How do you identify those parts of the documentation that might be of help?

This problem is difficult because

- Documentation, if present, is usually intended for the development team or the end users and as such is not immediately relevant for reengineering purposes. Worse, it is typically out of date with respect to the current state of affairs; thus it may contain misleading information.

- You do not yet know how the reengineering project will proceed; hence you cannot know which parts of the documentation will be relevant.

Yet, solving this problem is feasible because

- Some form of *documentation* is available, so at least there is a description that was intended to help the humans concerned with the system.

- Your reengineering project has a *clear goal,* so you can select those parts of the documentation that may be valuable and those parts that will be useless.

Solution Prepare a list summarizing those aspects of the system that seem interesting for your reengineering project. Then, match this list against the documentation, and meanwhile make a crude assessment of how up to date the documentation seems. Finally, summarize your findings in a short report, including

- a general assessment of whether the system documentation will be useful and why (not)
- a list of those parts of the documentation that seem useful and why (e.g., requirement specifications, desired features, important constraints, design diagrams, user and operator manuals)
- for each part, an impression of how up to date the description is

Hints

Depending on the goal of the reengineering project and the kind of documentation you have at your disposal, you may steer the reading process to match your main interest. For instance, if you want insight into the original system requirements, then you should look inside the system specification, while knowledge about which features are actually implemented should be collected from the end user manual or tutorial notes. If you have the luxury of choice, avoid spending too much time trying to understand the design documentation (e.g., class diagrams, database schemas); rather, record the presence and reliability of such documents since this will be of great help in the later stages of reengineering.

Check whether the documentation is outdated with respect to the actual system. Always compare version dates with the date of delivery of the system, and make note of those parts that you suspect are unreliable.

The fact that you are limited in time should force you to think how you can extract the most useful information. Here are some hints about things to look out for:

- A *table of contents* gives you a quick overview of the structure and the information presented.
- *Version numbers and dates* tell you how up to date that part of the documentation is.
- *Figures* are a good means to communicate information. A list of figures, if present, may provide a quick access path to certain parts of the documentation.
- *Screen dumps, sample printouts, sample reports, and command descriptions* reveal a lot about the functionality provided by the system.
- *Formal specifications* (e.g., state charts), if present, usually correspond with crucial functionality.
- An *index,* if present, contains the terms the author considers significant.

PATTERN 3.3 *continued*

Trade-offs   Pros

- *Provides a high abstraction level.* Documentation is supposed to be read by humans, thus at a certain level of abstraction. It may be that this abstraction level is not high enough for your reengineering project, but at least you can skip a few decoding steps.

- *Allows you to focus on relevant parts.* By preparing yourself with a list of what seems interesting, the reading session becomes goal oriented, as such increasing your chances of finding something worthwhile. Moreover, by making a quick assessment of how up to date the description is, you avoid wasting time on irrelevant parts.

Cons

- *You may miss crucial facts.* A quick read in overview mode is likely to miss crucial facts recorded in the documentation. However, you can counter this effect to some degree by preparing a list of what you would like to find.

- *You may find irrelevant information only.* There is a small chance that not a single part of the documentation will seem relevant for your reengineering project. Even in such a situation, the time spent on reading is worthwhile because now you can justify not worrying about the documentation.

Difficulties

- *Targets a different audience.* Documentation is costly to produce and hence is written for the end users (e.g., user manuals) or the development team (e.g., design). Documentation is also costly to maintain; hence only the stable parts of the system are documented. Consequently, the information you find may not be directly relevant and will require careful interpretation.

- *Documentation contains inconsistencies.* Documentation is almost always out of date with respect to the actual situation. This is quite dangerous during the early phases of a reengineering project because you lack the knowledge to recognize such inconsistencies. Consequently, avoid making important decisions based on documentation only—first verify your findings by other means (in particular, Read All the Code in One Hour, Pattern 3.2, and Interview during Demo, Pattern 3.4).

Example   After your informal chat with Dave and your code-reading sessions, you have some general idea of what the interesting aspects of the system are. You decide to skim through the documentation to see whether it contains relevant information.

You prepare yourself by compiling a list of aspects you would like to read about. Besides obvious items like design diagrams, class interface descriptions (javadoc?), and database schemas, the list includes the Euro (does the user manual say something about Euro conversions?) and the specification of Internet protocol.

Next, you go to Dave and ask him for all of the documentation concerning the software system. Dave looks at you with a small grin on his face: "You're not really gonna read all of that, are you?" "Not exactly," you say to him, "but at least I want to know whether we can do something with it." Dave looks in the box he has given you earlier and hands you three folders full of paper—the design documentation—and one booklet—the user manual.

You start with the user manual and . . . bingo! In the index you discover an entry for Euro. Turning to the corresponding pages, you see that the Euro is actually a chapter on its own consisting of about five pages, so you mark those page numbers for further study. Next you skim through the table of contents, and there you notice a title "Switching to French/German." Reading these pages you see that localizing the software is a documented feature. Localizing wasn't in your checklist, but it is still important, so you gladly add a note about it. All of this looks rather promising, so you verify the release date of the user manual and you see that it is quite recent. A good start indeed!

Opening the first folder (entitled "Classes") of the design documentation, you find more or less what you were expecting: a printout of the class interface as generated by javadoc. Not that interesting to read on paper, but you continue to leaf through the pages anyway. Your first impression is that the actual descriptions coming with each of the classes and methods are quite shallow—an impression that gets confirmed when you examine three random pages in more detail. Next, you look for descriptions for those classes interfacing with the C code implementing the Internet protocol, and there you even find empty descriptions. The litmus test with the release date of the documentation reveals that this documentation is quite old, so you make a note to check the online documentation.

The second folder contains a nice surprise: it is a generated description of the database schema, describing for each table what the purpose of each column is. Just as with the javadoc class interface descriptions, the documentation itself is quite shallow, but at least you have a way of finding what each record in the database is supposed to represent. Here as well, the litmus test with the document release date tells you to verify the online version of the same documentation.

PATTERN 3.3 *continued*

At first glance, the third folder seems to contain rubbish: various copies of miscellaneous documents that seem only vaguely related with your project. The first document is a price list for medicines; the next ten are extracts from the health care legislation. Still you continue to leaf through the pages, and you stumble upon some finite state diagrams that appear to describe the Internet protocol used to communicate with the health insurance companies. Apparently, the document is a copy from some pages out of a technical specification, but unfortunately no references to the original are included. Even the release date for this document is missing, so you don't have the means to verify whether this specification is outdated.

You conclude the reading session with the following report:

- User manual is clear and up to date: good source for black-box description of functionality.

- Euro is provided for (pp. 513–518); localization as well (pp. 723–725).

- Class interface descriptions are generated; shallow but verify on line.

- Documentation for database schema is generated; shallow, but verify on line.

- Finite state machines for the Internet protocol? Status questionable; verify with Dave.

- One folder containing miscellaneous documents (price lists, instruction leaflets, and so on).

Rationale   It is not unusual for a software development organization to spend as much as 20 or 30 percent of all software development effort on documentation.

[Pres94]

Documentation, as opposed to source code, is intended to explain the software system at an abstraction level well suited for humans. Therefore, the documentation will certainly contain information "nuggets"; the only problem is how to find the relevant ones. Finding relevant information is made difficult because of two typical circumstances present in almost all reengineering projects.

All of the case-studies face the problem of non-existent, unsatisfactory or inconsistent documentation.

[Deme97]

First of all, the documentation is likely to be out of sync with respect to the actual situation. For the five case studies we investigated during the

FAMOOS project, "insufficient documentation" was the only problem all maintainers complained about. Nevertheless, even outdated information may be useful because at least it tells you how the system was supposed to behave in the past. This is a good starting point to infer how it is used today.

> The documentation that exists for these systems usually describes isolated parts but not the overall architecture. Moreover, the documentation is often scattered throughout the system and on different media.
>
> [Wong95]

Second, documentation is normally produced in a forward engineering context and hence is not intended for reengineering purposes. Generated design documentation (e.g., database schemas, javadoc), for instance, is typically quite up to date, yet too fine-grained to be useful during the initial phases of a reengineering project. User manuals are black-box descriptions of the software system, and thus cannot serve as blueprints of what's inside the boxes. Here as well you should see the documentation as a good starting point to infer what you're really interested in.

Known Uses A study by Fjeldstadt and Hamlen reported that "in making an enhancement, maintenance programmers studied the original program about three-and-a-half times as long as they studied the documentation, but just as long as they spent implementing the enhancement" ([Corb89] quoting [Fjel79]). This equation gives a good impression of the relative importance that studying the documentation should have.

> The case-study began with an effort to understand the existing design of CTAS in general and the CM in particular. . . . The documentation for CTAS includes motivation and architecture overview, software structures, user manuals and research papers on the underlying algorithms. However, there appears to be no document that explains in high-level terms what the system computes or what assumptions it makes about its environment. Nor is there a design document that explains the relationship between the CTAS components: how they communicate, what services they offer, and so forth. We were forced to infer this information from the code, a challenge common to many commercial development efforts.
>
> [Jack00]

The above quotation summarizes quite well that you need to study the documentation yet it will not tell you all you need to know. The case study they are referring to concerns an air-traffic control system (CTAS) where they reverse- and reengineered a key component, CommunicationsManager (CM), of about 80 kilo lines of code (KLOC) C++ code.

PATTERN 3.3 *continued*

The following anecdote reveals how documentation might mislead you. In one of the FAMOOS case studies we were asked to evaluate whether a distributed system connecting about a dozen subsystems could be scaled up to connect approximately a hundred subsystems. During this evaluation, we studied the class responsible for maintaining all of the TCP/IP connections where the comments described how all of the open connections were maintained in a kind of lookup table. We did find a lookup table in the code, but we were unable to map the description of how it worked back to operations manipulating the table. After half a day of puzzling, we gave up and decided to ask the maintainer. His matter-of-fact response was, "Ah, but this class comment is obsolete. Now that you mention it, I should have deleted it when I redesigned that class."

What Next   You may want to Read All the Code in One Hour (Pattern 3.2) immediately after you Skim the Documentation to verify certain findings. It may also be worthwhile to Chat with the Maintainers (Pattern 3.1) and Interview during Demo (Pattern 3.4) to confirm certain suspicions.

At the end of your first contact with the system, you should decide on how to proceed with (or cancel) the project. Once you have discovered relevant documentation, you know that at least you do not have to reproduce this information. Even better, for those parts of the documentation that are relevant but seem inaccurate, you have some good starting points for further exploration (for instance, Analyze the Persistent Data, Pattern 4.1, and Speculate about Design, Pattern 4.2).

PATTERN

3.4   Interview during Demo

Intent: Obtain an initial feeling for the appreciated functionality of a software system by seeing a demo and interviewing the person giving the demo.

Problem   How can you get an idea of the typical usage scenarios and the main features of a software system?

This problem is difficult because

• Typical usage scenarios vary quite a lot depending on the type of user.

- If you ask the users, they have a tendency to complain about what's wrong, while for reverse engineering purposes you're mainly interested in what's valuable.

- The system is large, so there is too much data to inspect for an accurate assessment.

- You're unfamiliar with the software system, so you do not know how to filter out what's relevant.

Yet, solving this problem is feasible because

- You can exploit the presence of a working system and a few users who can *demonstrate* how they use the software system.

Solution Observe the system in operation by seeing a demo and interviewing the person who is demonstrating. Note that the interviewing part is at least as enlightening as the demo.

After this demo, take about the same amount of time to produce a report about your findings, including

- some typical usage scenarios

- the main features offered by the system and whether they are appreciated or not

- the system components and their responsibilities

- bizarre anecdotes that reveal the folklore about using the system

Hints

The user who is giving the demo is crucial to the outcome of this pattern, so take care when selecting the person. In fact, you may want to do the demonstration several times with different people giving the demo. This way you will see variations in what people find important, and you will hear different opinions about the value of the software system. Always be wary of enthusiastic supporters or fervent opponents: although they will certainly provide relevant information, you must spend extra time to look for complementary opinions in order to avoid prejudices.

Here are some hints concerning people you should be looking for, what kind of information you may expect from them, and what kind of questions you should ask. Which people you should talk to depends very much on the goal of your reengineering project and the kind of organization surrounding it; hence this list is provided as a starting point only.

- An *end user* should tell you what the system looks like from the outside and explain some detailed usage scenarios based on the daily working practices. Ask about the working habits before the software system was introduced to assess the scope of the software system within the business processes.

- A *manager* should inform you how the system fits within the rest of the business domain. Ask about the business processes around the system to check for unspoken motives concerning your reengineering project. This is important, as reengineering is rarely a goal in itself; it is just a means to achieve another goal.

- A person from the *sales department* ought to compare your software system with competing systems. Ask for a demo of the functionality most requested by the users (this is not necessarily the same as most appreciated!) and ask how this has evolved in the past and how it might evolve in the future. Use the opportunity to get insight into the various types of end users that exist and the way the software system is likely to evolve.

- A person from the *help desk* should demonstrate to you which features cause most of the problems. During this part of the demo, ask how they explain it to their users because this may reveal mismatches between the actual business practices and the way it is modeled by the software system. Try to get them to divulge bizarre anecdotes to get a feeling for the folklore around the software system.

- A *system administrator* should show you all that is happening behind the scenes of the software system (e.g., start-up and shutdown, back-up procedures, data archiving, etc.). Ask for past horror stories to assess the reliability of the system.

- A *maintainer/developer* may demonstrate to you some of the subsystems. Ask how this subsystem communicates with the other subsystems and why (and by whom!) it was designed that way. Use the opportunity to get insight into the architecture of the system and the trade-offs that influenced the design.

Variant

Demonstrate to Yourself. A scaled-down variant of Interview during Demo entails the *reverse engineer* demonstrating the system to him- or herself via a trial-and-error process. Such a demonstration obviously lacks the group dynamics that boosts the demonstration, but on the other hand may serve as a preparation technique for a discussion with the designers/ maintainers.

Trade-offs Pros

- *Focuses on valued features.* The fact of giving a demo will gently coerce the interviewee to demonstrate those features that are appreciated. As a reverse engineer, that's your main interest.

- *Provides lots of qualitative data.* Conducting an interview typically results in a wealth of relevant information, which is very hard to extract by other means.

- *Increases your credibility.* Performing an interview shows to the interviewee that there is a genuine interest in his or her opinions about that system. The interview thus provides a unique opportunity to enlarge the end users' confidence in the result of your reengineering project.

Cons

- *Provides anecdotal evidence only.* The information you obtain is anecdotal at best, just as it is when you Chat with the Maintainers (Pattern 3.1). Interviewees will almost certainly omit important facts, either because they forgot or because they deemed them uninteresting. This effect will be countered to some degree by demonstration, yet prepare to complement the information you obtained by other means (see, for instance, Skim the Documentation, Pattern 3.3; Read All the Code in One Hour, Pattern 3.2; and Do a Mock Installation, Pattern 3.5).

- *Time may be lacking.* At least one person should be able to do the demonstration. This seems a simple requirement but may be hard to achieve in practice. Some systems (embedded systems, for example) just don't have human users and—given the "time is scarce" principle—sometimes it will take too long to make an appointment with someone who is willing to demonstrate the system.

Difficulties

- *Requires interviewing experience.* The way the questions are phrased has considerable impact on the outcome of the interview. Unfortunately, not all reverse engineers have the necessary skills to conduct good interviews. When you're inexperienced, rely on the flow of the demonstration to trigger the right kind of questions.

- *Selecting interviewees may be difficult.* You should avoid interviewing enthusiastic supporters or fervent opponents. Unfortunately, in the beginning of a reengineering project you lack the knowledge to make a good selection. Consequently, rely on other people's opinions to make the selection, but prepare to adjust the results based on the enthusiasm (or lack of it) of the interviewees.

PATTERN 3.4 *continued*

- *Handling real-time software can be difficult.* For certain kinds of systems (especially real-time systems), it is impossible to answer questions while operating the software system. In such a situation, jot down your questions while seeing the demo, and do the actual interview afterward.

Example   Now that you checked the source code and the documentation, you're almost convinced that reengineering the XDoctor system will be feasible. However, you still have some doubts about precisely what should be reverse engineered because you don't really know what the users appreciate in the system. Via the sales department, you get in touch with one of the current users, and you make an appointment for the next day. You're also worried about the state of the Internet protocol (including the state chart specification you discovered in the documentation) and the way it fits in with the rest of the system, so you go to Dave and ask him whether he can give you a demo of the Internet protocols.

Dave is quite pleased to show you his work and immediately starts to type on his keyboard. "See, now I launched the server," he says, pointing at a little console window that appeared on the screen. "Wait a second," you reply, "what command did you type there?" "LSRV. You know, for Launch Server." A bit surprised, you ask Dave if there is some kind of manual explaining how to start up and shut down this server. Dave explains that there isn't, but that it is quite easy to infer from the batch file starting the whole system. He even tells you that there are some command-line options associated with LSVR and that they are all documented in a READ.ME file and via the -h(elp) option. Next, Dave starts a test program (yes, it is invoked via LSVRTST), and in the console window you see that the server is actually receiving traffic, while the test program is spitting out a long log of all the messages sent and received. Of course, you ask him how he knows that the test succeeded, and to your dismay he states that this is done by manually inspecting the log. You decide to switch topics and ask him why this subsystem is called a server because you would guess that it is actually running on the client machine. This question triggers a heated discussion that eventually leads to an architecture diagram like the one depicted in Figure 3.2, showing a remote server (managed by the health insurance companies and accepting requests), a local server (the *L* in LSVR probably stands for "local" and not "launch"), and some local clients. From this discussion you kind of understand how the complete system is working. The basic idea is that there are several client computers on various desks connected to a local server via a LAN network. The local server maintains the database and the Internet connections to the health insurance companies.

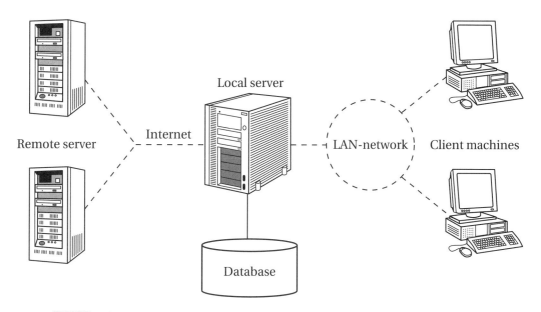

Local server

Remote server

Internet

LAN-network

Client machines

Database

FIGURE **3.2** The architecture diagram as you inferred it from the discussion with the maintainer.

With the diagram on a little sheet of paper, you ask Dave where this Internet protocol originated. This question again triggers a long story that reminds you that the protocol is designed in Germany (hence the reason why it's documented with state charts) and now adopted by the national health insurance companies.

The next day, you put on your suit and drive off to have a meeting with Dr. Mary Johanssen. While introducing yourself, you get the impression that she is not so pleased. You explain the reason for your visit, and during the conversation you understand that the doctor is quite worried about your company taking over the XDoctor software. You do your very best to assure her that the main purpose of the demonstration and interview is precisely to learn how your company may best serve the current users and that they do not intend to stop supporting it. Reassured, she starts the actual demonstration. Not surprisingly, the most appreciated feature is the automatic transaction processing with the health insurance companies because "it means that I can save on a secretary to do the paperwork." However, Dr. Johanssen also shows you some other features you were not aware of: built-in email, export to spreadsheet ("I just email this file to my bookkeeper"), and payments in multiple currencies ("Real good to deal with Euros"). During the course of the demo she tells you that in the beginning the system was a bit unstable (apparently she served as a beta tester) and that there are some weird mistakes (the list of patients is sorted by first

PATTERN 3.4 *continued*

name instead of family name), but all in all she is very pleased with the system.

Once you are back in your office you write a small report that includes the sequence of commands for testing the local server, plus the usage scenarios for the automatic transaction processing and the payment with multiple currencies. Your report also includes the architecture diagram (Figure 3.2) and the following observations:

- Testing of Internet protocols is manual; investigate regression tests.
- Internet protocol spec comes from a consortium of German health insurance companies.
- Sorting of patient list: by first name instead of last name.

Rationale　　The ability to respond flexibly to the interviewee's responses is one of the reasons why interviews are so widely used.

> [Benn99]

> Interviews are well suited to exploratory studies where one does not know yet what one is looking for, since the interviewer can adjust the interview to the situation.
>
> [Niel93]

Interviewing people working with a software system is essential to getting a handle on the important functionality and the typical usage scenarios. However, asking predefined questions does not work because in the initial phases of reengineering you do not know what to ask. Merely asking what people like about a system will result in vague or meaningless answers. On top of that, you risk getting a very negative picture because users have a tendency to complain about a legacy system.

> The real challenge of analysis begins when the expert must communicate the concept to someone else—to an analyst . . . Since the concept is often very rich and expansive, it is generally not possible for experts adequately to communicate their entire understanding in a single, holistic expression.
>
> [Gold95]

Compared with a forward engineering situation, a reverse engineer has one major advantage: there is a working software system available and you can exploit its presence. In such a situation it is safe to hand over the initiative to the user by requesting a demo. First of all, a demo allows users to tell the story in their own words, yet it is comprehensible because the demo imposes some kind of tangible structure. Second, because users must start from a working system, they will adopt a more positive attitude explaining what works. Finally, during the course of the demo, the interviewer can ask lots of precise questions and get lots of precise answers, and in this way dig out the expert knowledge about the system's usage.

Known Uses
The main idea of this pattern—let the user explain the system while using it—is commonly used for evaluating user interfaces: "Thinking aloud may be the single most valuable usability engineering method. Basically, a thinking-aloud test involves having a test subject use the system while continuously thinking out loud" [Niel93]. The same idea is also often applied during rapid prototyping for requirements elicitation [Somm96].

One anecdote from the very beginning of the FAMOOS project—an application of the Demonstrate to Yourself variant of this pattern—shows how ignorant questions arising from seeing a software system in action may trigger dormant expertise within the maintenance team. For one of the case studies—a typical example of a three-tiered system with a database layer, domain objects layer, and user interface layer—we were asked "to get the business objects out." Two separate individuals were set to that task: One took a source code browser and a CASE tool and extracted some class diagrams that represented those business objects. The other installed the system on his local PC and spent about an hour playing around with the user interface (that is, he demonstrated the system to himself) to come up with a list of 10 questions about some strange observations he made. Afterward, a meeting was organized with the chief analyst/designer of the system and the two individuals who tried to reverse engineer the system. When the analyst/designer was confronted with the class diagrams, he confirmed that these were indeed the business objects, but he couldn't tell us whether there was something missing, nor did he tell us anything about the rationale behind his design. It was only when we asked him the 10 questions that he launched off into a very enthusiastic and very detailed explanation of the problems he was facing during the design—he even pointed to our class diagrams during his story! After having listened to the analyst/designer, the first reaction of the person that extracted the class diagrams from the source code was "Gee, I never read that in the source code."

Related Patterns
A lot of good advice concerning how to interact with end users is embodied in the "Customer Interaction Patterns" [Risi00]. The main message of these patterns is that "it's a relationship, not a sale," emphasizing that your contacts with the end users should aim to develop a relationship of trust.

What Next
For optimum results, you should carry out several attempts of Interview during Demo with different kinds of people. Depending on your taste, you

PATTERN 3.4 *continued*

may perform these attempts before, after, or interwoven with Read All the Code in One Hour (Pattern 3.2) and Skim the Documentation (Pattern 3.3). Afterward, you may want to Chat with the Maintainers (Pattern 3.1) to verify some of your findings.

At the end of your first contact with the system, you should decide on how to proceed with (or cancel) the project. By seeing the demonstrations, you get a feeling for how the people use the system and which features are appreciated. Thus you know the valuable parts of the software system, and these are probably the ones that must be reverse engineered. The usage scenarios will also serve as an input for patterns like Speculate about Design (Pattern 4.2) and Record Business Rules as Tests (Pattern 6.5).

PATTERN
3.5   Do a Mock Installation

Intent: Check whether you have the necessary artifacts available by installing the system and recompiling the code.

Problem   How can you be sure that you will be able to (re)build the system?

This problem is difficult because

- The system is new to you, so you do not know which files you need to build the system.
- The system may depend on libraries, frameworks, and patches, and you're uncertain whether you have the right versions available.
- The system is large and complex, and the exact configuration under which the system is supposed to run is unclear.
- The maintainers may answer these questions, or you may find the answers in the manual, but you still must verify whether this answer is complete.

Yet, solving this problem is feasible because

- You have access to the *source code* and the necessary build tools (i.e., the makefiles, compilers, linkers).
- You have the ability to *reinstall* the system in an environment that is similar to that of the running system (i.e., the installation CD and a computer with the right operating system).

- Maybe the system includes some kind of *self-test* (see "Tests: Your Life Insurance!," Chapter 6), which you can use to verify whether the build or install succeeded.

Solution Try to install and build the system in a clean environment during a limited amount of time (at most one day). Run the self-test if the system includes one.

Hints

The main idea is to verify whether you are able to replicate the install and build processes, not to understand them completely.

Log all small failures you encounter during the build and installation process and the way you solved them, because this will tell you about the configuration of the system and its dependencies on libraries, frameworks, and patches. For example, you may learn that the system cannot be compiled on a certain location, needs an old legacy library only accessible from a particular machine, or needs a particular patch of the libraries.

It is possible that at the end of the day you did not succeed in building or installing the system completely. This corresponds to a high probability/high impact risk for your reengineering project and therefore, before you continue, you must plan to study the build and install procedures and adapt them where necessary.

After this build and install experiment, prepare a report containing

- *version numbers* of libraries, frameworks, and patches used
- *dependencies* between the infrastructure (database, network toolkits, ports, etc.)
- *problems* you encountered and how you tried to solve them
- suggestions for *improvement*
- (in case of incomplete installation or build) your *assessment* of the situation, including possibilities for solutions and workarounds

Trade-offs Pros

- *Is an essential prerequisite.* The ability to (re)build or (re)install the system is essential for a reengineering project; therefore you must assess this issue early on. If building or installing proves to be difficult or impossible, plan the necessary corrective actions.
- *Demands precision.* Replicating the build and installation process forces you to be precise about the components required. Especially for

PATTERN 3.5 *continued*

migration projects, this information is crucial because all the components must be available on the target platform as well.

- *Increases your credibility.* After the build or install you will have first-hand experience with the steps that prove to be difficult. It should be easy to offer some concrete suggestions for improvement, which will undoubtedly increase your credibility with the maintenance team.

Cons

- *Tedious activity.* You will feel very unproductive while you are busy tracking down the causes behind your failures to install the system, especially since most of the problems depend on trivial details that do not interest you right now. You can counter this effect to some extent by limiting the amount of time you devote to Do a Mock Installation, but then you will feel even more unproductive because you will not have succeeded in building or installing the system.

- *No certainty.* Although this pattern demands precision, there is no guarantee that you will actually succeed in building the system after you have reengineered some of its components. Especially when a reliable self-test is missing, you cannot verify whether your build or install was complete.

Difficulties

- *Easy to get carried away.* Building or installing a complex system may easily fail due to external factors (missing components, unclear installation scripts). It is tempting to continue fixing these annoying problems due to the "next time it will work" effect. Rather than getting carried away with these details, it is important not to lose sight of the main goal, which is not to build the system, but to gain insight into the build process. Consequently you should limit the time you spend and focus on documenting the problems that arise so you can address them later.

Example   You have carried out an Interview during Demo (Pattern 3.4) with some end users and consequently have a feeling for the important features that should be preserved during your reengineering project. However, before accepting the project, you still must verify whether you will be able to change the system. Hence, you decide to do a quick experiment to see whether you should carry out a clean build of the system.

From the box that Dave has left in your office, you take the second CD containing all the source code. Browsing the directories you notice one top-level makefile, and you decide to give it a try. You copy all the files to the Linux partition of your system and type the command make all at the prompt. Everything goes smoothly for a while, and the system reports numerous successful java compilations. Unfortunately, after a few minutes the make fails due to a missing library java.sql. You realize that you still have a JDK1.1 installed, while you remember that the documentation mentioned that it should have been JDK1.3. Reluctantly, you trash the whole directory structure, uninstall JDK1.1, download and install a JDK1.3 (downloading takes forever so you fetch yourself a cup of real coffee), and then start again. This time the make proceeds smoothly until the compiling of the C code starts. The first compilation immediately fails due to a missing library file, and you open the C file to see what exactly is causing this failure. Apparently something must be wrong with the search paths because assert.h is a standard library you know is available in your system. By then it is almost lunchtime, and since you planned to finish this build experiment today, you decide to leave the whole C compilation for later. Dave is here anyway, and since he wrote this C code he will surely be able to show you how to compile it.

After lunch, you want to verify whether what you built is OK. A grep "void main(" reveals that the XDoctor.java file contains the main entry so you type java XDoctor to launch the system. And indeed, the start-up screen you recognize from the demonstration appears, and a little status window appears telling you that "the system is connecting to the database." Immediately thereafter, the system fails with a "something unexpected happens" message, and you suspect this is due to the missing database. You decide to investigate this issue later and turn your attention to the installation procedure.

You put the installation CD in the CD drive of your Macintosh to see whether you are able to install the system. Automatically, the typical installation window appears, and you proceed through the installation process smoothly. After the installation process completes, the installer asks you to reboot your computer before launching the system. You make a note to verify which system extensions are installed, reboot your computer, and then double-click the XDoctor icon that appeared on your desktop. Unfortunately, a window appears that asks you to provide a license key. Studying the CD box you read that you must have received the license key in a separate letter, which of course you did not receive. "Too bad," you think. "It would have been nice to run a demo version of the system when no license key is provided, just as we do with our proDoc." Frustrated, you decide to give up and write the following report:

- Make with a JDK1.3 appears to work; could not verify whether this build was complete.

- C compilation fails; request Dave to demonstrate the build.

PATTERN、3.5 *continued*

- Investigate licensing in further detail: how is the system protected?
- *Suggestion:* If no license key is provided, run in demo mode (compare with proDoc).
- *Suggestion:* Verify preconditions when calling XDoctor.main(); system exits with "something unexpectedly happens" after a fresh build.

Known Uses In one of the FAMOOS case studies, we had to reengineer a distributed system that was communicating over sockets with a central server by means of a little command language. We received a tape containing a tar file that—according to the letter attached—"contains everything that is required." Rebuilding and reinstalling the system proved to be difficult, however, and we had to dive into the installation scripts and ask the maintainers for clarification. In the end, we could not communicate with the central server due to security and connection problems, but we were able to test the system in simulation mode. Although the experiment did not succeed completely, it gave us insights into the system's architecture. In particular, the way the simulation mode mimicked the central server and the way this was encoded in the source code and the makefiles provided us with information that turned out to be crucial during the rest of the project.

Toward the end of the first day of an auditing project we carried out, we requested to see a clean install the following morning. We considered this to be an innocent request meant to prepare things for an Interview during Demo (Pattern 3.4), but during the installation we discovered that one maintainer had to stay overnight to prepare the installation CD. From the subsequent discussion we learned that the system wasn't meant to be installed: the user base was fixed and the system was designed to download weekly updates over the Internet. This explained many peculiarities we observed during a previous effort to Read All the Code in One Hour (Pattern 3.2) and helped us a lot to expose the design issues during the remainder of the auditing project.

When working with a configuration management system, it is a good idea to first try to import the code into a clean configuration before recompiling it. In the case of a Smalltalk system, for instance, one general piece of advice is to first try to load the Envy configuration maps that compose the system and then load the code into a clean image [Pelr01].

What Next It can be a good idea to Chat with the Maintainers (Pattern 3.1) before you report your conclusions. They may be able to confirm your findings and clear up some misconceptions. Concrete suggestions for improvement are best discussed with the maintainers because it is the best way to convince them that you really mean to help them.

When the build or installation fails completely, you may want to combine Interview during Demo (Pattern 3.4) with Do a Mock Installation. In that case, invite a maintainer to demonstrate the build or installation process and ask questions about those steps you have found unclear.

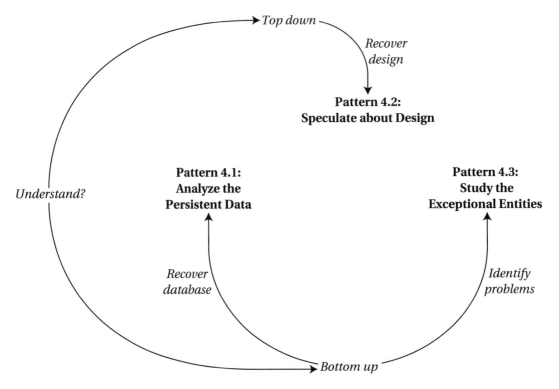

FIGURE **4.1**   Obtain an Initial Understanding of a software system and cast it into a higher-level representation.

## CHAPTER 4

Initial Understanding

Your company develops and distributes a medical information system named proDoc for use by doctors. Now the company has bought a competing software product, XDoctor, that provides Internet support to perform transactions with various health insurance companies. The two products should be merged into a single system.

A first evaluation of XDoctor has revealed that a few components should somehow be recovered and integrated into yours. Of course, to successfully recover a software component, you must understand its inner structure as well as its connections with the rest of the system. For instance, your company has promised that customers "won't lose a single byte of data"; hence you must recover the database contents and consequently understand the database structure and how the upper layers depend on it. Also, your company has promised to continue and even expand the transaction support with health insurance companies; hence you must recover the network communication component used to communicate with these remote services.

Forces

Situations similar to this one occur frequently in reengineering projects. "After the First Contact" (Chapter 3) with the system and its users, it is clear what kind of functionality is valuable and why it must be recovered. However, you lack knowledge about the overall design of the software system, so you cannot predict whether this functionality can be lifted out of the legacy system and how much effort that will cost you. Such initial understanding is crucial for the success of a reengineering project, and this chapter will explain how to obtain it.

The patterns in "First Contact" (Chapter 3) should have helped you to get some first ideas about the software system. Now is the right time to refine those ideas into an initial understanding and to document that understanding in order to support further reverse engineering activities. The main priority at this stage of reverse engineering is to set up a reliable foundation for the rest of your project; thus you must make sure that your discoveries are correct and properly documented.

How to properly document your discoveries depends largely on the scope of your project and the size of your team. A complicated reverse engineering project involving more than ten developers demands some standard document templates and a configuration management system. At the other extreme, a run-of-the-mill project involving fewer than three people may be able to manage just fine with some loosely structured files shared on a central server. However, there are a few inherent forces that apply to any situation:

- *Data is deceptive.* To understand an existing software system you must collect and interpret data and summarize it in a coherent view. There is usually more than one way to interpret data, and when choosing between alternatives you will make assumptions that are not always backed up by concrete evidence. *Consequently, double-check your sources to make sure you build your understanding on a solid foundation.*

- *Understanding implies iteration.* Understanding occurs inside the human brain and thus corresponds to a kind of learning process. Reverse engineering techniques must support the way our minds assimilate new ideas and hence be very flexible and allow for a lot of iteration and backtracking. *Consequently, plan for iteration and feedback loops in order to stimulate a learning process.*

- *Knowledge must be shared.* Once you understand the system, it is important to share this knowledge with your colleagues. Not only will it help them to do their job, it will also result in comments and feedback that may improve your understanding. *Therefore, put the map on the wall:* publish your discoveries in a highly visible place and make explicit provisions for feedback. How to do this will depend on the team organization and working habits. Team meetings in general are a good way to publish information (see Speak to the Round Table, Pattern 2.3), but a large drawing on the wall near the coffee machine may serve just as well.

- *Teams need to communicate.* Building and documenting your understanding of a system is not a goal; it is a means to achieve a goal. The real goal of understanding the system is to communicate effectively with the other people involved in the project; thus the way you document your understanding must support that goal. There is, for instance, no point in drawing UML class diagrams if your colleagues only know how to read ER diagrams; there is no point in writing use cases if your end users can't understand their scope. *Consequently, use their language:* choose the language for documenting your understanding so that your team members can read, understand, and comment on what you have documented.

Overview

When developing your initial understanding of a software system, incorrect information is your biggest concern. Therefore these patterns rely mainly on source code because this is the only trustworthy information source.

In principle, there are two approaches for studying source code: one is top down; the other is bottom up (see Figure 4.1 on page 64). In practice, every reverse engineering approach must incorporate a little bit of both, but still it is worthwhile to make the distinction. With the top-down approach, you start from a high-level representation and verify it against the source code (as, for instance, described in Speculate about Design, Pattern 4.2). In the bottom-up approach, you start from the source code, determine what's relevant, and cast the relevant entities into a higher-level representation. This is the approach used in Analyze the Persistent Data (Pattern 4.1) and Study the Exceptional Entities (Pattern 4.3)

There is no preferred order in which to apply each of these patterns. It may be natural to first Analyze the Persistent Data (Pattern 4.1), then refine the resulting model via Speculate about Design (Pattern 4.2), and finally exploit this knowledge to Study the Exceptional Entities (Pattern 4.3). Therefore the patterns are presented in that order. However, large parts of your system won't have anything to do with a database (some systems lack any form of persistent data), and then Speculate about Design (Pattern 4.2) must be done without having studied the database. And when you lack the inspiration to start with Speculate about Design (Pattern 4.2), then Study the Exceptional Entities (Pattern 4.3) will surely provide you with an initial hypothesis.

The amount of time you should devote to each of these patterns depends largely on the goal of your reengineering project. In principle, none of these patterns will take long, but each of them should be applied several times. You cannot predict how many cycles will be necessary because the assessment of whether your team understands enough to proceed with the rest of the project can only be done after the patterns have been applied. Therefore these patterns must be applied on a case-by-case basis.

What Next

You should make sure to reflect your increased understanding in the project plan. For instance, Analyze the Persistent Data (Pattern 4.1) and Speculate about Design (Pattern 4.2) will document parts of the system, and this documentation must be added to the opportunities. On the other hand, Study the Exceptional Entities (Pattern 4.3) will reveal some suspicious components, and these must be added to the risks.

Once you have obtained a solid foundation for your understanding, you should fill in the details for those components that are important for the rest of your project. Activities described in "Detailed Model Capture" (Chapter 5) may help you to fill in those details.

P A T T E R N

4.1   Analyze the Persistent Data

Intent: Learn about objects that are so valuable they must be kept inside a database system.

Problem   Which object structures represent the valuable data?

This problem is difficult because

- Valuable data must be kept safe on some external storage device (e.g., a file system, a database). However, such data stores often act as an attic: they are rarely cleaned up and may contain lots of junk.

- When loaded in memory, the valuable data is represented by complex object structures. Unfortunately there is a big gap between the data structures provided by external storage devices and the object structures living in main memory. Inheritance relationships, for instance, are seldom explicitly provided in a legacy database.

- "Valuable" is a relative property. It is possible that large parts of the saved data are irrelevant for your reengineering project.

Yet, solving this problem is feasible because

- The software system employs some form of a *database* to make its data persistent. Thus there exists some form of database schema providing a static description of the data inside the database.

- The database comes with the *necessary tools* to inspect the actual objects inside the database, so you can exploit the presence of legacy data to fine-tune your findings.

- You have some *expertise* with mapping data structures from your implementation language onto a database schema, enough to reconstruct a class diagram from the database schema.

- You have a *rough understanding* of the system's functionality and the goals of your project (for example, obtained via "First Contact," Chapter 3), so you can assess which parts of the database are valuable for your project.

Solution   Analyze the database schema and assess which structures represent valuable data. Derive a class diagram representing those entities to document that knowledge for the rest of the team.

Steps

The following steps assume that the system makes use of a *relational database,* which is commonly the case for object-oriented applications. However, in case you're confronted with another kind of database system, many of these steps may still be applicable. The steps themselves are guidelines only; they must be applied iteratively, with liberal doses of intuition and backtracking.

Prepare model. To derive a class diagram from a relational database schema, first prepare an initial model representing the tables as classes. You may do this by means of a software tool, but a set of index cards may serve just as well.

1. Enumerate all table names, and for each one, create a class with the same name.

2. For each table, collect all column names and add these as attributes to the corresponding class.

3. For each table, determine candidate keys. Some of them may be read directly from the database schema, but usually a more detailed analysis is required. Certainly check all (unique) indexes because they often suggest candidate keys. Naming conventions (names including ID or #) may also indicate candidate keys. In case of doubt, collect data samples and verify whether the candidate key is indeed unique within the database population.

4. Collect all foreign key relationships between tables and create an association between the corresponding classes. Foreign key relationships may not be maintained explicitly in the database schema, and then you must infer these from column types and naming conventions. Careful analysis is required here, as homonyms (= identical column name and type, yet different semantics) and synonyms (= different column name or type, yet identical semantics) may exist. To cope with such difficulties, at least verify the indexes and view declarations because these point to frequent traversal paths. If possible, verify the

join clauses in the SQL statements executed against the database. Finally, confirm or refute certain foreign key relationships by inspecting data samples.

Incorporate inheritance. After the previous steps, you will have a set of classes that represents the tables being stored in the relational database. However, because relational databases cannot represent inheritance relationships, you have to infer these from the foreign keys. (The terminology for the three representations of inheritance relations in steps 5–7 stems from [Fros94].)

5. *One to one* (Figure 4.2(a)). Check tables where the primary key also serves as a foreign key to another table, as such foreign keys may represent inheritance relationships. Examine the SELECT statements that are executed against these tables to see whether they usually involve a join over this foreign key. If this is the case, analyze the table names and the corresponding source code to verify whether this foreign key indeed represents an inheritance relationship. If it does, transform the association that corresponds with the foreign key into an inheritance relationship.

6. *Rolled down* (Figure 4.2(b)). Check tables with common sets of column definitions, since these probably indicate a situation where the class hierarchy is spread over several tables, each table representing one nonabstract class. Define a common superclass for each cluster of duplicated column definitions and move the corresponding attributes inside the new class. Check the source code for the name applicable for the newly created classes.

7. *Rolled up* (Figure 4.2(c)). Check tables with many columns and lots of optional attributes because these may indicate a situation where a complete class hierarchy is represented in a single table. If you have found such a table, examine all the SELECT statements that are executed against this table. If these SELECT statements explicitly request subsets of the columns, then you may break this one class into several classes depending on the subsets requested. For the names of these classes, check for an encoding of subtype information like, for instance, a "kind" column holding an enumeration type number.

Incorporate associations. Note that the class diagram extracted from the database may be too small: it is possible that classes in the actual inheritance hierarchy have been omitted in the database because they did not define any new attributes. Also, table and column names may sound bizarre. Therefore, consider verifying the class diagram against the source

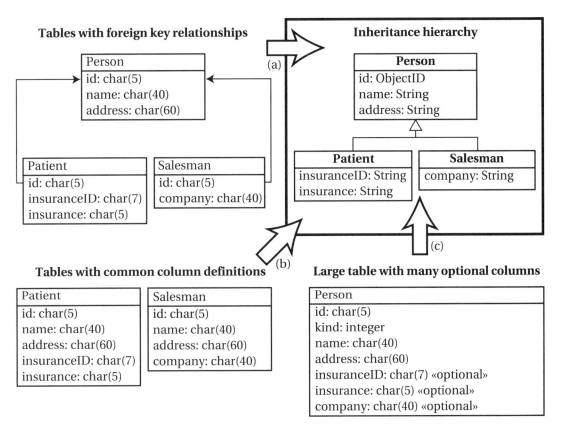

FIGURE **4.2** Mapping a series of relational tables onto an inheritance hierarchy: (a) one to one; (b) rolled down; (c) rolled up.

code (see Speculate about Design, Pattern 4.2) because this may provide extra insight. Afterward, refine the remaining associations.

8. Determinate association classes—classes that represent the fact that two objects are associated. The most common example is a many-to-many association, which is represented by a table having a candidate key consisting of two foreign keys. In general, all tables where the candidate keys are concatenations of multiple foreign keys are potential cases of an association class.

9. Merge complementary associations. Sometimes class A will have a foreign key association to class B, and class B, an inverse foreign key to class A. In that case, merge the two associations into a single association navigable in both directions.

10. Resolve foreign key targets. When inheritance hierarchies have been rolled up or down in the database, foreign key targets may become

ambiguous after the table has been decomposed into its constituent classes. Foreign key targets may be too high or too low in the hierarchy, in which case the corresponding association will have too little or too many participating classes. Resolving such situations typically requires analyzing data samples and SQL statements to see which classes actually participate in the association.

11. Identify qualified associations—associations that can be navigated by providing a certain lookup key (the qualifier). Common examples are ordered one-to-many associations, where the ordering number serves as the qualifier. In general, all tables where the candidate key combines a foreign key with extra columns are potential qualified associations; the extra columns then represent the qualifier.

12. Note multiplicities for the associations. Since all associations are derived from foreign key relationships, all associations are by construction optional one-to-many associations. However, by inspecting non-null declarations, indices, and data samples, you can often determine the minimum and maximum multiplicities for each of the roles in the association.

Verification. Note the recurring remark that the database schema alone is too weak as a basis to derive a complete class diagram. Fortunately, a legacy system has a populated database and programs manipulating that database. Hence, data samples and embedded SQL statements can be used to verify the reconstructed classes.

- *Data samples.* Database schemas only specify the constraints allowed by the underlying database system and model. However, the problem domain may involve other constraints not expressed in the schema. By inspecting samples of the actual data stored in the database, you can infer other constraints.

- *SQL statements.* Tables in a relational database schema are linked via foreign keys. However, it is sometimes the case that some tables are always accessed together, even if there is no explicit foreign key. Therefore, it is a good idea to check which queries are actually executed against the database engine. One way to do this is to extract all embedded SQL statements in the program. Another way is to analyze all executed queries via the tracing facilities provided with the database system.

Incorporate operations. It should be clear that the class diagram you extract from a database will only represent the data structure, not the operations used to manipulate those structures. As such, the resulting class diagram is necessarily incomplete. By comparing the code with the model extracted from the database (see Speculate about Design, Pattern 4.2, and Look for the Contracts, Pattern 5.4), it is possible to incorporate the operations for the extracted classes.

Trade-offs Pros

- *Improves team communication.* By capturing the database schema you will improve the communication within the reengineering team and with other developers associated with the project (in particular the maintenance team). Moreover, many if not all of the people associated with the project will be reassured by the fact that the data schema is present because lots of development methodologies stress the importance of the database design.

- *Focuses on valuable data.* A database provides special features for backup and security and is therefore the ideal place to store the valuable data. Once you understand the database schema, it is possible to extract the valuable data and preserve it during future reengineering activities.

Cons

- *Has limited scope.* Although the database is crucial in many of today's software systems, it involves but a fraction of the complete system. As such, you cannot rely on this pattern alone to gain a complete view of the system.

- *Contains junk data.* A database will contain a lot more than the valuable data, and depending on how old the legacy system is, a lot of junk data may be stored just because nobody took time to remove it. Therefore, you must match the database schema you recovered against the needs of your reengineering project.

- *Requires database expertise.* The pattern requires a good deal of knowledge about the underlying database plus structures to map the database schema into the implementation language. As such, the pattern should preferably be applied by people having expertise in mappings from the chosen database to the implementation language.

- *Lacks behavior.* The class diagram you extract from a database is very data oriented and includes little or no behavior. A truly object-oriented class diagram should encapsulate both data and behavior, so in that sense the database schema shows only half of the picture. However, once the database model exists, it is possible to add the missing behavior later.

P A T T E R N 4.1 *continued*

Difficulties

- *Polluted database schema.* The database schema itself is not always the best source of information to reconstruct a class diagram for the valuable objects. Many projects must optimize database access and often sacrifice a clean database schema. Also, the database schema itself evolves over time and will slowly deteriorate. *Therefore, it is quite important to refine the class diagram via analysis of data samples and embedded SQL statements.*

Example While taking over XDoctor your company has promised to continue to support the existing customer base. In particular, you have guaranteed customers that they won't lose a single byte of data, and now your boss asks you to recover the database structure. From experience with your own product, you know that doctors care a lot about their patient files and that it is unacceptable to lose such information. Therefore you decide that you will start by analyzing the way patient files are stored inside the database.

You start by browsing all table names looking for a table named Patient, but unfortunately you don't find one. However, there is a close match in a table named Person, where column names like insuranceID suggest that at least some patient information is stored. Nevertheless, many column names are optional, so you suspect a rolled-up representation, where patient information is mixed with information from other kinds of people. Therefore, you check the source code and look for all embedded SQL statements querying the table Person (i.e., grep "SELECT * Person"). Indeed, there are two classes where such a query is used, namely, Patient and Salesman, and from the subsets of columns queried in each class, you infer the inheritance hierarchy depicted in Figure 4.2.

Now that you recovered the Patient, you start looking for the table that stores the treatments a patient received. And indeed there is a table Treatment, which has a foreign key to the table Person. However, since you have decomposed Person into the classes Patient and Salesman, it is necessary to resolve the target of the foreign key. You join the tables Person and Treatment over patientID (SELECT DISTINCT name, kind FROM Person, Treatment WHERE Person.id = Treatment.patientID) and see that all selected persons indeed have a kind that corresponds to a Patient. Therefore, you set the target of the foreign key leaving from Treatment to Patient (see left side of Figure 4.3). Next, you verify the indices defined on Treatment and notice that there is a unique index on the columns patientID-date-nr, which makes you conclude that these columns serve as a candidate key. Since the candidate key on Treatment consists of a foreign key combined with two extra columns, you suspect a qualified association. To confirm this assump-

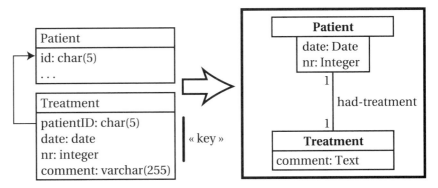

4.3   Identify a qualified association via a key consisting of a foreign key (`patientID`) and two extra columns (`date, nr`).

tion you analyze a data sample (`SELECT name, date, nr FROM Person, Treatment WHERE Person.id = Treatment.patientID ORDER BY name, date, nr`) and see that the date and the number uniquely identify a treatment for a given patient. As a consequence, you transform the foreign key into a qualified association `had-treatment` with a multiplicity of one on each role.

Rationale   The object model is important for database applications because it concisely describes data structure and captures structural constraints.

> [Blah98]

Having a well-defined central database schema is a common practice in larger software projects that deal with persistent data. Not only does it specify common rules on how to access certain data structures, it is also a great aid in dividing the work between team members. Therefore, it is a good idea to extract an accurate model of the database before proceeding with other reverse engineering activities.

Note that extracting a database model is essentially a bottom-up approach: you start from the rough information contained in the database schema and you polish it up until you have a satisfactory class diagram. A bottom-up approach works quite well in such a situation because a database schema is already an abstraction from a more detailed representation.

All data should be hidden within its class.

> [Riel96], Heuristic 2.1

Information hiding is an important design principle, and most authors agree that for a class this implies that all data should be encapsulated within the class and only accessed via the operations defined on that class. Unfortunately, the class diagram you extract from a database will expose

PATTERN 4.1 *continued*

all of its data because that's the nature of a database. Therefore, this class diagram is just a first step toward a well-designed interface to the database.

Known Uses The reverse engineering and reengineering of database systems is a well-explored area of research [Arno92] [Mull00]. Several experiments indicate that it is feasible to recover the database structure, even for database systems that are poorly designed. [Prem94], for instance, reports on an experiment concerning the reverse engineering of a data dictionary of a leading RDBMS vendor, as well as a production database storing data about mechanical parts. [Hain96] describes a prototype database reverse engineering toolkit, as well as five industrial cases where the toolkit has been applied. To illustrate the unpredictable nature of database reverse engineering, [Jahn97] reports on the use of a fuzzy reasoning engine as the core of a tool that extracts class diagrams out of relational database schemas.

What Next Analyze the Persistent Data results in a class diagram for the persistent data in your software system. Such a class diagram is quite rough and is mainly concerned with the structure of the data and not with its behavior. However, it may serve as an ideal initial hypothesis to be further refined by applying Speculate about Design (Pattern 4.2) and Look for the Contracts (Pattern 5.4).

If you need to migrate to another database, you should cast your understanding of the database model in a test suite as explained in "Tests: Your Life Insurance!" (Chapter 6).

Note that there exist patterns, idioms, and pattern languages that describe various ways to map object-oriented data structures to relational database counterparts [Brow96b] [Kell98]. Consulting these may help you when you are reverse engineering a database schema.

PATTERN

4.2   Speculate about Design

Intent: Progressively refine your model of the system by checking hypotheses about the design against the source code.

Problem How do you recover the way design concepts are represented in the source code?

This problem is difficult because

- There are many design concepts, and there are countless ways to represent them in the programming language used.
- Much of the source code won't have anything to do with the design but rather with implementation issues (glue code, user interface control, database connections, etc.).

Yet, solving this problem is feasible because

- You have a *rough understanding* of the system's functionality (for example, obtained via Skim the Documentation, Pattern 3.3, and Interview during Demo, Pattern 3.4), and you therefore have an initial idea which design issues should be addressed.
- You have *development expertise,* so you can imagine how you would design the problem yourself.
- You are *somewhat familiar* with the main structure of the source code (for example, obtained by Read All the Code in One Hour, Pattern 3.2) so that you can find your way around.

Solution Use your development expertise to conceive a hypothetical class diagram representing the design. Refine that model by verifying whether the names in the class diagram occur in the source code and by adapting the model accordingly. Repeat the process until your class diagram stabilizes.

Steps

1. With your understanding of the system, develop a class diagram that serves as your initial hypothesis of what to expect in the source code. For the names of the classes, operations, and attributes, make a guess based on your experience and potential naming conventions (see Skim the Documentation, Pattern 3.3).

2. Enumerate the names in the class diagram (that is, names of classes, attributes, and operations) and try to find them in the source code, using whatever tools you have available. Take care as names inside the source code do not always match with the concepts they represent.[1] To counter this effect, you may rank the names according to the likelihood that they would appear in the source code.

---

1. In one particular reverse engineering experience, we were facing source code that was a mixture of English and German. As you may expect, this complicates matters a lot.

3. Keep track of the names that appear in source code (confirm your hypothesis) and the names that do not match with identifiers in the source code (contradict your hypothesis). Remember that mismatches are positive because they will trigger the learning process that you must go through in trying to understand the system.

4. Adapt the class diagram based on the mismatches. Such adaptation may involve

   (a) *renaming,* when you discover that the names chosen in the source code do not match with your hypothesis.

   (b) *remodeling,* when you find out that the source code representation of the design concept does not correspond with what you have in your model. For instance, you may transform an operation into a class, or an attribute into an operation.

   (c) *extending,* when you detect important elements in the source code that do not appear in your class diagram.

   (d) *seeking alternatives,* when you do not find the design concept in the source code. This may entail trying synonyms when there are few mismatches but may also entail defining a completely different class diagram when there are lots of mismatches.

5. Repeat steps 2–4 until you obtain a class diagram that is satisfactory.

Variants

Speculate about Business Objects. A crucial part of the system design is the way concepts of the problem domain are represented as classes in the source code. You can use a variant of this pattern to extract those so-called business objects.

One way to build an initial hypothesis is to use the noun phrases in the requirements as the initial class names and the verb phrases as the initial method names. (See [Wirf90] [Bell97] [Booc94] for in-depth treatments of finding classes and their responsibilities.) You should probably augment this information via the usage scenarios that you get out of Interview during Demo (Pattern 3.4), which may help you to find out which objects fulfill which roles. (See [Jaco92] [Schn98] for scenarios and use cases and [Reen96] [Rieh98] for role modeling.)

Speculate about Patterns. Patterns are "recurring solutions to a common design problem in a given context." Once you know where a certain pattern has been applied, it reveals a lot about the underlying system design. This variant verifies a hypothesis about occurrences of architectural [Busc96], analysis [Fowl97], or design patterns [Gamm95].

Speculate about Architecture. "A software architecture is a description of the subsystem and components of a software system and the relationships between them" [Busc96] (a.k.a. Components and Connectors [Shaw96]). The software architecture is typically associated with the coarse-level design of a system, and as such it is crucial in understanding the overall structure. Software architecture is especially relevant in the context of a distributed system with multiple cooperating processes, an area where reverse engineering is quite difficult.

This variant builds and refines a hypothesis about which components and connectors exist, or in the context of a distributed system, which processes exist, how they are launched, how they get terminated, and how they interact. Consult [Busc96] for a catalogue of architectural patterns and [Shaw96] for a list of well-known architectural styles. See [Lea96] for some typical patterns and idioms that may be applied in concurrent programming and [Schm00] for architectural patterns in distributed systems.

Trade-offs   Pros

- *Scales well.* Speculating about what you'll find in the source code is a technique that scales up well. This is especially important because for large object-oriented programs (over 100 classes), a bottom-up approach quickly becomes impractical.

- *Investment pays off.* The technique is quite cheap in terms of resources and tools, especially when considering the amount of understanding you obtain.

Cons

- *Requires expertise.* A large repertoire of knowledge about idioms, patterns, algorithms, and techniques is necessary to recognize what you see in the source code. As such, the pattern should preferably be applied by experts.

- *Consumes much time.* Although the technique is quite cheap in terms of resources and tools, it requires a substantial amount of time before you derive a satisfactory representation.

Difficulties

- *Maintain consistency.* You should plan to keep the class diagram up to date while your reverse engineering project progresses and your understanding of the software system grows. Otherwise your efforts will be wasted. *Therefore, make sure that your class diagram relies heavily on the naming conventions used in the source code and that the class diagram is under the control of the configuration management system.*

PATTERN 4.2 *continued*

Example   While taking over XDoctor, your company has promised to continue to support the existing customer base. And since Switzerland will be joining the Euro region within six months, the marketing department wants to make sure that Euro conversions will be supported properly. A first evaluation has revealed that the Euro is supported to some degree (i.e., it was described in the user manual and there exists a class named Currency). Now, your boss asks you to investigate whether they can meet the legal obligations, and if not, how long it will take to adapt the software.

From a previous code review, you learned that the design is reasonably good, so you suspect that the designers have applied some variant of the Quantity pattern (Pattern A.16). Therefore, you define an initial hypothesis in the form of the class diagram, depicted in Figure 4.4(a). There is one class Money holding two attributes; one for the amount of money (a floating point number) and one for the currency being used (an instance of the Currency class). You assume operations on the Money class to perform the standard calculations like addition, subtraction, multiplication, and so on, plus one operation for converting to another currency. Currency should have subclasses for every currency supported and then operations to support the conversion from one currency into another. Of course, some questions are left unanswered, and you note them down on your class diagram:

1. What is the precision for an amount of Money?
2. Which calculations are allowed on an instance of Money?
3. How do you convert an instance of Money into another currency?
4. How is this conversion done internally? How is the support from the Currency class?
5. Which are the currencies supported?

To answer these questions you verify your hypothesis against the source code and you adapt your class diagram accordingly. A quick glance at the filenames reveals a class Currency but no class named Money; a grep search on all of the source code confirms that no class Money exists. Browsing which packages import Currency, you quickly find out that the actual name in the source code is Price, and you rename the Money class accordingly.

Looking inside the Price class reveals that the amount of money is represented as a fixed-point number. There is a little comment line stating:

```
Michael (Oct 1999)--Bug Report #324--Replaced Float by BigDecimal
due to rounding errors in the floating point representation.
Trimmed down the permitted calculation operations as well.
```

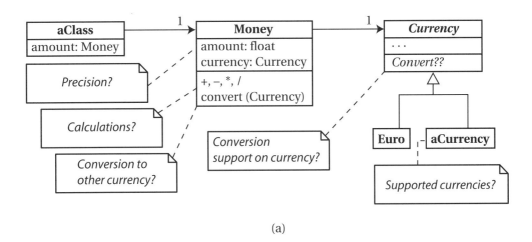

(a)

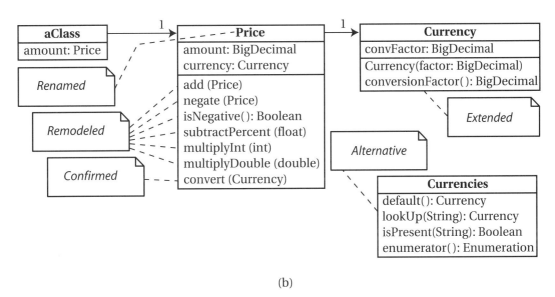

(b)

FIGURE **4.4** Refining the hypotheses concerning the Euro representation. (a) An initial hypothesis where the open questions are inserted as Notes (subclasses for the different currencies) and (b) a refined hypothesis after verification against the source code (flyweight approach); the modifications are shown as Notes.

Checking the interface of the Price class you see that the calculation operations are indeed quite minimal: only addition and negation (apparently subtraction must be done via an addition with a negated operand) and some extra operations to take percentages and multiply with other numbers. However, you also spot a convert operation, which confirms your hypothesis concerning the conversion of prices.

PATTERN 4.2 *continued*

Next you look for subclasses of Currency, but you don't seem to find any. Puzzled, you start thinking about alternative solutions, and after a while you consider the possibility of a Flyweight (Pattern A.14). After all, having a separate subclass for each currency is a bit of an overhead because no extra behavior is involved. Moreover, with the flyweight approach you can save a lot of memory by representing all occurrences of the Euro currency with a single Euro object. To verify this alternative, you look for all occurrences of constructor methods for Currency. A grep 'Currency(' does the trick—and you actually discover a class Currencies that encapsulates a global table containing all currencies accepted. Looking at the initialize method, you learn that the actual table contains entries for two currencies: the Euro and the Swiss franc.

Finally, you study the actual conversion in a bit more detail by looking at the Price.convert operation and the contents of the Currency class. After some browsing, you discover that each Currency has a single conversion factor. This makes you wonder: isn't conversion supposed to work in two ways and between all possible currencies? But then you check all invocations of the conversionFactor method, and you deduce that the conversion is designed around the notion of a default currency (i.e., the Currencies.default() operation) and that the conversionFactor is the one that converts the given currency to the default one. Checking the Price.convert operation, you see that there is indeed a test for default currency, in which case the conversion corresponds to a simple multiplication. In the other case, the conversion is done via a two-step calculation involving an intermediate conversion to the default currency.

You're quite happy with your findings and you adapt your class diagram to the one depicted in Figure 4.4(b). That model is annotated with the modifications you made to the original hypothesis; thus you store both the original and refined models into the configuration management system so that your colleagues can reconstruct your deductive process. You also file the following report summarizing your findings.

Conversion to Euro: Facilities for Euro conversion are available, but extra work is required. One central class (Currencies) maintains a list of supported currencies, including one default currency (Currencies.default). To convert to Euro, the initialization of this class must be changed so that the default becomes Euro. All prices stored in the database must also be converted, but this is outside the scope of my study.

Follow-up actions:

- Adapt initialization of class Currencies so that it reads the default currency and conversion factors from the configuration file.
- Check the database to see how Prices should be converted.

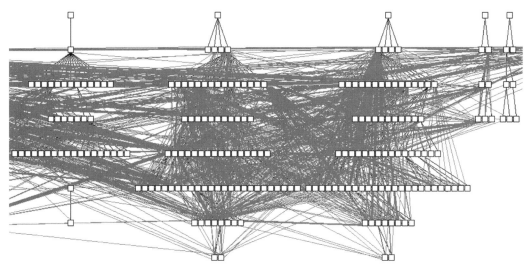

FIGURE **4.5** White noise obtained by a bottom-up design extraction approach. The figure shows a fragment of an inheritance hierarchy augmented with all method invocations and attribute accesses for a medium-sized system. The visualization is performed by CodeCrawler [Deme99] [Lanz99].

Rationale The naive approach to design extraction is bottom up: first build a complete class diagram from source code and afterward condense it by removing the noise. Unfortunately, the bottom-up approach does not work for large-scale systems because you typically get a lot of white noise to start from (see, for example, Figure 4.5, showing an inheritance hierarchy with associations for a medium-sized system). Moreover, such a bottom-up approach does not improve your understanding very much because it forces you to focus on the irrelevant noise instead of the important concepts.

> We get things wrong before we get things right.
>
> [Cock93]

In order to gain a true understanding of the legacy problem, you must go through a learning process. Speculate about Design is intended to stimulate such a learning process, and therefore evidence that contradicts your hypothesis is as valuable as evidence that confirms it. Indeed, mismatches force you to consider alternative solutions and assess their pros and cons, and that is the moment when true understanding emerges.

Known Uses In [Murp97] there is a report of an experiment where a software engineer at Microsoft applied this pattern (it is called "the Reflection Model" in the paper) to reverse engineer the C code of Microsoft Excel. One of the nice

PATTERN 4.2 *continued*

sides of the story is that the software engineer was a newcomer to that part of the system and that his colleagues could not spend too much time to explain it to him. Yet after a brief discussion he could come up with an initial hypothesis and then use the source code to gradually refine his understanding. Note that the paper also includes a description of a light-weight tool to help in specifying the model, mapping from the model to the source code, and checking of the code against the model.

The articles [Bigg89] [Bigg93] [Bigg94] report several successful uses of this pattern (there it is called the "concept assignment problem"). In particular, the authors describe a tool prototype named DESIRE, which includes advanced browsing facilities, program slicing, and a Prolog-based query language. The tool has been used by a number of people in different companies to analyze programs of up to 220 KLOC. Other well-known applications are reported by the Rigi group which, among others, has applied this pattern on a system consisting of over 2 million lines of PL/AS code [Wong95].

It has been shown that such an approach can be used to map an object-oriented design onto a procedural implementation purely based on a static analysis of the source code [Gall99] [Weid98]. Nevertheless, newer approaches try to exploit richer and more diverse information sources. DALI, for instance, also analyzes information from makefiles and profilers [Bass98] [Kazm98] [Kazm99]. Gaudi, on the other hand, verifies the hypothesis against a mixture of the static call graphs with run-time traces [Rich99].

What Next   After this pattern, you will have a class diagram representing a part of the design. You may want to Study the Exceptional Entities (Pattern 4.3) to get an impression of the design quality. If you need a more refined model, consider the patterns in "Detailed Model Capture" (Chapter 5). When your reverse engineering efforts are part of a migration or reengineer project, you should cast your understanding of design in a test suite as explained in "Tests: Your Life Insurance!" (Chapter 6).

PATTERN

4.3   ## Study the Exceptional Entities

Intent: Identify potential design problems by collecting measurements and studying the exceptional values.

Problem How can you quickly identify potential design problems in large software systems?

This problem is difficult because

- There is no easy way to discern problematic from good designs. Assessing the quality of a design must be done in the terms of the problem it tries to solve and thus can never be inferred from the design alone.

- To confirm that a piece of code represents a design problem, you must first unravel its inner structure. With problematic code this is typically quite difficult.

- The system is large. Thus a detailed assessment of the design quality of every piece of code is not feasible.

Yet, solving this problem is feasible because

- You have a *metrics tool* at your disposal, so you can quickly collect a number of measurements about the entities in the source code.

- You have a *rough understanding* of the system's functionality (for example, obtained via "First Contact," Chapter 3), so you can assess the quality of the design in the system context.

- You have the necessary *tools to browse* the source code, so you can verify manually whether certain entities are indeed a problem.

Solution Measure the structural entities forming the software system (i.e., the inheritance hierarchy, the packages, the classes, and the methods) and look for exceptions in the quantitative data you collected. Verify manually whether these anomalies represent design problems.

Hints

Identifying problematic designs in a software system via measurements is a delicate activity that requires expertise in both data collection and interpretation. Here are some hints you might consider to get the best out of the raw numbers:

- *Which tool to use?* There are many tools—commercial as well as public domain—that measure various attributes of source code entities. Nevertheless, few development teams make regular use of such tools, and therefore it is likely that you will have to look for a metrics tool before applying this pattern.

  In principle, start by looking at the tools used by the development team and see whether they can be used to collect data about the code. For

PATTERN 4.3 *continued*

instance, a code verification tool such as `lint` can serve as a basis for your measurements. Start looking for a metrics tool only when none of the development tools currently in use may collect data for you. If that's the case, simplicity should be your main tool adoption criterion, as you do not want to spend your precious time on installing and learning. The second tool adoption criterion is how easily the metrics tool integrates with the other development tools in use.

- *Which metrics to collect?* In general, it is better to stick to the simple metrics, since the more complex ones involve more computation, yet will rarely perform better.

  For instance, to identify large methods it is sufficient to count the lines of code by counting all carriage returns or new lines. Most other method-size metrics require some form of parsing, and this effort is usually not worth the gain.

- *Which metric variants to use?* Usually, it does not make a lot of difference which metric variant is chosen, as long as the choice is clearly stated and applied consistently. Here as well, it is preferable to choose the most simple variant, unless you have a good reason to do otherwise.

  For instance, while counting the lines of code, you should decide whether to include or exclude comment lines, or whether you count the lines after the source code has been normalized via pretty printing. However, when looking for potential design problems, it usually does not pay off to make the extra effort of excluding comment lines or normalizing the source code.

- *Which thresholds to apply?* Due to the need for reliability, it is better *not* to apply thresholds.[2] First, selecting threshold values must be done based on the coding standards applied in the development team, and you do not necessarily have access to these. Second, thresholds will distort your perspective on the anomalies inside the system since you will not know how many normal entities there are.

- *How to interpret the results?* An anomaly is not necessarily problematic, so care must be taken when interpreting the measurement data. To assess whether an entity is indeed problematic, it is a good idea to simultaneously inspect different measurements for the same entity. For instance, do not limit yourself to the study of large classes, but combine the size of the class with the number of subclasses and the number of

---

2. Most metric tools allow you to focus on special entities by specifying some threshold interval and then only displaying those entities where the measurements fall into that interval.

superclasses, because this says something about where the class is located in the class hierarchy.

However, formulas that combine different measurements into a single number should be avoided as you lose the sense of the constituting elements. Therefore it is better to present the results in a table, where the first column shows the name of the entity, and the remaining columns show the different measurement data. Sorting these tables according to the different measurement columns will help you to identify exceptional values.

- *How to identify anomalies quickly?* Although it is possible to identify exceptional values in a tabular representation of measurement data, such an approach is tedious and error prone. Most metric tools include some visualization features (histograms, scatter plots, etc.) to help you scan large volumes of measurements, and this is usually a better way to quickly focus on potential design problems.

- *Should I browse the code afterward?* Measurements alone cannot determine whether an entity is truly problematic: some human assessment is always necessary. Metrics are a great aid in quickly identifying entities that are potential problems, but code browsing is necessary for confirmation. Note that large entities are usually quite complicated; thus understanding the corresponding source code may prove to be difficult.

- *What about normal entities?* Experienced programmers tend to distribute important functionality over a number of well-designed components. Conversely, exceptional entities are quite often irrelevant as truly important code would have been refactored. Therefore, you should be aware that you are only applying a heuristic; it is possible that you are studying code that does not represent a design problem simply because it is deemed unimportant.

Trade-offs Pros

- *Scales well.* Metrics are readily applicable to large-scale systems, mainly because with metric tools about 20% of all the entities require further investigation. When different metrics are combined properly (preferably using some form of visualization), you can deduce quite rapidly which parts of the system represent potential design problems.

- *Overview mode is appealing.* With proper tool support you can produce visual representations of the metrics data that provide immediate insight into the good as well as the problematic parts of the design.

PATTERN 4.3 *continued*

Cons

- *Results are inaccurate.* Some of the entities having exceptional measurements will turn out not to be problematic. Metrics are only a heuristic, and false positives are likely to occur. Moreover, the metric may reveal problems that are not worth solving because the solutions will not contribute to your reengineering goal. Unfortunately, you will only know this after you have analyzed the source code.

- *Priorities may be missing.* Identifying a potential problem is easy; the real difficult part is assessing the severity of the problem. Especially during a reengineering project, you identify far more problems than you have time to solve. Prioritizing the list requires a good understanding of both the system and the reengineering project.

Difficulties

- *Data is tedious to interpret.* To measure the quality of a piece of code, you must collect several measurements. Interpreting and comparing such multivalued tuples is quite tedious, especially when dealing with large software systems. *Therefore, use visualizations that allow you to analyze different measurements simultaneously.*

- *Requires expertise.* The interpretation of measurement data is difficult and requires a lot of expertise. Fortunately, part of this expertise is documented in the form of design heuristics (see among others [Riel96] [Lore94]) and the rest *can be acquired on the job.*

Example The analysis of the database and the design of XDoctor was quite reassuring. Although there were some things to improve, the overall quality was quite good. Yet you want to confirm this feeling and therefore plan to collect a number of quality metrics and visualize them. (Of course the visualization can be done with ordinary spreadsheets, but in this case you decide to use the CodeCrawler tool [Deme99b] [Lanz99].)

Class Size Overview

As a starter, you get an impression of the raw physical size of all the classes constituting XDoctor. You measure the class size in terms of number of lines of code (LOC) and number of instance variables (NIV) and use a *checkers graph* to show the relative proportion of the sizes. In such a graph all nodes are shown as squares, where the size of the square is proportional to one size (here LOC) and the gray value is proportional to another size (here NIV).

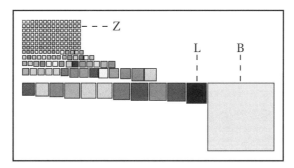

FIGURE **4.6**   Class size overview with node size showing the number of lines of code and gray value showing the number of instance variables.

Figure 4.6 shows the checker graph for XDoctor. The picture reveals that the class size is distributed quite evenly—which is reassuring—with a few noteworthy exceptions. For instance, class B is the largest in terms of lines of code (with 1495) and class L has most instance variables and second most lines of code. The classes in row Z are exceptional in the sense that they are very small; some of them are even empty.

Class Inheritance

Next, you get a feeling for the way inheritance is used by studying the various subtrees in the inheritance hierarchy. Therefore, you measure the classes in terms of hierarchy nesting level (HNL) and number of descendant classes (NDC). You include size measurements as well to assess the magnitude of the classes within the inheritance tree. Therefore, you collect the number of methods (NOM), number of instance variables (NIV), and number of lines of code (LOC) as well. You use an *inheritance tree* to visualize the various subtrees and the proportion of class sizes inside each of them. All nodes in such a tree have a rectangular shape where the height, width, and gray values of each node show three measurements.

Figure 4.7 shows such an inheritance tree for XDoctor, where the height, width, and gray values of each node represent NOM, NIV, and LOC. To the left, you observe several normal inheritance trees, namely, small ones where the size of the classes is quite similar. One exceptional value is the same B you noticed earlier; however, you now see that it also has a large superclass A (defining 70 methods), making it even more suspicious. The L you've seen before appears here as a solitary class. The hierarchies rooted in K, F, and G seem quite interesting: they go deep (four levels of inheritance) and have one large root class plus many smaller subclasses. H and I, plus M and N, are cases of large sibling classes, which may imply that too little is inherited from the common superclass. This must be verified via code browsing, however.

PATTERN 4.3 *continued*

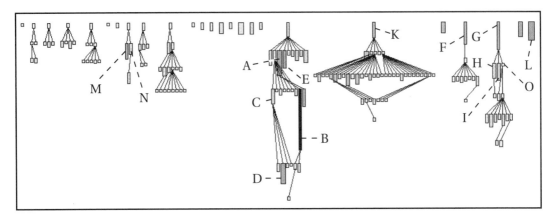

FIGURE **4.7** Inheritance tree focusing on class size. The node width shows the number of instance variables, the node height shows the number of methods, and the gray value shows the number of code lines.

Method Inheritance

To analyze particular inheritance trees in further detail, you investigate how methods in a subclass relate to methods in their superclass. Therefore, you produce a table showing for each class the number of methods overriding a method defined in a superclass (NMO), the number of methods added to the superclass (NMA), and the number of methods extending a method defined in a superclass (NME). Here as well you use an inheritance tree to identify exceptional values in the measurements.

Figure 4.8 shows the A, G, and F subtrees identified earlier, but now the height, width, and gray values of each node represent NMO, NMA, and NME. The root classes are displayed as narrow white rectangles, which is normal as root classes can neither override nor extend. As far as the subclasses are concerned, you observe two phenomena. On the one hand, the subclasses of A add a lot, yet override very little, which suggests that code reuse is the main purpose of this inheritance tree. On the other hand, the subclasses of F and G override more methods than they add, which suggests a lot of hook methods and an inheritance tree aimed at specializing behavior. Here as well, these assumptions must be verified by code browsing.

Method Size Overview

An example of how to identify potential problems in the method bodies concerns the ratio of lines of code (LOC) and the number of messages sent (MSG). In most method bodies, these two measurements will correlate, but

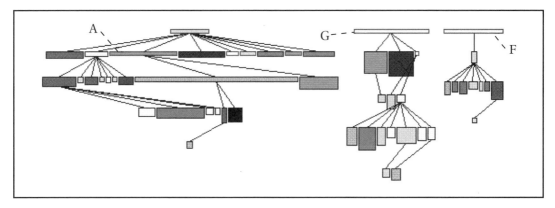

FIGURE **4.8**   Inheritance tree focusing on method inheritance. The node width shows the number of methods added, the node height shows the number of methods overridden, and the gray value shows the number of methods extended.

methods where this correlation does not hold typically represent special code.

To study this correlation relationship, you might divide the two measurements.[3] However, then you lose the sense of the constituting measurements, which makes interpretation difficult. Therefore, you visualize the relationship by means of a correlation graph, where each method is shown as a small square and where the x, y position shows the measurements that are supposed to correlate. In such a graph, the nodes where the measurements correlate cluster around a diagonal, while the exceptions are farther from the diagonal.

Figure 4.9 shows a correlation graph where the horizontal axis (left to right) represents the number of messages sent and the vertical axis (top to bottom) the number of lines of code. You observe a big cluster in the top-left corner, where most nodes are superimposed on each other. This is reassuring because it implies that most methods have fewer than 15 lines of code and 10 messages sent. The exceptions appear at the edges of the picture. For instance, node A is a large method with 99 messages packed in 45 lines of code. Node D and its neighbors are also methods where many messages are packed in a single line of code. Via code browsing you see that many of them are initialization methods. At the other side of the diagonal there is node B, which represents a method with 16 lines of code yet no messages sent. Code browsing reveals that it is a case where the whole method body has been commented out.

---

3. Metrics theory prohibits arbitrary manipulations of numbers; you should first verify whether the scale of the measurement permits the calculation [Fent96]. However, both are counting measurements having a ratio scale and then division is permitted.

PATTERN 4.3 *continued*

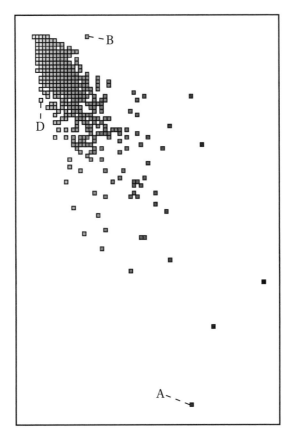

FIGURE **4.9** Correlation graph, with the *x*-position showing the number of messages sent and the *y*-position showing the lines of code.

Rationale   You cannot control what you cannot measure.

[DeMa82]

In several places in the literature it is mentioned that measuring source code helps in problem identification (see among others, [Lore94] [Fent96] [Mayr96] [Nesi98]). Most metric tools applied during these experiments visualize information by means of histograms and Kiviat diagrams. However, little research has studied the impact of thresholds while identifying exceptional entities; our own experience is that thresholds don't really matter [Deme99a].

Unfortunately, the current research is inconclusive with regard to the accuracy of the results. Up until now, no experiments exist that count how many problems remain undiscovered, nor is there any work on assessing the severity of the problems discovered. As such it is impossible to assess the reliability of metrics for reverse engineering.

Known Uses

During the FAMOOS project one event provided anecdotal evidence for how well a simple approach may outperform more specialized and complex approaches. Once we visited a business unit for a few days to demonstrate our CodeCrawler tool. At first the developers were quite skeptical because they felt that they would see "yet another metrics tool." The first surprise came when we showed them results the very first day. They told us that other tools would typically require several days' configuration time before they could parse their C++ code because it made such heavy use of special C++ features and macros. Moreover, and this was the second surprise, this simplicity did not diminish the quality of our results. The programmers confirmed most of the design anomalies we discovered, yet were intrigued by some observations we made. During the subsequent discussions they at least considered design alternatives.

What Next

Applying this pattern will result in an overall impression of design quality and the identification of a few potential design problems. With this knowledge you should at least reconsider whether the goal of your reengineering project is still attainable. If it is, you will probably want to solve some of these design problems, for instance, using patterns in "Redistribute Responsibilities" (Chapter 9) and "Transform Conditionals to Polymorphism" (Chapter 10). Solving some of these problems may require a more detailed understanding of that design, which may be obtained by patterns in "Detailed Model Capture" (Chapter 5).

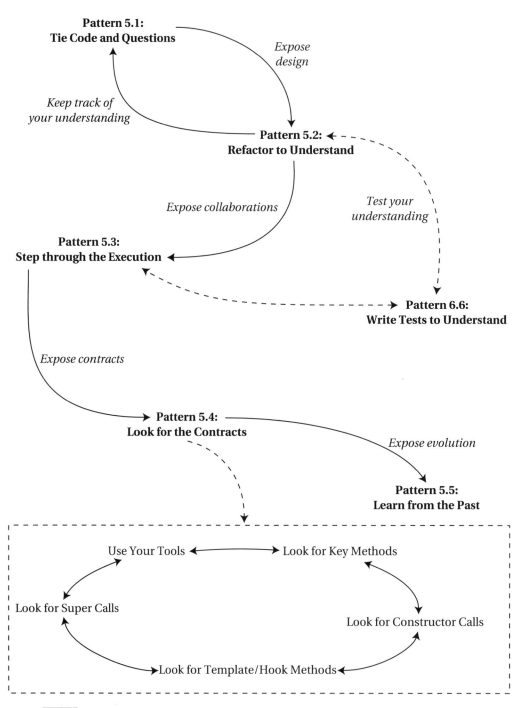

FIGURE **5.1** The patterns of "Detailed Model Capture" help you to expose the design of the software system and keep track of your understanding.

CHAPTER 5

Detailed Model Capture

The patterns in "First Contact" (Chapter 3) should have helped you to get acquainted with the software system, while those in "Initial Understanding" (Chapter 4) should have helped you to understand which are the most important entities in the system. Your main priority now is to build up a detailed model of those parts of the system that will be important for your reengineering effort.

Most of the patterns concerned with "Detailed Model Capture" entail considerably more technical knowledge, use of tools, and investment of effort than the patterns we have applied up to now. This is only natural, since only after you have built up your "Initial Understanding" can you determine whether more intensive investment of effort will pay off.

Forces

Although you already have an impression of the system, there are several forces at play that may make it difficult to extract a more detailed model:

- *Details matter.* As argued by Brooks [Broo87], software engineering is different from other engineering disciplines because of the inherent lack of abstraction barriers. Other engineering disciplines rely on the laws of nature to hide irrelevant details, but software engineering must build on less solid foundations. *Consequently, it is essential to pay attention to the details.* The only question is how to filter out those details that do not matter because you cannot possibly investigate everything.

- *Design remains implicit.* As you read the code, many design decisions will become apparent to you, but it will not be clear why and how these decisions were made. In particular, it will be hard to tell which design decisions were easy to make, and which of them created a lot of grief.

Nevertheless, such knowledge is crucial during a reengineering project because you want to avoid making the same mistakes over and over again. *Consequently, once you discover the underlying design rationale, make sure that it is properly recorded.* This way, your successors will be able to build on your discoveries rather than be forced to reinvent the wheel.

- *Design does evolve.* Change is an essential ingredient of a successful system, and certainly in object-oriented development processes with their emphasis on iterative development. As a consequence, design documents will always be out of date with respect to the actual situation. However, this also implies that change itself is the key to understanding how and why the design of a system has evolved the way it has. *Consequently, assume that important design issues will be reflected in the source code and in the way this code has changed over time.*

- *Static structure versus dynamic behavior.* Object-oriented source code tells you which classes are defined, and how they are arranged in a class hierarchy. It is much harder to see which *objects* are instantiated at run time and how they collaborate to support the system. On a fine-grained level, however, the latter is much more relevant than the former, especially due to the use of polymorphism. *Consequently, to extract the detailed design you must inevitably study the dynamic behavior.*

Overview

The patterns of "Detailed Model Capture" propose a series of activities that help you to expose design artifacts that are hidden in the code. Although some of these patterns, in particular Tie Code and Questions (Pattern 5.1), are lightweight, most of them entail considerable effort, so you should evaluate carefully how much you expect to get out of applying them.

Figure 5.1 on page 94 suggests some possible relationships between the patterns. Tie Code and Questions (Pattern 5.1) is perhaps the most fundamental of these patterns, and the easiest to apply. As you work through the source code, keep track of comments, questions, hypotheses, and possible actions to perform by directly annotating the source code *at the point where the comment applies.* This pattern works well with the other patterns in this cluster and can be productively applied throughout a reengineering project.

Refactor to Understand (Pattern 5.2) helps you to expose the design of cryptic code. It is important to understand that the intent of this pattern is *not* to improve the code base itself, but only to improve your understanding. It might well be that you decide to keep the results of your refactorings, but this should not be your goal at this point. Your refactorings should instead be treated as experiments to tests various hypotheses concerning the code.

Since the source code gives you only a very static view of the class hierarchy, it is useful to Step through the Execution (Pattern 5.3) to learn what objects are instantiated at run time and how they interact.

Although it is very easy to extract the interfaces of the classes in the system, this will not tell you very much about how these interfaces can or should be used. What you really need to do is Look for the Contracts (Pattern 5.4) supported by each class. The contracts tell you which client-supplier relationships exist, and how the public interface of a class supports that relationship. Idiomatic coding practices and design patterns typically express such contracts in a direct way, so you should train yourself to recognize them.

Finally, although you may be able to extract various design artifacts from the source code, you will not necessarily be able to get an insight into *how* the system evolved that way. In particular, you may wonder whether certain design decisions were really justified, or whether they were arbitrary, and you may wonder how stable parts of the design are. By comparing different versions of the code base and focusing on places where functionality was *removed* or refactored, you will be able to Learn from the Past (Pattern 5.5).

What Next

Now that you have mastered the details of a part of your system, it is a good time to prepare for the actual reengineering by applying the patterns in "Tests: Your Life Insurance!" (Chapter 6). In particular, as you Refactor to Understand (Patten 5.2), it is a good idea to Write Tests to Understand (Pattern 6.6), as this will give you confidence in your experiments. Also, patterns like Step through the Execution (Pattern 5.3), Look for the Contracts (Pattern 5.4), and Learn from the Past (Pattern 5.5) help you to see which components implement what functionality; this knowledge must be used to Test the Interface, Not the Implementation (Pattern 6.4) and to Record Business Rules as Tests (Pattern 6.5).

PATTERN

5.1   **Tie Code and Questions**

Intent: Keep the questions and answers concerning your reengineering activities synchronized with the code by storing them directly in the source files.

Problem   How do you *keep track of your understanding* about a piece of code and the questions that you have, keep these *remarks synchronized with the code* during its future evolution, and *share them* with the other members of your team?

This problem is difficult because

- Writing up what you know and don't know about the system you are analyzing is tedious and time-consuming.
- Your understanding is a moving target, so it is hard to keep a written document up to date.
- If you don't write down your questions and insights as soon as they occur to you, you will not be able to keep track of them.
- You want to *share* your knowledge with the team to maximize its value.
- Logging questions and answers in log files, bulletin boards, or email distribution lists may be convenient for disseminating knowledge within the team, and may provide a convenient searchable history of the team's understanding, but when you are looking at a piece of code, it will be hard to tell what questions and answers pertain to it.

Yet, solving this problem is feasible because

- You can annotate the code and therefore record your understanding *physically close* to the code element it refers to.

Solution   While you are working on the code, annotate it directly and immediately with the questions you are facing.
In principle there are two ways to annotate the code.

- *Comment-based annotations.* This approach uses the commenting conventions of the programming language and as such is better suited for a text-oriented environment. A few conventions are needed to distinguish the normal comments from the annotations.

```
/*  #to: John #by: SD #on: 3/12/99 ********************
    Screws up when we have nested IFs. */
```

Basic tools that are a part of your program environment can then be used to search and modify annotations. With a little bit of extra effort you can easily build tools to query, extract, and cross-index all comment-based annotations.

- *Method-based annotations.* This approach exploits the possibility of querying which method invokes a given method, a feature provided by many of today's programming environments. The idea is to declare a global method accepting a few strings as an argument and having an empty method body. Each time you want to annotate a particular piece of code, you invoke that method, passing your annotations as a parameter.

```
this.annotateCode("#to: John #by: SD #on: 3/12/99,"
    "Screws up when we have nested IFs.");
```

You can then use the querying and browsing facilities of your programming environment to identify the locations where this special method is invoked and thus where the annotations occur. Most programming environments can be extended by means of little scripts, in which case it is possible to develop tools to generate reports about all annotations.

Note that the less you change the code, the less likely it is that you will introduce errors. This makes the comment-based version safer than the method-based version.

Hints

- Record your annotations *as close as possible* to the code to which they refer.

- Annotations may be *questions, hypotheses, "to do"* lists, or simply *observations* about the code that you wish to record for future reference.

- Use conventions to *identify your annotations.* In a team context, include, for example, the initials of the developer that made the comments and the date the comment was entered. This way you can easily query them.

- *Follow the corporate practices.* If comments are written in a language other than English, continue if you can. However, if you have the choice, never write your annotations in a language different from that in which the source code is written (English in most cases). Otherwise, you create a different context and force the reader to switch between them.

PATTERN 5.1 *continued*

- When you discover the *answer* to any one of your questions, *immediately update* the annotation for the benefit of future readers, or simply *delete* the question if it is no longer relevant.

Tradeoffs   Pros

- *Improves synchronization.* You keep the code and the annotations in close physical proximity, and you thereby improve your chances of keeping them in sync. While modifying the code, you will more naturally modify the annotations, or remove them if they become obsolete.

- *Improves team communication.* Tie Code and Questions avoids forcing team members to open an extra communication channel (email, bulletin boards, etc.). They must read the code they work with anyway, so you can multiplex the code as a communication channel.

- *Minimizes context description.* When you annotate the code you are immediately in context. This way you will minimize the need to describe the context of your questions and keep your effort low while documenting your questions and annotations.

Cons

- *Passive in nature.* Questions that you enter are not necessarily directed to anyone, and even if they are, it is not certain that the addressee will read them or answer them in time. Additional tools are needed to collect the annotations and maybe even notify the appropriate people.

- *Incompatible with some processes.* Many companies are organized around a hierarchical reporting structure. Tie Code and Questions may be rejected by these organizations because it circumvents the normal communication channels. Also, some corporate practices impose strong constraints on what programmers are allowed to do with the code, which may limit the potential of this pattern. For instance, if annotations cannot be removed when they become obsolete, they will create too much noise to be useful.

Difficulties

- *Finding the right granularity.* As with any kind of comments, you should take care to introduce just the right amount of detail. Terse or cryptic annotations quickly lose their value, and verbose annotations will distract the reader from the code itself.

- *Motivating the programmers to write comments.* Programmers generally do not like to write comments or documentation. One way of motivating them is to use the annotations during code reviews or status meetings; this way the comments have an immediate benefit.

- *Quality of the answers.* As with any other kind of documentation, it may happen that wrong answers are given. One way to deal with this situation is to review the annotations regularly within the team.

- *Eliminating the annotations.* On certain occasions you may wish to remove the annotations—for instance, if you must deliver a "clean" version of the source code to your customer, or if your compiler isn't smart enough to remove an invocation of an empty method body. In that case, make sure that you have the proper tools to filter out the annotations.

Rationale This pattern has its roots in *literate programming* [Reen89] [Knut92]. A literate program reverses the usual relationship between program text and comments: executable code is embedded within documentation, not the other way around. Literate programming puts the emphasis on keeping the code and its documentation physically close. The physical proximity reduces the effort spent in keeping the code and its documentation in sync.

Known Uses Comment-based annotations

Various programming environments provide implicit support for managing annotations within the code. Emacs, for example, has a built-in tool, called e-tags, which allows you to easily generate a cross-reference database of a set of files [Came96]. The Eiffel environment, on the other hand, allows you to assign different levels of visibility to your comments (and your code). If you assign private scope to your annotations, you can easily separate the annotations yet make sure that they will not be seen externally.

The company MediaGeniX—a Belgian company operating in the multimedia sector—uses a systematic code tagging mechanism to record information about changes. The programming environment was altered in such a way that every change to the code is automatically annotated with a tag describing the motivation for the code change (bug fix, change request, new release), the name of the developer, and the time of the modification. Only the last tag is kept in the code, but via the configuration management system it is possible to inspect previous tags and changes. The tag also includes a free field where the developers may write what they want and is often used for questions and answers.

PATTERN 5.1 *continued*

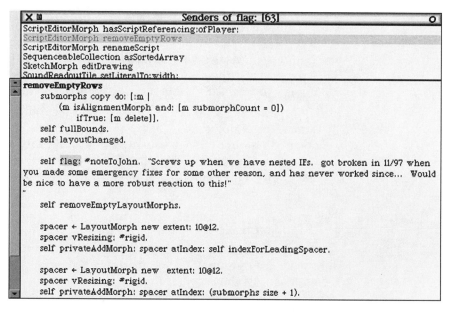

```
removeEmptyRows
    submorphs copy do: [:m |
        (m isAlignmentMorph and: [m submorphCount = 0])
            ifTrue: [m delete]].
    self fullBounds.
    self layoutChanged.

    self flag: #noteToJohn. "Screws up when we have nested IFs. got broken in 11/97 when
you made some emergency fixes for some other reason, and has never worked since... Would
be nice to have a more robust reaction to this!"

    self removeEmptyLayoutMorphs.

    spacer ← LayoutMorph new extent: 10@12.
    spacer vResizing: #rigid.
    self privateAddMorph: spacer atIndex: self indexForLeadingSpacer.

    spacer ← LayoutMorph new  extent: 10@12.
    spacer vResizing: #rigid.
    self privateAddMorph: spacer atIndex: (submorphs size + 1).
```

FIGURE **5.2**   Finding all senders of a message in Squeak.

Method-based annotations

The Squeak development team [Inga97] used this technique not so much to keep track of questions but as a means to facilitate communication in an open-source development project. In this team comments were introduced by invoking the method flag: defined in the class Object. Developers can query all senders of the flag: message to locate annotations. Furthermore, the method is defined to accept a *symbol* as its argument. This makes it possible to search more specifically, for example, for all the annotations flagged with the symbol #noteForJohn.

```
Object>>flag: aSymbol
  "Send this message, with a relevant symbol as argument, to flag
  a message for subsequent retrieval. For example, you might put
  the following line in a number of messages:
    self flag: #returnHereUrgently
  Then, to retrieve all such messages, browse all senders of
  #returnHereUrgently."
```

Figure 5.2 shows, on the top pane, all the senders of the flag: message in the Squeak 2.7 environment. The bottom pane then shows the code of the method `removeEmptyRows` that contains a call to the method `flag:` high-lighted. The `flag:` message is sent with argument `#noteToJohn`. The actual content of the annotation follows as a comment.

Related Patterns

Tie Code and Questions works well in tandem with Refactor to Understand (Pattern 5.2). Questions in the code may often be resolved by refactoring it. Conversely, as you Refactor to Understand, new questions will be raised and can be entered as annotations.

PATTERN

5.2   Refactor to Understand

Intent: Iteratively refactor a part of a software system in order to validate and reflect your understanding of how it works.

Problem

How can you understand a cryptic piece of code?

This problem is difficult because

- Cryptic code is difficult to read, and hence to understand.
- You may have some idea how the code works, but it is hard to verify because the code does not reflect your ideas.

Yet, solving this problem is feasible because

- The piece of code is *relatively small* and has clearly defined boundaries.
- Your development tools allow for *rapid edit-compile cycles,* so you can make some small changes and check whether you're still able to compile the source code or whether your tests still run.
- You have a *source code browser* that allows you to query dependencies between source code entities (e.g., which methods invoke a given operation, which methods access a given attribute, etc.), so that you can infer its purpose.

Solution

Iteratively rename and refactor the code to introduce meaningful names and to make sure the structure of the code reflects what the system is actually doing. Run regression tests after each change if they are available, or else compile often to check whether your changes make sense. Decide what to do with the code after you have refactored it.

Hints

Your primary goal here is to *understand the system,* not to improve the code. The changes you make to the code should therefore be treated as "experiments" to test your understanding of the code. As a consequence, you should *make a copy of the code* before you start. After you have refactored the code, it is possible that you will release any of the changes you make, but you do not want to make that decision up front. Perhaps your refactoring experiments will actually improve the code, but it is just as likely that you will make a mess of things since you do not yet understand the code. It does not really matter at this stage. After a first experience you will be in a better position to do a proper job of refactoring.

It is hard to do a good job of refactoring without having tests in place to verify that your changes have not broken anything. If adequate tests do not exist, you should *not* seriously consider keeping the results of your refactoring experiments. However, consider applying Write Tests to Understand (Pattern 6.6) in tandem with Refactor to Understand.

You should select refactoring operations that will make design decisions more explicit in the code. The typical refactorings applied during this iterative restructuring are Rename Attribute (Pattern A.7), Rename Method (Pattern A.8), and Extract Method (Pattern A.5).

The following guidelines will help you to find out where and how to apply these refactorings to improve the readability of the code. Many of these guidelines are considered to be just good, standard practice in Smalltalk programming [Beck97]. They apply, however, equally well to other programming languages. They can be applied in any order; each of them participates in the understanding of the others.

- *Rename attributes to convey roles.* Focus on attributes with cryptic names. To find out about their roles, look at all the attribute accesses (including invocations of accessor methods). Afterward, rename the attribute and its accessors according to its role, update all references, and recompile the system.

- *Rename methods to convey intent.* To retrieve the intent of a method that does not have an intention-revealing name, investigate all invocations and attribute uses, and deduce the method's responsibility. Afterward, rename the method according to its intent, update all invocations, and recompile the system.

- *Rename classes to convey purpose.* To capture the purpose of a class having an unclear name, investigate clients of the class by examining who is invoking its operations or who is creating instances of it. Afterward, rename the class according to its purpose, update all references, and recompile the system.

- *Remove duplicated code.* If you identify duplicated code, try to refactor it into a single location. As such, you will identify slight differences that you probably would not have noticed before refactoring and that are likely to reveal some subtle design issues.

- *Replace condition branches by methods.* If you encounter conditions with large branches, extract the leaves as new (private) methods. To name these methods, study the condition until you understand it well enough to choose an intention-revealing name.

- *Define method bodies with same level of abstraction.* Long method bodies with comments separating blocks of code violate the rule of thumb that all statements in a single method body should have the same level of abstraction. Refactor such code by introducing a new (private) method for each separated block of code; name the method after the intent recorded in the comment.

Trade-offs   Pros

- *Exposes design.* Not only will the refactoring process improve your understanding of the code, but this understanding will also become explicit in the structure of the code. This will make it easier to further document that understanding by means of Tie Code and Questions (Pattern 5.1) or Write Tests to Understand (Pattern 6.6).

- *Validates incremental approach.* Normally, understanding does not arise as part of a single revelation, but as the result of an iterative process in which earlier understanding is the base for the next iteration. Refactor to Understand encourages such an approach because of its emphasis on small steps and frequent verification (either by running tests or by compiling often).

Cons

- *Risks introducing errors.* The less you change the code, the smaller your chances of introducing errors. Small refactorings should be behavior preserving, but it may be nontrivial to verify that even simple refactorings do not break the code. If you do not have adequate regression tests in place, it can be risky to introduce changes, or costly to develop the needed tests. For these reasons it is important to attempt to Refactor to Understand only on a working copy of the software.

Difficulties

- *Tool support.* Manually refactoring code can be tedious and risky [Fowl99]. Various tools, like the Refactoring Browser [Robe97], greatly

PATTERN 5.2 *continued*

simplify the task of refactoring, and especially help to apply nontrivial refactorings such as Extract Method.

- *Acceptance of changes.* Refactoring someone else's code may prove a lot harder than refactoring your own. A lot of companies have a strong culture of code ownership, so improving someone else's code is often considered an insult. That is one of the reasons why you should not necessarily release the refactored version to the rest of the team.

- *Knowing when to stop.* It is often difficult to stop changing code when you identify problems. Remember that your primary goal here is just to understand the system. When you have achieved that goal, it is time to stop.

Known Uses   Don Roberts and John Brant coined the term "Refactor to Understand" at ESUG'97 and Smalltalk Solution'97 during a demonstration of the Refactoring Browser. They showed how they gradually understood an algorithm by renaming and refactoring its code. During the subsequent iterations of the pattern, the code slowly started to make sense, and the design gradually became explicit in the code.

We applied this pattern ourselves during a FAMOOS case study. We had to understand a single method of about 3000 lines of C++, which was a deeply nested conditional. We first replaced the leaf condition branches by methods, gradually working our way up the nesting structure. After several iterations, we discovered that this method was actually implementing a complete parser for a small command language.

Harry Sneed reports several reengineering projects where a large Cobol program was refactored by removing all goto statements. However, he was later forced to reintroduce the goto statements because the developers rejected his changes [Snee99].

Related Patterns   "Arranging the furniture" [Tayl00] is a pattern to help newcomers feel at home when they start in a new project. The pattern solution is "An adopter should be encouraged to 'move in' by cosmetically arranging the code."

What Next   Refactor to Understand works well in tandem with Tie Code and Questions (Pattern 5.1). Refactorings are more expensive to implement than simply annotating the code, so first annotate, and then refactor. Also, consider applying Write Tests to Understand (Pattern 6.6) as you refactor. These two activities reinforce each other since tests document your understanding of how a software artifact works, and refactoring helps you to expose its design. Furthermore, tests will help you to verify that your refactorings didn't break anything.

When you have finished a round of Refactor to Understand, you must decide what to do with your changes. If you discard the experimental code, you should consider applying Tie Code and Questions (Pattern 5.1) to annotate the code base with the knowledge you have acquired.

PATTERN

5.3 Step through the Execution

Intent: Understand how objects in the system collaborate by stepping through examples in a debugger.

Problem   How do you discover which objects are instantiated at run time and how they collaborate?

This is a difficult problem because

- The source code exposes the class hierarchy, not the objects instantiated at run time and how they interact.
- Collaborations are typically spread out through the code. Although it is easy to see which classes and methods are defined in a system, it can be hard to tell by reading the source code alone which sequence of events will lead to an object being created or a method being invoked.
- In the presence of polymorphism, it can be especially difficult to tell which objects are clients of which service providers. Just because an object uses a certain interface that another object provides does not mean that the former is actually a client of the latter.
- Reading the code will not tell you what concrete scenarios can take place. The actual flow of execution will depend on the internal state of all participating objects, and this cannot be inferred directly from the source code.
- The source code will not tell you which objects are long-lived and which are ephemeral (i.e., local to the execution of a single method).

Yet, solving this problem is feasible because

- You are aware of some typical usage scenarios.
- You can run the code inside a debugger.
- Your attention is focused on a specific part of the system.

PATTERN 5.3 *continued*

Solution   Run each of the scenarios and use your debugger to step through the code. Observe which objects collaborate and how they are instantiated. Afterward, generalize these observations and record your knowledge for future reference, possibly by means of Tie Code and Questions (Pattern 5.1) and Record Business Rules as Tests (Pattern 6.5).

Hints

It is too time-consuming to step through every single statement of a running system. The assumption here is that you are focused on some specific aspect of the system that is difficult to understand.

- Set *breakpoints* to interrupt execution when the system enters the code you are interested in.
- Change the *internal state* of the objects to see how alternative execution paths are triggered.
- *Restart a method* currently on the execution stack to quickly verify a similar scenario.

Trade-offs   Pros

- *Provides a realistic view.* By stepping through the running program, you get a precise picture of how the scenario unfolds. Moreover, you can inspect the internal state of the objects involved, see how new objects are created, and observe which objects collaborate under which circumstances.
- *Handles complexity.* On a small scale it is possible to infer object collaborations from analyzing the source code. Slicing tools, for instance, may tell you which statements of the source code are affected by a given variable. For large and complex systems, however, the number of possibilities and interactions is just too large. Therefore, the only reasonable way to learn how objects collaborate is to study the execution traces.

Cons

- *Scenario based.* You must restrict yourself to a limited set of scenarios; hence the observed object collaborations are necessarily incomplete. Of course you must do your best to choose representative scenarios. Unfortunately, this choice brings you back to square one, because the only way to be sure that you have a representative set of scenarios is to verify whether they cover all possible object collaborations.

- *Restricted applicability.* For systems where time plays a crucial role, stepping through the execution will give you an unrealistic view of the system's behavior. Worse, for concurrent or distributed systems, the mere fact of stepping through concurrent code may perturb the execution of the system itself. As such, you get the same effects as in Heisenberg's uncertainty experiments, where determining exact positions of quantum particles implies that other attributes about these particles become uncertain.

Difficulties

- *Dependency on tools.* You need to have good debugger to Step through the Execution. Not only must it allow the setting and removal of breakpoints dynamically, it also should provide the means to examine the state of the objects involved. And to easily verify alternative paths, the debugger should allow you to change the internal state of an object or even restart a method currently on the execution stack.

What Next You will need concrete scenarios in order to Step through the Execution (possibly inferred from Interview during Demo, Pattern 3.4). Consider encoding these scenarios as test cases. You can then iteratively Write Tests to Understand (Pattern 6.6) as you Step through the Execution since the insights you gain into the states of collaborating objects can then be formulated as concrete tests.

As you Step through the Execution, it is a good idea to keep an eye on the way collaborating objects use each other's interface. Afterward, you can exploit the knowledge you have gained to Look for the Contracts (Pattern 5.4).

PATTERN

5.4   Look for the Contracts

Intent: Infer the proper use of a class interface by studying the way clients currently use it.

Problem How do you determine which *contracts* a class supports? That is, how do you know what a class expects from its client classes in order to function as intended?

PATTERN 5.4 *continued*

This problem is difficult because

- Client/supplier relationships and contracts are only implicit in the code. Although interfaces are easy to extract from the code, they do not necessarily tell you how to use them properly. If not explicitly documented, it can be hard to guess (1) the proper sequence in which methods should be invoked, (2) the valid parameters that should be supplied, (3) which methods should be invoked by which clients, and (4) which methods should be overridden by subclasses.

- Typing and scoping rules often force programmers to compromise the provider's interface. Moreover, encapsulation constructs (e.g., public/private declarations) are frequently misused to cope with implementation issues. For instance, database and user interface toolkits often require the presence of public accessor methods.

Yet, solving this problem is feasible because

- You have a *good understanding* of the system's structure (for example, obtained via "Initial Understanding," Chapter 4), so you can distinguish key classes from less important ones.

- You trust that the class is being used properly by its clients and its subclasses.

Solution   Look for common programming idioms that expose the way clients make use of the class interface. Generalize your observations in the form of *contracts*—explicit declarations of what a class expects from its clients.

Hints

Your goal here is to understand how classes collaborate by exposing the *way* in which the interface to a class is used by its different clients. Since an exhaustive analysis of the code will probably exhaust you, you need some way to expose the contracts without stepping through every single line of code.

Although contracts are only implicit in the code, most frequently there will be hints in the code that a particular relationship exists between various classes. These hints may manifest themselves as idioms particular to the programming language in use, conventions in use by the development team, or even common design patterns.

What precisely you should look for will depend on the context, but here are a few *examples* that are generally useful:

Use Your Tools. To get an overview of the relationships between classes, make the best use you can of the available tools. Although you could analyze the code by hand to infer relationships between classes, the process is tedious when applied to *more than a couple of classes.*

Many organizations use design extraction or round-trip engineering tools to document their systems. You can easily generate a draft view of the system you are analyzing without investing too much time. However, be prepared to be flooded with "boxes and arrows" diagrams containing irrelevant detail. Nevertheless, design extraction tools let you specify filters and ways to interpret code, so once your mappings are defined you can reuse them over multiple extractions.

The design overview can help you to identify key classes in the hierarchy (i.e., abstract classes that many other classes inherit from), part-whole relationships, and so on.

Look for Key Methods. Focus on the most important methods. With your knowledge of the system, you will recognize key methods based on their signature:

- *Method names.* Key methods are likely to bear intention-revealing names [Beck97].

- *Parameter types.* Methods taking parameters with types corresponding to key classes in the system are likely to be important.

- *Recurring parameter types.* Parameters represent temporary associations between objects. When the same parameter types often recur in method signatures, they are likely to represent important associations.

Look for Constructor Calls. To understand how and when to instantiate objects of a particular class, look for methods in other classes invoking the constructors.

Pay particular attention to which parameters are passed to the constructor, and whether the parameters are shared or not. This will help you determine which instance variables are parts of the constructed object and which are merely references to shared objects.

Invocations of constructor methods may reveal a *part-whole relationship.* When a client stores the result of a constructor method in an attribute, then this client will probably serve as the whole. On the other hand, when a client passes itself as an argument to a constructor method, it is likely to act as a part.

Invocations of a constructor method may also expose a Factory Method (Pattern A.13) or even an Abstract Factory (Pattern A.10). If they do, then you know that you will be able to extend the system by subclassing the class under study.

PATTERN 5.4 *continued*

Look for Template/Hook Methods. To understand how to specialize a class, look for (protected) methods that are overridden by subclasses, and identify the public methods that call them. The public calling method is almost certainly a Template Method (Pattern A.21). Check the class hierarchy to determine whether the overridden method is *abstract,* in which case subclasses must implement it, or whether a default implementation is provided. In the latter case, it is a *hook method,* and subclasses may choose to override it or be happy with the default.

For each template method check all the other methods it invokes, as these are likely to represent other hook methods.

Look for Super Calls. To understand what assumptions a class makes about its subclasses, look for super calls. Super calls may be used by subclasses to extend an inherited method in an ad hoc way. But very often super calls express the fact that a particular method *must not be overridden by subclasses* unless the overridden method is explicitly invoked by a super call.

This idiom is heavily used in Java by classes that define multiple constructors. Any subclass of `java.lang.Exception`, for example, is expected to define both a default constructor and a constructor that takes a `String` argument. Those constructors should do nothing in particular except invoke the super constructor so that the exception subclass will be correctly initialized.

Trade-offs   Pros

- *Reliable.* You can trust the source code more than the documentation.

Cons

- *Bad habits linger.* Just because certain practices appear in the code doesn't mean that's the right way to do things. The contracts that clients and subclasses adhere to are not necessarily the ones that the class actually supports.

- *Noisy.* Browsing the source code is like mining—once in a while you will find a gem, but you will have to dig through a lot of dirt first. By focusing your attention on idiomatic usages, you should be able to reduce the noise factor to a large degree.

Known Uses   Many researchers have investigated ways to analyze how clients use a class interface. For instance, Brown [Brow96a], Florijn [Flor97], and Wuyts [Wuyt98] have all shown that it is possible to find symptoms of design patterns in code. Also, Schauer et al. [Scha99] report about a technique to semiautomatically detect hook methods based on analysis of overridden methods. The latter technique scales quite well, due to their particular way of visualizing class hierarchies and emphasizing classes where many methods are overridden and hence are likely to define hook methods. Additionally, Steyaert et al. [Stey96] have shown that it is possible to capture how subclasses depend on their superclasses (they have named these dependencies *reuse contracts*) and afterward detect potential conflicts when the superclasses gets changed.

What Next One way to validate the contracts you have identified is to Step through the Execution (Pattern 5.3). Conversely, as you Step through the Execution you will uncover collaborations between various objects. At that point you may Look for the Contracts that govern those collaborations.

If the code is hard to read, you may wish to Refactor to Understand (Pattern 5.2) before you Look for the Contracts. To understand how the contracts evolved to their current state, you might Learn from the Past (Pattern 5.5).

PATTERN

5.5 Learn from the Past

Intent: Obtain insights into the design by comparing subsequent versions of the system.

Problem How can you discover *why the system is designed the way it is?* How can you learn which parts of the system are stable and which parts aren't?

This problem is difficult because

- The lessons learned during a development process are rarely recorded in documentation. Furthermore, the developers' perceptions and memory of design decisions tend to warp over time. Therefore, you can only rely on source code and must reconstruct the learning process from there.

- The system is large and has been released in successive versions, and therefore you have a large quantity of source code to analyze. Text comparison tools (such as Unix diff) will not scale up for the sizes you're dealing with.

PATTERN 5.5 *continued*

- Even if you have a tool to identify the changes between two subsequent releases, most of the changes will concern adding *new* functionality. For the reconstruction of the learning process and how this consolidated into the class design, your main interest lies in what happened with the *old* functionality.

Yet, solving this problem is feasible because

- You have a *good understanding* of the system's structure (for example, obtained via "Initial Understanding," Chapter 4), so you're able to focus on appropriate subsystems.
- You have access to the *subsequent releases* of the system, so you can reconstruct the changes by comparing the source code of the versions.
- You have the means to examine what happened with individual source code entities. For instance, you have a *metrics tool* at your disposal, which allows you to quantify the size of entities in the source code and use these numbers as a basis for comparison. As an alternative, you have a *configuration management system* that can provide you with information about particular changes to source code entities.
- You have enough *expertise with refactorings* in the implementation language being used, so you are able to recognize refactorings from their effects on source code. Moreover, once you know which refactorings have been applied, you can use this expertise to make an educated guess at the underlying design rationale.
- You have a *source code browser* that allows you to query which methods invoke a given operation (even for polymorphic operations), so you can find out dependencies between classes and investigate how they are affected by the refactorings.

Solution   Use the metrics or configuration management tool to find entities where functionality has been *removed* because such entities are a sign of a consolidating design. Also, look for entities that change often, as these may point you to an unstable part of the design.

Hints

Your goal is to get a feeling for how and why the system has evolved to its current state. In particular, you want to understand which parts of the system have been heavily refactored, which parts have become stable, and which parts are hot spots of activity.

Portions of the software system that have been heavily extended are simply a sign of growth, not of evolution of the design. On the other hand, portions where software has been *removed* are signs that the design of the system has been altered. By understanding how it has been altered, you can obtain insights into the stability of the design.

Unstable design. If you detect repeated growth and refactoring in the same portion of the system, that should be a sign that the design is unstable. It may indicate opportunities to redesign that portion of the system to better accommodate the kinds of changes and extensions that habitually take place.

Mature and stable design. A mature subsystem will exhibit some growth and refactoring, followed by a period of stability. Early versions of the subsystem will show growth followed by refactoring, followed by a period in which only new classes and subclasses are added. As the hierarchy stabilizes, classes near the top of the hierarchy will exhibit only moderate growth, but little refactoring.

Trade-offs Pros

- *Concentrates on important design artifacts.* The changes point you to those places where the design is expanding or consolidating, and this in turn provides insight into the underlying design rationale.

- *Provides an unbiased view of the system.* You do not have to formulate assumptions about what to expect in the software (in contrast to top-down techniques like Speculate about Design, Pattern 4.2).

Cons

- *Requires considerable experience.* The reverse engineer must be well aware of how the refactorings interact with the coding idioms in the particular implementation language.

- *Requires considerable tool support.* You need (1) a metrics tool or a configuration management system and (2) a code browser that is able to trace back polymorphic method invocations.

Difficulties

- *Imprecise for many changes.* When too many changes have been applied on the same piece of code, it becomes difficult to reconstruct the change process.

PATTERN 5.5 *continued*

- *Sensitive to renaming.* If one identifies classes and methods via their name,[1] then rename operations will show up as removals and additions, which makes interpreting the data more difficult.

Rationale   Many object-oriented systems came into being via a combination of iterative and incremental development (see [Booc94] [Gold95] [Jaco97] [Reen96]). That is, the original development team recognized their lack of problem domain expertise and therefore invested in a learning process where each learning phase resulted in a new system release. It is worthwhile to reconstruct that learning process because it will help you to understand the rationale embodied in the system design.

One way to reconstruct the learning process is to recover its primitive steps. In object-oriented parlance, these steps are called refactorings, and consequently this pattern tells you how to recover refactorings as they have been applied in the past. The technique itself compares two subsequent releases of the source code, identifying entities that decrease in size, because that's the typical symptom of functionality that has been moved elsewhere.

Known Uses   We ran an experiment on three medium-sized systems implemented in Smalltalk. As reported in [Deme00], these case studies suggest that some simple heuristics can support the reverse engineering process by focusing attention on parts of the system where functionality has been removed. This way we could, for instance, detect where a class had been split or where methods had been moved to a sibling class. Of course these refactorings must be examined in further detail to guess the intent behind the refactoring. This is never easy, but in our experience it has proven worthwhile. In one particular case, for instance, we discovered several classes where methods had been moved to sibling classes. Closer examination revealed that the reengineer was moving these methods to break circular dependencies and was in fact introducing a layer.

Other researchers also report on examining changes to support the reverse engineering process. For instance, Ball and Eick annotate code views with colors showing code age [Ball96]. On the other hand, Jazayeri et al. use a three-dimensional visual representation for examining a system's software release history [Jaza99]. The same people have also investigated which

---

1. Note that some configuration management systems keep track of renaming operations, which will of course alleviate the problem.

change requests affect which software modules to detect logical dependencies between software modules [Gall98].

What Next   Now that you have discovered some stable parts in the design, you will probably want to reuse them. In that case take some precautions: first document the interfaces of that part (see Look for the Contracts, Pattern 5.4) and then write the corresponding test cases (see Test the Interface, Not the Implementation, Pattern 3.1).

On the other hand, the unstable parts of the design should probably be dismissed. Nevertheless, if the unstable part seems crucial for your reengineering project, then you must seek which change requests caused the instability. In that case, Chat with the Maintainers (Pattern 3.1) or even Interview during Demo (Pattern 3.4), and based on this knowledge decide how to restructure that part so that it is better suited for the kind of change requests that come in.

PART **2**

Reengineering

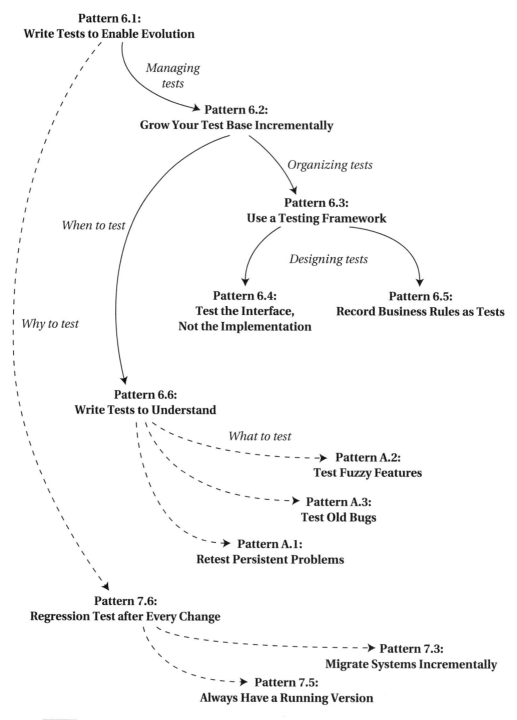

Pattern 6.1:
Write Tests to Enable Evolution

Managing tests

Pattern 6.2:
Grow Your Test Base Incrementally

Organizing tests

Pattern 6.3:
Use a Testing Framework

When to test

Designing tests

Pattern 6.4:
Test the Interface,
Not the Implementation

Pattern 6.5:
Record Business Rules as Tests

Why to test

Pattern 6.6:
Write Tests to Understand

What to test

Pattern A.2:
Test Fuzzy Features

Pattern A.3:
Test Old Bugs

Pattern A.1:
Retest Persistent Problems

Pattern 7.6:
Regression Test after Every Change

Pattern 7.3:
Migrate Systems Incrementally

Pattern 7.5:
Always Have a Running Version

FIGURE **6.1** When, why, how, and what to test.

## CHAPTER 6

Tests: Your Life Insurance!

You are at the beginning of a reengineering project. You know that you will have to perform radical surgery on many parts of a valuable legacy system. You are wondering how you will be able to minimize the risks of changing a system on which your business depends: the risk of *breaking features* that used to work, the risk of *spending too much effort on the wrong tasks,* the risk of *failing to integrate needed new functionality* into the system, and the risk of *further increasing maintenance costs.*

The patterns presented in this cluster present effective ways of using tests in a reengineering context to reduce the risks posed by reengineering changes.

Caveat: Testing is a rich and important subject that can scarcely be covered in any depth in the few pages we devote to it in this chapter. We have done no more than identify a few of the more significant testing patterns that are especially relevant to reengineering projects, and briefly sketch out some of the key issues. Binder, for example, devotes an entire book to testing object-oriented systems [Bind99].

Forces

These patterns share common forces that concern various elements of risk for the evolution of the legacy system. Each pattern addresses some of these forces in order to achieve a certain balance between effort and risk. Certain forces are inherent to reengineering:

- Legacy systems often do not have test procedures defined.

- Changing parts of a system without introducing new bugs is a challenging task.

Other forces concern system development:

- Not every aspect of a system can be tested.

- Certain aspects like concurrency and user interfaces are difficult to test.

- Under time pressure, writing tests is always the task that is eliminated first.

- Having all the knowledge of a system concentrated in only a few people poses a high risk for the future of the project.

Customers come into a project with certain expectations:

- Customers ultimately do not pay for tests but for new features in the system.

- An unstable or buggy system is not acceptable for customers.

Testing is not typically a programmer's prime concern:

- Programmers believe they do not need tests, since they write good code.

- Programmers are not motivated by long-term goals, since they may leave the project a month from now.

- Programmers are more interested in tools and processes that can reduce the time they are losing in identifying problems.

- Fixing bugs is not fun.

- Writing tests is not considered to be a noble task.

Overview

As shown in Figure 6.1 on page 120, Write Tests to Enable Evolution (Pattern 6.1) is the root of this cluster. It explains why systematic tests are critical to reengineering projects and what kinds of tests are necessary. It is based on Grow Your Test Base Incrementally (Pattern 6.2), which advocates strategies for introducing new tests as you need them.

In order to effectively manage the incremental introduction of tests, it is important to Use a Testing Framework (Pattern 6.3) to structure and organize suites of tests. The testing framework should support you in designing certain styles of tests. In particular, if you Test the Interface, Not the Implementation (Pattern 6.4) of components, by using black-box testing strategies, then your tests will tend to be more useful in the face of system changes. Furthermore, if you can Record Business Rules as Tests (Pattern 6.5), then you will have an effective way to keep the business rules explicitly represented and continuously synchronized with the running system even in the presence of radical changes.

Tests may be introduced at various times for various reasons. Write Tests to Understand (Pattern 6.1) advocates investing testing effort in those parts of the system that you need to understand in order to implement changes. More specifically, it is a good idea to Test Fuzzy Features (Pattern A.2), to Test Old Bugs (Pattern A.3), and especially to Retest Persistent Problems (Pattern A.1).

The patterns in this cluster directly support "Migration Strategies" (Chapter 7) for reengineering: Regression Test after Every Change (Pattern 7.6) helps you build confidence by ensuring that everything still runs after every incremental change to the system. In effect, tests are a necessary precondition to Always Have a Running Version (Pattern 7.5), and they enable you to Migrate Systems Incrementally (Pattern 7.3).

PATTERN
6.1 Write Tests to Enable Evolution

Intent: Protect your investment in the legacy code by imposing a systematic testing program.

Problem How do you minimize the risks of a reengineering project, specifically, the risks of

- failing to simplify the legacy system
- introducing yet more complexity to the system
- breaking features that used to work
- spending too much effort on the wrong tasks
- failing to accommodate future change?

This problem is difficult because

- The impact of changes cannot always be predicted because parts of the system may not be well understood or may have hidden dependencies.
- Any change to a legacy system may destabilize it due to undocumented aspects or dependencies.

Yet, solving this problem is feasible because

- You have a running system, so you can determine what works and what doesn't work.
- You know which parts of the system are stable, and which are subject to change.

PATTERN 6.1 *continued*

Solution   Introduce a testing process based on tests that are *automated, repeatable,* and *stored.*

Hints

Well-designed tests exhibit the following properties:

- *Automation.* Tests should run without human intervention. Only fully automated tests offer an efficient way to check after every change to the system whether it still works as it did before. By minimizing the effort needed to run tests, developers will hesitate less to use them.

- *Persistence.* Tests must be stored to be automatable. Each test documents its test data, the actions to perform, and the expected results. A test succeeds if the expected result is obtained; otherwise it fails. Stored tests document the way the system is expected to work.

- *Repeatability.* Confidence in the system is increased if tests can be repeated after any change is implemented. Whenever new functionality is added, new tests can be added to the pool of existing tests, thereby increasing the confidence in the system.

- *Unit testing.* Tests should be associated with individual software components so that they identify clearly which part of the system they test [Davi95].

- *Independence.* Each test should minimize its dependencies on other tests. Dependent tests typically result in avalanche effects: when one test breaks, many others break as well. It is important that the number of failures represent quantitatively the size of the detected problems. This minimizes distrust in the tests. Programmers should believe in tests.

Trade-offs   Pros

- Tests increase your confidence in the system and improve your ability to change the functionality, the design, and even the architecture of the system in a behavior-preserving way.

- Tests document how artifacts of a system are to be used. In contrast to written documentation, running tests are an always up-to-date description of the system.

- Selling testing to clients who are concerned with security and stability is not usually a problem. Assuring the long-term life of the system is also a good argument.

- Tests provide the necessary climate for enabling future system evolution.
- Simple unit testing frameworks exist for all the main object-oriented languages like Smalltalk, Java, C++, and even perl.

Cons

- Tests do not come free. Resources must be allocated to write them.
- Tests can only demonstrate the presence of defects. It is impossible to test all the aspects of a legacy system (or any system, for that matter).
- Inadequate tests will give you false confidence. You may think your system is working well because all the tests run, but this might not be the case at all.

Difficulties

- A plethora of testing approaches exists. Choose a simple approach that fits your development process.
- Testing legacy systems is difficult because they tend to be large and undocumented. Sometimes testing a part of a system requires a large and complex set-up procedure, which may seem prohibitive.
- Management may be reluctant to invest in testing. Here are some arguments in favor of testing:
  - Testing helps to improve the safety of the system.
  - Tests represent a tangible form of confidence in the system functionality.
  - Debugging is easier when automated tests exist.
  - Tests are simple documentation that is always in sync with the application.
- Developers may be reluctant to adopt testing. Build a business case to show them that tests will not only speed up today's development, but they will speed up future maintenance efforts. Once we talked with a developer who spent one day fixing a bug and then three more days checking if the changes he made were valid. When we showed him that automated tests could help him in his daily work to debug his program more quickly, he was finally convinced.
- Testing can be boring for developers, so at least use the right tools. For unit testing, SUnit and its many variants are simple, free, and available for Smalltalk, C++, Java, and other languages [Beck98].

PATTERN 6.1 *continued*

Example   The following code illustrates a unit test written using JUnit in Java [Beck98]. The test checks that the add operation defined on a class Money works as expected, namely, that 12 + 14 = 26.

```java
public class MoneyTest extends TestCase {
  // ...
    public void testSimpleAdd() {
      Money m12CHF= new Money(12, "CHF");          // (1)
      Money m14CHF= new Money(14, "CHF");
      Money expected= new Money(26, "CHF");
      Money result= m12CHF.add(m14CHF);            // (2)
      assert(result.currency().equals(expected.currency())
        && result.amount() == expected.amount());   // (3)
    }
}
```

This satisfies the properties that a test should have:

- This test is *automated:* it returns the boolean value true if the action is the right one and false otherwise.

- It is *stored:* it is a method of a test class, so it can be versioned like any other code.

- It is *repeatable:* its initialization part (1) produces the context in which the test can be run and rerun indefinitely.

- It is *independent* of the other tests.

Using tests with these properties helps you to build a test suite for the long term. Every time you write a test, either after a bug fix or after adding a new feature, or to test an already existing aspect of the system, you are adding *reproducible* and *verifiable* information about your system into your test suite. Especially in the context of reengineering a system, this fact is important because this reproducible and verifiable information can be checked after any change to see if aspects of a system are compromised.

Rationale   Tests represent confidence in a system because they specify how parts of the system work in a *verifiable* way, and because they can be run at any time to check if the system is still consistent.

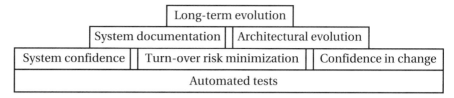

FIGURE **6.2** Automated tests are the *foundation* of reengineering. They establish your confidence in the system, reduce risks, and improve confidence in your ability to change the system.

> . . . testing simply exposes the presence of flaws in a program; it cannot be used to verify the absence of flaws. It can increase your confidence that a program is correct.
>
> [Davi95], Principle 111

Systematic testing is heavily promoted by Extreme Programming [Beck00] as one of the basic techniques necessary to be able to adapt programs quickly to changing requirements. Changing legacy systems is risky business. Will the code still work after a change? How many unexpected side effects will appear? Having a set of automated, repeatable tests helps to reduce this risk (see Figure 6.2).

- A set of running tests provides confidence in the system. ("Are you really sure this piece of code works?" "Yes. Look, here I have the tests that prove it.")

- A set of running tests represents *reproducible* and *verifiable* information about your system and is at all times in sync with the application. This is in contrast to most of the written documentation, which is typically slightly outdated already the next day.

- Writing tests increases productivity because bugs are found much earlier in the development process.

Related Patterns Write Tests to Enable Evolution is a prerequisite to Always Have a Running Version (Pattern 7.5). Only with a comprehensive test program in place can you Migrate Systems Incrementally (Pattern 7.3).

Grow Your Test Base Incrementally (Pattern 6.2) and Test the Interface, Not the Implementation (Pattern 6.4) introduce a way to incrementally build a test suite while a system is evolving.

PATTERN

| 6.2 | **Grow Your Test Base Incrementally** |

Intent: Balance the costs and the benefits of tests by incrementally introducing just the tests you need at a given point in time.

Problem   When should you start to introduce tests? When can you stop?

This problem is difficult because

- In a reengineering project, you cannot afford to spend too much time on writing tests.
- Legacy systems tend to be huge, so testing everything is impossible.
- Legacy systems tend to be poorly documented and poorly understood.
- The original developers may have left, and the system maintainers may have only limited knowledge of the system's inner workings.

Yet, solving this problem is feasible because

- We know where the fragile parts or the parts that we would like to change are.
- We can convince programmers that they can benefit from tests.

Solution   Introduce tests incrementally for parts of the system you are working on.

Hints

- Carefully assess your priorities and initially develop tests only for the most critical components. As you reengineer the system, introduce tests for the new features, parts of the legacy that may be affected, and any bugs you identify along the way.
- Keep a snapshot of the old system handy so you can later introduce tests that should run against both the original system and its new incarnation.
- Focus on business values. Start to write tests for the parts of your system that have the most important artifacts. Try to Record Business Rules as Tests (Pattern 6.5).
- If you have the history of bug fixes or problems, apply Test Old Bugs (Pattern A.3) as a starting point.

- If you have acceptable documentation and some original developers of the system at hand, consider applying Test Fuzzy Features (Pattern A.2).

- Apply Test the Interface, Not the Implementation (Pattern 6.4), start to test big abstractions, and then refine tests if time allows. For example, if you have a pipeline architecture, start to write tests that ensure you that the output of the full pipeline is right given the right input. Then write tests for the individual pipeline components.

- Black-box test parts (subsystems, classes, methods) that are likely to change their implementation in the future.

Trade-offs Pros

- You save time by only developing the tests that you need.
- You build up a base of the most critical tests as the project progresses.
- You build confidence as you go along.
- You streamline future development and maintenance activities.

Cons

- You may guess wrong which aspects are critical to test.
- Tests can give you false confidence—untested bugs can still lurk in the system.

Difficulties

- Setting up the proper context for the tests may require considerable time and effort.
- Identifying the boundaries of the components to test is just hard. Deciding which parts to test and how fine-grained these tests should be requires a good understanding of the system and the way you intend to reengineer it.

Example Initially introduce tests only for the subsystems and components you intend to change. In Figure 6.3 we introduce some tests for subsystem ABC and for its component B. We apply Test the Interface, Not the Implementation (Pattern 6.4) to ensure that the tests for B should also pass for newB.

Note that if we only introduce tests for component B, then we fail to test its integration with A and C. In any case, it may be that we fail to test all important aspects, so it is important to incrementally add new tests as bugs are detected and repaired.

PATTERN 6.2 *continued*

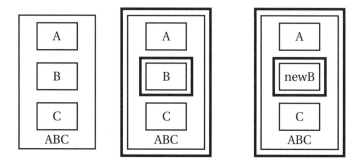

FIGURE **6.3**   Introduce tests for the parts of the system you intend to change.

Rationale   An incremental testing strategy allows you to start reengineering efforts before all the tests are in place. By focusing on just those tests that concern the parts of the system you are currently changing, you enable change with a minimal investment in testing, while you help your team build confidence as you grow your test base.

Related Patterns   Use a Testing Framework (Pattern 6.3) to organize your tests.

Test the Interface, Not the Implementation (Pattern 6.4) provides a strategy for developing tests at arbitrary granularities. Record Business Rules as Tests (Pattern 6.5) provides another strategy for testing components that implement business logic. Write Tests to Understand (Pattern 6.6) helps you prime a test base while you are still reverse engineering the system.

PATTERN

6.3   **Use a Testing Framework**

Intent: Encourage developers to write and use regression tests by providing a framework that makes it easy to develop, organize, and run tests.

Problem   How do you encourage your team to adopt systematic testing?

This problem is difficult because

- Tests are boring to write.
- Tests may require considerable test data to be built up and torn down.

- It may be hard to distinguish between test failures and unexpected errors.

Yet, solving this problem is feasible because

- Most tests follow the same basic pattern: create some test data, perform some actions, see if the results match your expectations, clean up the test data.
- Very little infrastructure is needed to run tests and report failures and errors.

Solution Use a testing framework that allows suites of tests to be composed from individual test cases.

Steps

Unit testing frameworks, like JUnit and SUnit [Beck98], and various commercial test harness packages are available for most programming languages. If a suitable testing framework is not available for the programming language you are using, you can easily brew your own according to the following principles:

- The user must provide test cases that set up test data, exercise them, and make assertions about the results.
- The testing framework should wrap test cases as tests that can distinguish between assertion failures and unexpected errors.
- The framework should provide only minimal feedback if tests succeed. Assertion failures should indicate precisely which test failed. Errors should result in more detailed feedback (such as a full stack trace).
- The framework should allow tests to be composed as test suites.

Trade-offs ### Pros

- A testing framework simplifies the formulation of tests and encourages programmers to write tests and use them.

Cons

- Testing requires commitment, discipline, and support. You must convince your team of the need and benefits of disciplined testing, and you must integrate testing into your daily process. One way of supporting this discipline is to have one testing coach in your team; consider this when you Appoint a Navigator (Pattern 2.2).

PATTERN 6.3 *continued*

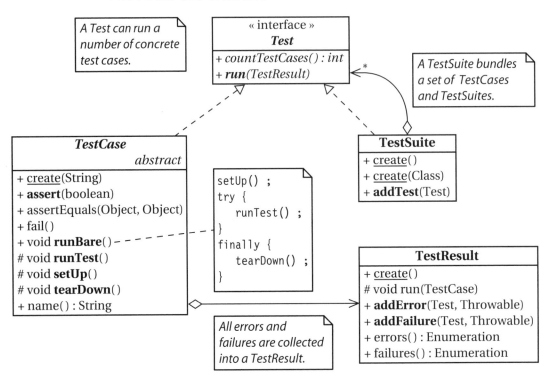

FIGURE **6.4**   JUnit is a popular testing framework for Java that offers much more flexibility than the minimal scheme described earlier.

Example   JUnit is a popular testing framework for Java, which considerably enhances the basic scheme described previously. Figure 6.4 shows that the framework requires users to define their tests as subclasses of TestCase. Users must provide the methods setUp(), runTest(), and tearDown(). The default implementations of setup() and tearDown() are empty, and the default implementation of runTest() looks for and runs a method that is the name of the test (given in the constructor). These user-supplied hook methods are then called by the runBare() template method.

JUnit manages the reporting of failures and errors with the help of an additional TestResult class. In the design of JUnit, it is an instance of TestResult that actually runs the tests and logs errors or failures. In Figure 6.5 we see a scenario in which a TestCase, in its run method, passes control to an instance of TestResult, which in turn calls the runBare template method of the TestCase.

TestCase additionally provides a set of different kinds of standard assertion methods, such as assertEquals, assertFails, and so on. Each of

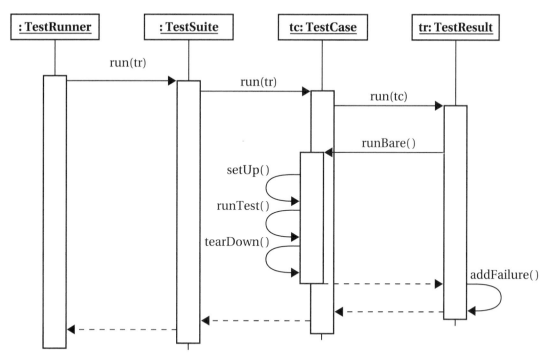

FIGURE **6.5** In JUnit, tests are actually run by an instance of TestResult, which invokes the runBare template method of a TestCase. The user only needs to provide the setUp() and tearDown() methods and the test method to be invoked by runTest().

these methods throws an AssertionFailedError, which can be distinguished from any other kind of exception.

In order to use the framework, we will typically define a new class, say, TestHashtable, that bundles a set of test suites for a given class, Hashtable, that we would like to test. The test class should extend junit.framework.TestCase:

```
import junit.framework.*;
import java.util.Hashtable;
public class TestHashtable extends TestCase {
```

The instance variables of the test class will hold the *fixture*—the actual test data:

```
private Hashtable boss_;
private String joe = "Joe";
private String mary = "Mary";
private String dave = "Dave";
private String boris = "Boris";
```

PATTERN 6.3 *continued*

There should be a constructor that takes the name of a test case as its parameter. Its behavior is defined by its superclass:

```
public TestHashtable(String name) {
  super(name);
}
```

The setUp() hook method can be overridden to set up the fixture. If there is any cleanup activity to be performed, we should also override tearDown(). Their default implementations are empty.

```
protected void setUp() {
  boss_ = new Hashtable();
}
```

We can then define any number of test cases that make use of the fixture. Note that each test case is independent and will have a fresh copy of the fixture. (In principle, we should design tests that not only exercise the entire interface, but the test data should cover both typical and boundary cases. The sample tests shown here are far from complete.)

Each test case should start with the characters "test":

```
public void testEmpty() {
  assert(boss_.isEmpty());
  assertEquals(boss_.size(), 0);
  assert(!boss_.contains(joe));
  assert(!boss_.containsKey(joe));
}

public void testBasics() {
  boss_.put(joe, mary);
  boss_.put(mary, dave);
  boss_.put(boris, dave);

  assert(!boss_.isEmpty());
  assertEquals(boss_.size(), 3);
  assert(boss_.contains(mary));
  assert(!boss_.contains(joe));
  assert(boss_.containsKey(mary));
  assert(!boss_.containsKey(dave));
  assertEquals(boss_.get(joe), mary);
  assertEquals(boss_.get(mary), dave);
  assertEquals(boss_.get(dave), null);
}
```

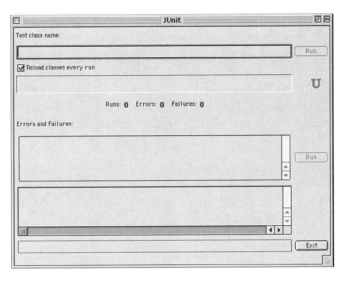

FIGURE **6.6** An instance of java.ui.TestRunner.

You may provide a static method `suite()` that will build an instance of `junit.framework.TestSuite` from the test cases defined by this class:

```
public static TestSuite suite() {
  TestSuite suite = new TestSuite();
  suite.addTest(new TestHashtable("testBasics"));
  suite.addTest(new TestHashtable("testEmpty"));
  return suite;
  }
}
```

The test case class should be compiled, together with any class it depends on.

To run the tests, we can start up any one of a number of *test runner* classes provided by the JUnit framework, for instance `junit.ui.TestRunner` (see Figure 6.6).

This particular test runner expects you to type in the name of the test class. You may then *run* the tests defined by this class. The test runner will look for the suite method and use it to build an instance of `TestSuite`. If you do not provide a static `suite` method, the test runner will automatically build a test suite assuming that all the methods named test* are test cases. The test runner then runs the resulting test suite. The interface will report how many tests succeeded (see Figure 6.7). A successful test run will show a green display. If any individual test fails, the display will be red, and details of the test case leading to the failure will be given.

PATTERN 6.3 *continued*

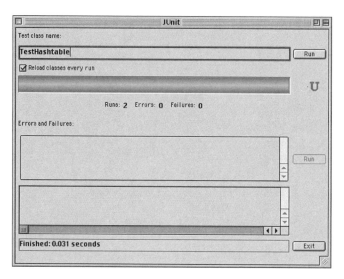

FIGURE   **6.7**   A successful test run.

Rationale   A testing framework makes it easier to organize and run tests.
Hierarchically organizing tests makes it easier to run just the tests that concern the part of the system you are working on.

Known Uses   Testing frameworks exist for a vast number of languages, including Ada, ANT, C , C++, Delphi, .Net (all languages), Eiffel, Forte 4GL, GemStone/S, Jade, JavaScript, k language (ksql, from kbd), Objective C, Open Road (CA), Oracle, perl, Php, PowerBuilder, Python, Rebolþ Ruby, Smalltalk, Visual Objects, and Visual Basic.
Beck and Gamma give a good overview in the context of JUnit [Beck98].

PATTERN

6.4   **Test the Interface, Not the Implementation**

Also Known As: Black-Box Testing [Pres94]

Intent: Build up reusable tests that focus on external behavior rather than on implementation details and that thereby will survive changes to the system.

Problem How can you develop tests that not only protect your software legacy, but also will continue to be valuable as the system changes?

This problem is difficult because

- Legacy systems have many features that should continue to function as the system evolves.
- You cannot afford to spend too much time writing tests while reengineering the system.
- You do not want to waste effort in developing tests that will have to be changed as you change the system.

Yet, solving this problem is feasible because

- The interfaces to the components of the system tell you what should be tested.
- Interfaces tend to be more stable than implementations.

Solution Develop black-box tests that exercise the public interface of your components.

Hints

- Be sure to exercise boundary values (i.e., minimum and maximum values for method parameters). The most common errors occur here.
- Use a top-down strategy to develop black-box tests if there are many fine-grained components that you do not initially have time to develop tests for.
- Use a bottom-up strategy if you are replacing functionality in a very focused part of the legacy system.

Trade-offs Pros

- Tests that exercise public interfaces are more likely to be reusable if the implementation changes.
- Black-box tests can often be used to exercise multiple implementations of the same interface.
- It is relatively easy to develop tests based on a component's interface.
- Focusing on the external behavior reduces considerably the possible tests to be written while still covering the essential aspects of a system.

PATTERN 6.4 *continued*

Cons

- Back-box tests will not necessarily exercise all possible program paths. You may have to use a separate coverage tool to check whether your tests cover all the code.

- If the interface to a component changes, you will still have to adapt the tests.

Difficulties

- Sometimes the class does not provide the right interface to support black-box testing. Adding accessors to sample the state of the object can be a simple solution, but this generally weakens encapsulation and makes the object *less* of a black box.

Example   Let's look back at the test presented in Write Tests to Enable Evolution (Pattern 6.1). The code we saw earlier was supposed to check whether the add operation defined on a class Money works as expected. However, we see that the assert in line (3) actually depends on the internal implementation of the Money class because it checks for equality by accessing the two attributes.

```
public class MoneyTest extends TestCase {
  //...
    public void testSimpleAdd() {
      Money m12CHF= new Money(12, "CHF");            // (1)
      Money m14CHF= new Money(14, "CHF");
      Money expected= new Money(26, "CHF");
      Money result= m12CHF.add(m14CHF);              // (2)
      assert(result.currency().equals(expected.currency())
        && result.amount() == expected.amount());    // (3)
    }
}
```

However, if the class Money would override the default equals operation defined on Object (doing so would also require overriding hashCode), the last assert statement could be simplified and would become independent of the internal implementation.

```
public class MoneyTest extends TestCase {
  //...
    public void testSimpleAdd() {
```

```
        Money m12CHF= new Money(12, "CHF");          // (1)
        Money m14CHF= new Money(14, "CHF");
        Money expected= new Money(26, "CHF");
        Money result= m12CHF.add(m14CHF);            // (2)
        assert(expected.equals(result));             // (3)
      }
    }
```

Rationale   The interface of a component is a direct consequence of its collaborations with other components. Black-box tests therefore have a good chance of exercising the most important interactions of a system.

Since interfaces tend to be more stable than implementations, black-box tests have a good chance of surviving major changes to the system, and they thereby protect your investment in developing tests.

Known Uses   Black-box testing is a standard testing strategy [Somm96].

Related Patterns   Record Business Rules as Tests (Pattern 6.5) adopts a different strategy to develop tests that focuses on exercising business rules. This is fine if the components to be tested are the ones that implement the business logic. For most other components, Test the Interface, Not the Implementation will likely be more appropriate.

Components that implement complex algorithms may not be well suited to black-box testing, since an analysis of the interface alone may not reveal all the cases that the algorithm should handle. White-box testing [Somm96] is another standard technique for testing algorithms in which test cases are generated to cover all possible paths through an algorithm.

PATTERN

6.5   Record Business Rules as Tests

Intent: Keep the system in sync with the business rules it implements by encoding the rules explicitly as tests.

Problem   How do you keep the *actual business rules,* the *documentation* about those business rules, and the system *implementation* in sync, while all three are changing?

PATTERN 6.5 *continued*

This problem is difficult because

- Written documentation gets out of date quickly and does not ensure you that your system really implements the description of the business rules you have.
- Business rules tend to be implicit in the code. It may not be obvious which pieces of software are responsible for computing a given business rule.
- Developer turnover introduces a high risk for your business by having more and more people knowing less and less about the system.
- Most of the time only one programmer or user knows specific rules, and that person could be leaving tomorrow.
- Business rules are likely to change due to external factors, such as the introduction of a new law, so it is important to represent them explicitly.

Yet, solving this problem is feasible because

- Most business rules are well expressed by sets of canonical examples, each of which requires certain well-defined actions to be taken and results in some clear, observable results.

Solution   Write executable tests that record the business rules as test cases, actions, and tests over the results. When tests break, you know that things are out of sync.

Hints

- Developers and clients can write tests. Developers may write tests associated with specific functionality or a piece of code. Users may also have to write integration tests in the form of use cases that bind together several unit tests [Davi95] [Beck00].
- Note that you are not interested in the implementation strategies or optimization aspects, but only the business rules.

Trade-offs   Pros

- The rules become explicit, thereby reducing dependency on human memory.

- You need to record the business rules anyway before you can reengineer the legacy system.

- Recording business rules as tests enables evolution: when new features must be added, you can check that the existing business rules are still correctly implemented by running the regression tests. On the other hand, when the business rules change, you can update the corresponding tests to reflect the changes.

Cons

- Tests can only encode concrete scenarios, not the actual logic of the business rules themselves.

- When the business logic must deal with an extremely large number of cases, it may be impractical to test them all.

Difficulties

- Recording business rules does not mean extracting them. Extracting business rules from code with the current technology is a pipe dream.

- Recording business rules can be difficult for a system whose original developers and users have all left.

Examples   In this example we compute the amount of additional money an employee receives for a child. The rule states that a person or couple gets an amount of money for every child he, she, or they raise. Basically parents get 150 Swiss francs per month for every child younger than 12 years, and 180 Swiss francs for every child between 12 and 18 and for every child between 18 and 25 as long as the child is not working and is still in the educational system. A single parent gets the full 100% of this money as long as he or she is working more than 50%. Couples get a percentage of the money that is equal to the summed working percentages of both partners.

   The following Smalltalk code shows a test that hardcodes the expected outcomes for the different computations. It allows for automatically checking the outcomes instead of having to print the outcomes and check by hand if they are right, and it acts as a regression test. It also documents the expected outcome of the different computations.

```
testMoneyGivenForKids
    | singlePerson80occupationWithOneKidOf5
      couplePerson40occupationWithOneKidOf5
      couplePerson100occupationWith2KsidOf5
      couplePersonWithOneKidOf14 |
```

PATTERN 6.5 *continued*

```
"cases are extracted from a database after the system has
performed the computation"

singlePerson80WithOneKidOf5 := extract....
couplePerson40occupationWithOneKidOf5 := extract....
couplePerson100occupationWithOneKidOf5 := extract....
couplePersonWithOneKidOf14 := extract....
"tests"
"We test that the right amount of money is computed correctly"

self assert: singlePerson80occupationWithOneKidOf5 moneyForKid = 150.
self assert: couplePerson40occupationWithOneKidOf5 moneyForKid = 150*4.
self assert: couplePerson100occupationWith2KidsOf5 moneyForKid = 150*2.
self assert: couplePersonWithOneKidOf14 moneyForKid = 180.
```

Rationale   Tests are a good way to document what the system does. By documenting business rules as tests, you guarantee that the description of the business rules will be in sync with the implementation.

The beginning of a reengineering project is a good point in time to set up a process to document knowledge about the system as explicit tests.

Related Patterns   While you are reverse engineering a legacy system, you may Write Tests to Understand (Pattern 6.6). During this process it will be natural to Record Business Rules as Tests. In this way you can prime your test base as you Grow Your Test Base Incrementally (Pattern 6.2).

PATTERN

6.6   **Write Tests to Understand**

Intent: Record your understanding of a piece of code in the form of executable tests, thus setting the stage for future changes.

Problem   How do you develop an understanding of a part of a legacy system that contains neither tests nor accurate and precise documentation?

This problem is difficult because

• Code is always difficult to understand.

- You would like to make hypotheses about what the code is really doing and validate them.

- You would like to specify as precisely as possible the behavior of the system.

- You would like to record your understanding to communicate it, but you do not want to waste your time writing documents that will be obsolete as soon as you start changing the code.

Yet, solving this problem is feasible because

- The piece of code is *relatively small* and has clearly defined boundaries.
- You have the possibility to specify tests and validate them.

Solution Encode your hypotheses and conclusions as executable tests.

Trade-offs Pros

- Tests help you to validate your understanding.

- Tests can provide a precise specification of certain aspects of the system. Tests cannot be fuzzy.

- Tests can be applied to gain different levels of understanding. For example, black-box tests can help you to refine your understanding of roles and collaborations, whereas white-box tests can help you to gain understanding of the implementation of complex logic.

- The tests that you develop will help to enable future reengineering efforts.

- Tests will force you to be precise about the creation and use of the objects under test.

Cons

- Writing tests is time-consuming.

Difficulties

- Obtaining a well-defined context in which you can test the objects is difficult, especially if the objects to be tested do not represent specific abstractions. Looking for the places where objects you want to understand are created can help.

- Concurrent systems are known to be difficult to test, so tests can miss important aspects (such as handling of race conditions).

PATTERN 6.6 *continued*

Rationale By writing automated tests, you exercise parts of the system you want to understand, while recording your understanding and setting the stage for future reengineering efforts.

Related Patterns Before writing any tests, you might want to Refactor to Understand (Pattern 5.2). As you write your tests, be sure to Tie Code and Questions (Pattern 5.1).

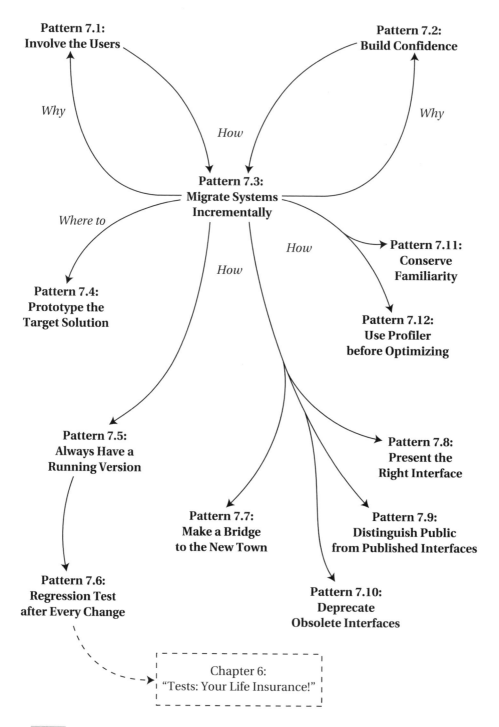

FIGURE **7.1** How, why, and whither to migrate legacy systems.

## CHAPTER 7

Migration Strategies

Your reengineering project is well underway. You have developed a good understanding of the legacy system, and you have started to Write Tests to Enable Evolution (Pattern 6.1). You have gone through a process of "Setting Direction" (Chapter 2) and have decided to tackle the Most Valuable First (Pattern 2.4).

How can you be sure that the new system will be accepted by users? How do you migrate to the new system while the old system is being used? How can you test and evaluate the new system before it is finished?

Forces

The strategies you adopt to migrate from the legacy system to the new solution must resolve the following forces:

- Big-bang migration carries a high risk of failure.
- Introducing too many changes at once may alienate users.
- Constant feedback helps you stay on track, although it may be difficult and costly to achieve.
- Users have to get their work done; they don't want to be distracted by incomplete solutions.
- Legacy data must survive while the system is being used.

Overview

It is not enough to reengineer a legacy system and then deploy it. In fact, if you try this, you will surely fail (for the same reasons that big Waterfall projects in new territories often fail). You must be prepared to introduce the new solution gradually, to gain the confidence and collaboration of the users, and you must adopt a strategy for migrating gradually and painlessly from the existing system, *while it is still being deployed,* to the new system.

The central message of this cluster is to Migrate Systems Incrementally (Pattern 7.3). This is, however, easier said than done. In Figure 7.1 on page 146 we can see that in order to Migrate Systems Incrementally, we should consider a large number of other patterns. Since there exists a vast literature on system migration, we do not attempt to cover the topic in great detail. We have selected, however, the patterns that we consider to be most important for reengineering object-oriented legacy systems, and we have summarized the main points. Where appropriate, we point you to further sources of information.

Although the central pattern of this cluster is Migrate Systems Incrementally, the key motivation is provided by Involve the Users and Build Confidence. These first three patterns are fundamental patterns for minimizing risk and increasing the chances of success:

- Involve the Users (Pattern 7.1) increases the chance that users will accept the new system by involving them closely in the entire reengineering process, getting them to use intermediate results, and providing them with strong support. It is easier to achieve if you Migrate Systems Incrementally and Build Confidence step by step.

- Build Confidence (Pattern 7.2) helps you overcome skepticism and doubt by regularly delivering results that are of value to the users.

- Migrate Systems Incrementally (Pattern 7.3) recommends that the old system be gradually and incrementally replaced by the new system. New results can then be integrated as you proceed, thus helping you to Build Confidence and Involve the Users.

It is very hard to Migrate Systems Incrementally unless you also adhere to the following practices:

- Prototype the Target Solution (Pattern 7.4) to test the new architecture and new technical risks. It is too easy to be tempted to think you don't need a prototype since you already have a running system, but this is almost always a mistake.

- Always Have a Running Version (Pattern 7.5) helps to keep changes in sync by ensuring that they are integrated frequently.

- Regression Test after Every Change (Pattern 7.6) helps you to Always Have a Running Version by making sure that everything that used to run still runs. It presupposes that you Write Tests to Enable Evolution (Pattern 6.1).

Depending on the circumstances, there are various practices that may help you to Migrate Systems Incrementally:

- Make a Bridge to the New Town (Pattern 7.7) introduces the metaphor of a (data) "bridge" to allow you to gradually migrate data from a legacy component to its replacement, while the two run in tandem. When all the data have been transferred, the legacy component can be retired.

- Present the Right Interface (Pattern 7.8) helps you to develop the target system in increments by wrapping the old functionality to export the abstractions you really want.

- Distinguish Public from Published Interfaces (Pattern 7.9) distinguishes between stable (public) and unstable (published) interfaces to facilitate parallel development within a reengineering team.

- Deprecate Obsolete Interfaces (Pattern 7.10) lets you gracefully retire obsolete interfaces without immediately invalidating clients.

Finally, the following two practices may help you avoid making radical but unnecessary changes:

- Conserve Familiarity (Pattern 7.11) warns you against introducing radical interface changes that may alienate users.

- Use Profiler before Optimizing (Pattern 7.12) reminds you to delay considering performance issues until you can demonstrate that you have a problem and can pinpoint the source of the problem.

PATTERN

7.1   Involve the Users

Also Known As: Engage Customers [Copl95]

Intent: Maximize acceptance of changes by involving the users at every step.

Problem   How can you be sure that users will accept the reengineered system?

This problem is difficult because

- The old system works. It is clunky, but the users know how it works and know how to get around the problems.

- People hate to have to learn something new unless it really makes their life simpler.

- User perceptions of what is needed to improve a system tend to change as the system evolves.

P A T T E R N 7 . 1 *continued*

- Users can have difficulty evaluating a paper design.
- It is hard to get excited about a new system that is not ready to use.

Yet, solving this problem is feasible because

- Users will try new solutions if they see that their needs are being seriously addressed.
- Users will give you feedback if you give them something useful to use.

Solution Get the users directly involved in the new development, and support them closely in using the new system.

Steps

Get the users to tell you where their priorities lie. Start with Most Valuable First (Pattern 2.4). Break the priorities down into small steps that can be delivered in regular increments, so you can Build Confidence (Pattern 7.2).

Create an environment that will encourage contact between users and developers. Physical location is important.

Establish simple procedures for delivering intermediate results on a regular basis and obtaining feedback. Early prototypes may help, especially to evaluate risky new technologies or approaches. A good strategy is to Migrate Systems Incrementally (Pattern 7.3) so that users can start using the new system as it is being built. You should Conserve Familiarity (Pattern 7.11) to avoid alienating users.

Trade-offs Pros

- Requirements will continuously be validated and updated, increasing your chances that you will move in the right direction.
- If the users feel they are getting useful results and they are being supported, they will put extra effort into giving useful feedback.
- Users will be involved throughout the effort, eliminating the need for a special training session late in the project.

Cons

- Developers may feel that supporting users is distracting them from the job of reengineering the system.

- If you succeed in involving the users, this will raise expectations and put extra pressure on your team. For instance, Yourdon mentions that prototypes can really raise expectations too much and that you should always make clear which parts are not yet working [Your97].

Difficulties

- It can be hard to involve the users initially, before you have shown any results.
- You can't involve everybody, and the users who are left out might feel neglected.

Rationale You need a feedback loop to ensure that you are addressing the real customer needs. By involving and supporting the users, you encourage this feedback loop.

Coplien points out: "Note that 'maintaining product quality' is not the problem being solved here. Product quality is only one component of customer satisfaction" [Copl95].

Related Patterns Virtually all of the patterns in this cluster support Involve the Users. Migrate Systems Incrementally (Pattern 7.3) to get the users working with the system as it is being reengineered and thereby Build Confidence (Pattern 7.2).

The Planning Game [Beck01] is an effective technique to Involve the Users by iteratively identifying stories, estimating costs, and committing to the stories to be released.

PATTERN

7.2 Build Confidence

Intent: Improve your chances of overall success by demonstrating results in regular increments.

Problem How can you overcome the high degree of skepticism that customers and team members often have for any kind of software project?

This problem is difficult because

- Few software projects meet requirements, come in on time, and stay within budget. The skepticism that accompanies most projects can easily lead to defeatism, and projects can fail as a self-fulfilling prophecy.

PATTERN 7.2 *continued*

- Users rarely get what they really want or need.
- It can be hard to convince the users or even your own team that the legacy system can really be salvaged.

Yet, solving this problem is feasible because

- You don't need to solve all the problems at once.

Solution Create a positive atmosphere by demonstrating some tangible results as early as you can, and continue to do so on a regular basis.

Steps

Pick short intervals for delivering new results. At each step, try to agree together with the users what are the smallest results that can demonstrate real value.

Trade-offs Pros

- Both users and developers can measure real progress.
- It is easier to estimate the cost of smaller steps.

Cons

- It takes time to frequently synchronize with the users.
- Users may resent the extra work it takes to use the new system in tandem with the old one.
- If you succeed in demonstrating good results early in the project, you may raise expectations too high.

Difficulties

- Some requirements can be hard to break down into small steps, particularly if they entail architectural changes to the system.
- Reengineering teams must be careful not to alienate the developers of the original system, since they are one of the most valuable sources of information.
- It is not enough to convince users—you must also take care to get commitment from management. It is hard to convince management in small steps. Plan big demos at regular intervals.

Rationale   By taking smaller steps, you reduce the risk that an individual step will fail. Frequent, positive results help to build confidence. By the same token, Extreme Programming advocates Small Releases [Beck00]. Even negative results help you to monitor progress and understand the situation better, and so help to build up confidence.

Related Patterns   Prototype the Target Solution (Pattern 7.4) and Make a Bridge to the New Town (Pattern 7.7) can make it easier to demonstrate results in small steps. It is easier to Build Confidence if you Involve the Users (Pattern 7.1).

PATTERN

7.3   Migrate Systems Incrementally

Also Known As: Chicken Little [Brod95]

Intent: Avoid complexity and risk of big-bang reengineering by deploying functionality in frequent increments.

Problem   When should you plan to deploy the new system?

This problem is difficult because

- Projects are often planned and funded on large time scales, with "big bang" requirements specified up front.
- The real requirements are often only clear in hindsight. Users will resist adopting a new system that is radically different from what they are used to, especially if it does not work flawlessly from the beginning.
- The longer you wait to deploy the new system, the longer you must wait to get user feedback.
- You cannot deploy an incomplete system. Users do not have time to waste on incomplete solutions.

Yet, solving this problem is feasible because

- You have a running system that can be extended and modified.

Solution   Deploy a first *update* of the legacy system as soon as you can, and migrate incrementally to the target system.

PATTERN 7.3 *continued*

Steps

- Decompose the legacy system into parts.
- Choose one part to tackle at a time.
- Put tests in place for that part and the parts that depend on it.
- Take appropriate steps to wrap, reengineer, or replace the legacy component.
- Deploy the updated component and obtain feedback.
- Iterate.

Trade-offs Pros

- You get user feedback early and Build Confidence (Pattern 7.2).
- You see immediately when things break.
- Users learn the new system as it's being built.
- The system is always deployed.
- The system is always being tested, so you can't skip testing.

Cons

- You will have to work harder to keep the system running while you are changing it.

Difficulties

- It can be difficult to migrate to a new architecture. You may want to Prototype the Target Solution (Pattern 7.4) to get the new architecture in place, and Present the Right Interface (Pattern 7.8) to the old system to hide the legacy interfaces while you migrate the underlying components.
- It is risky to change a running system. Be sure to Regression Test after Every Change (Pattern 7.6).

Rationale You get the best user feedback from a running system. Users are more motivated and involved with a system they use daily.

Known Uses Migrating Legacy Systems [Brod95] introduces this pattern under the name "Chicken Little" (to migrate incrementally means to "take Chicken

Little steps"). This book discusses in great detail strategies and techniques for incremental migration.

Related Patterns Apply Most Valuable First (Pattern 2.4) to select the legacy components to work on first. Appoint a Navigator (Pattern 2.2) to maintain architectural integrity.

Write Tests to Enable Evolution (Pattern 6.1), and Grow Your Test Base Incrementally (Pattern 6.2) as you migrate. Be sure to Test the Interface, Not the Implementation (Pattern 6.4) so you do not always have to rewrite your tests as you reengineer or replace legacy components. Regression Test after Every Change (Pattern 7.6) so you can Always Have a Running Version (Pattern 7.5).

Consider applying Present the Right Interface (Pattern 7.8) for legacy components that you do not intend to reengineer or replace.

You might consider applying Make a Bridge to the New Town (Pattern 7.7) if you need to migrate data from legacy components that you are replacing.

PATTERN
7.4 Prototype the Target Solution

Intent: Evaluate the risk of migrating to a new target solution by building a prototype.

Problem How do you know if your ideas for the new target system will work?

This problem is difficult because

- It is risky to make radical changes to a working system.
- It can be hard to anticipate how design changes will impact existing functionality.
- A solution that works is more believable than one that has not been tested.

Yet, solving this problem is feasible because

- You don't need to reengineer the whole legacy system to test the new ideas.

PATTERN 7.4 *continued*

Solution   Develop a prototype of the new concept and evaluate it with respect to the new, emerging requirements.

Steps

- Identify the biggest technical risks for your reengineering project. Typically they will concern things like
    - choice of a new system architecture
    - migration of legacy data to new system
    - adequate performance—or performance gains—with new technology or platform (for example, demonstrating that a certain transaction throughput can be achieved)
- Decide whether to implement an *exploratory* (i.e., throwaway) prototype that will serve purely to evaluate the feasibility of a technical option, or rather an *evolutionary* prototype that will eventually evolve into the new target system.
    - An exploratory prototype must be designed to answer very precise questions. These may be purely technical questions, such as whether the new platform can meet performance constraints set by the legacy system, or they may be usability questions that require participation of and evaluation by the users. The exploratory prototype does not need to be designed to address any other issues or questions and will not be part of the migrated system (although the answers it provides will influence the new system).
    - An evolutionary prototype, on the other hand, is intended to eventually *replace* a legacy component and must therefore reflect the target architecture. The new architecture must not only adequately support the legacy services, but also overcome the obstacles that limit the legacy solution's usefulness. The prototype must be designed to answer these risks first.

Trade-offs   Pros

- A prototype can be built quickly, since it does not have to implement all the functionality of the legacy system.
- You can hack parts of the legacy system to get your prototype running.
- You can learn quickly if your ideas for the target system are sound.

Cons

- Users may not be highly motivated to spend a lot of time evaluating a throwaway prototype.
- You may be tempted to continue to develop the throwaway prototype.

Difficulties

- It may be hard to convince yourself or your customer of the need for a prototype—after all, you already have a running system.
- It can take too much time to get an evolutionary prototype up to speed. Consider applying Present the Right Interface (Pattern 7.8) to legacy components to provide a good interface for legacy services to the prototype.

Rationale A prototype can tell you quickly whether a certain technical approach is sound or not. Brooks in *The Mythical Man-Month* [Broo75] advises us to "write one to throw away" since it is hard to get it right the first time.

Love [Love93] takes this one step further and warns us that for object-oriented systems we should "write two to throw away"! Foote and Yoder [Foot00] argue that, among other things, Throwaway Code is often the best way to clarify domain requirements, but they also warn that a prototype risks evolving into a "Big Ball of Mud."

Related Patterns You might consider applying Make a Bridge to the New Town (Pattern 7.7) to migrate legacy data to an evolutionary prototype.

PATTERN 7.5
Always Have a Running Version

Intent: Increase confidence in changes by regularly rebuilding the system.

Problem How do you convince your customer that you are on the right path?

This problem is difficult because

- It can be hard to demo a software system under development, or to discuss problems with users since there is often no stable, running version of the system available.

PATTERN 7.5 *continued*

- Integrating changes from multiple versions of a system can be slow and painful.

Yet, solving this problem is feasible because

- You don't have to wait until a component is "finished" before integrating it.

Solution   Institute a discipline of integrating new changes and developments on a daily basis.

Steps

- Have version management and configuration management systems in place.
- Make sure you have regression tests in place for the parts you are working on.
- Institute a discipline of short transactions for checking out system components and checking them back in again. Plan iterations to be as short as possible to allow changes to be integrated into a running system.

Trade-offs   Pros

- You always have a working version to demo.
- You can always have a working version to run your regression tests.
- You can quickly validate your changes, thereby helping you to Build Confidence (Pattern 7.2).

Cons

- You must continuously integrate changes.

Difficulties

- Large systems may have very long build times. You may need to re-architect the system first to enable shorter build times.
- It can be hard to break some kinds of large modifications into meaningful updates that can be individually integrated.

Rationale Many practitioners advocate a process of continuous integration as a way to avoid a risky and painful big-bang integration [Booc94].

Related Patterns Regression Test after Every Change minimizes the risk of defects creeping in during integration.

Continuous Integration [Booc94] [Beck00] is a proven way to Always Have a Running Version (Pattern 7.5).

PATTERN

7.6   Regression Test after Every Change

Intent: Build confidence by making sure that whatever worked before still works.

Problem How can you be sure that the last change you made won't break the system?

This problem is difficult because

- In a complex system, small changes can have unexpected side effects. A seemingly innocuous change may break something without this being immediately discovered.

Yet, solving this problem is feasible because

- You have written test suites that express how the system should behave.

Solution Run your regression test suite every time you think you have reached a stable state.

Trade-offs Pros

- It is easier to Always Have a Running Version (Pattern 7.5).
- It is easier to Build Confidence (Pattern 7.2) as you proceed.

Cons

- You must relentlessly write the tests.

PATTERN 7.6 *continued*

Difficulties

- The legacy system may not have adequate regression tests defined. To enable evolution, you will have to Grow Your Test Base Incrementally (Pattern 6.2).

- Tests can only show that defects are present, not that they are absent. You may have failed to test precisely the aspect that you have broken.

- Running the tests may be very time-consuming, so you might want to run only those tests that you think might be affected by your change. Categorize your tests to avoid ad hoc testing of changes, but run all the tests at least once a day.

Rationale   Regression tests tell you that whatever ran before still runs. If you consistently build up tests for defects you discover and new features, you will end up with a reusable test base that gives you confidence that your changes are sound and helps you detect problems earlier.

A Davis advocates, "Regression test after every change" [Davi95] as standard software development practice.

Related Patterns   You should have already started to Write Tests to Enable Evolution (Pattern 6.1).

A common practice in Extreme Programming is to write tests *before* you implement new functionality [Jeff01]. In the context of reengineering, you should consider writing tests that will fail before you make a change and will pass if the change is correctly implemented. (Unfortunately it is not generally possible to design tests that will *only* pass if the change is correct!)

Regression tests should help you to Retest Persistent Problems (Pattern A.1).

PATTERN
7.7   Make a Bridge to the New Town

Also Known As: The Bridge to the New Town [Kell00], Keep the Data—Toss the Code [Brod95]

Intent: Migrate data from a legacy system by running the new system in parallel, with a bridge in between.

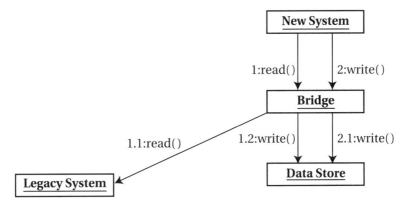

FIGURE **7.2** A bridge helps you to transparently transfer data to the new system.

Problem How do you incrementally migrate data from a legacy system to its replacement while the two systems are running in tandem?

This problem is difficult because

- Some components of the legacy system are beyond repair and should be replaced.
- Big-bang replacement of critical components is highly risky.
- The *data* manipulated by the legacy components must be kept available and alive during the migration.

Yet, solving this problem is feasible because

- You have a running legacy system.

Solution Make a (data) bridge that will incrementally transfer data from the legacy system to the replacement system as new components are ready to take the data over from their legacy counterparts (see Figure 7.2).

Steps

- Identify legacy and replacement components that deal with the same logical data entities.
- Implement a "data bridge" that is responsible for redirecting *read* requests from the new component to the legacy data source if the data have not already been migrated. The bridge is responsible for any necessary data conversion. The new component should not be aware of the bridge.

P A T T E R N 7 . 7 *continued*

- Adapt the legacy component to redirect *write* requests to the new component, so that the new data stay up to date.
- When all the data have been transferred, remove the bridge and the legacy component.

Trade-offs Pros

- You can start using the new system without migrating all the legacy data.

Cons

- A data bridge can be tricky to implement correctly if there is not a simple mapping between the legacy data and the new data.
- Once some of the data has been transferred, it can be hard to go back.
- The data bridge will add a performance overhead that may or may not be acceptable.

Difficulties

- "Stepwise migration schemes have proven very effective in large, layered business systems. They are not common in let's say CAD applications that have check in/check out persistence and a tightly coupled and very woven object net" [Kell00].

Known Uses Brodie and Stonebraker discuss much more thoroughly the use of data bridges and gateways in *Migrating Legacy Systems* [Brod95].

Keller in "The Bridge to the New Town" [Kell00] focuses more on the technical issue of migrating legacy data, and he points out numerous examples of the pattern successfully being applied.

There are many possible variants of this pattern, depending on whether the entire legacy system is to be replaced or only a component, and whether users should be able to have access to both systems at the same time or not.

Rationale A bridge between the old and new systems allows you to let users start using features of the new system before it is complete. The bridge isolates the two systems from each other so that the new system can be developed according to a new architectural vision without influence from the legacy system.

Related Patterns A bridge helps you Migrate Systems Incrementally (Pattern 7.3) and thereby Build Confidence (Pattern 7.2).

PATTERN

7.8   **Present the Right Interface**

Also Known As: Semantic Wrapper [Ocal00], Sweeping It under the Rug [Foot00]

Intent: Wrap a legacy system to export the right abstractions, even if they are not reflected in the existing implementation.

Problem How should the new target system access legacy services during the migration process?

This problem is difficult because

- The target system is not yet complete so you must rely on legacy services during the migration.
- The legacy system does not present the interfaces you need for the target system.
- Implementing new components directly in terms of legacy components will bias the target toward the legacy architecture and design.

Yet, solving this problem is feasible because

- You don't have to access the legacy services directly.

Solution Identify the abstractions that you want to have in the new system, and wrap up the old software to emulate the new abstractions.

Hints

Consider, for example, a procedural graphics library that will be used within an object-oriented system. It will be too costly and time-consuming to reimplement the library in an object-oriented way. It would be easier to wrap it as a utility class (i.e., as a class with static methods but no instances), but it would be wiser to write a slightly thicker wrapper that presents a truly object-oriented interface but is implemented using the underlying procedural abstractions. In this way the new system will not be polluted by legacy abstractions.

Trade-offs Pros

- It is easier to wean the target system from legacy services if they can use appropriate abstractions from the start.

PATTERN 7.8 *continued*

- You reduce the risk that the legacy design will adversely influence the new target.

Cons

- The new interface may not be stable, so developers may be reluctant to use it.

Difficulties

- It can be hard to resist the temptation to simply wrap the procedural abstractions as utility classes.

Known Uses   Alan O'Callaghan [Ocal00] presents this pattern as "Semantic Wrapper" briefly in the context of the ADAPTOR pattern language, which addresses the migration of large-scale, business-critical legacy systems to object-oriented and component-based technology.

Rationale   Present the Right Interface frees you from thinking in terms of the legacy design and makes it easier to consider alternative approaches.

Related Patterns   Present the Right Interface superficially resembles an Adapter (Pattern A.11), since both use wrappers as their implementation technique. An Adapter, however, adapts an incompatible interface to another interface expected by its clients. Present the Right Interface, on the other hand, introduces a new, more suitable interface to a legacy component.

Be sure to Deprecate Obsolete Interfaces (Pattern 7.10).

If the new interface implemented by Present the Right Interface is not stable, you should Distinguish Public from Published Interfaces (Pattern 7.9).

PATTERN

7.9   Distinguish Public from Published Interfaces

Also Known As: Published Interface [Ocal00]

Intent: Facilitate parallel development by distinguishing unstable "published interfaces" from stable "public interfaces."

Problem   How do you enable migration from legacy interfaces to new target interfaces while the new interfaces are still under development?

This problem is difficult because

- You want to enable migration to the new target system as early as possible.
- You do not want to freeze the interfaces of new target components too early.
- Changing the interface to a component that is widely used will slow down development.

Yet, solving this problem is feasible because

- You can control the status of the interfaces you provide.

Solution   Distinguish between public interfaces of components that are available to the rest of the system, and unstable "published" interfaces of components that are available within a subsystem but are not yet ready for prime time.

Hints

Since "published" interfaces are not supported by any programming language, you may have to use naming conventions or abuse other features to achieve the desired effect.

- In Java, consider declaring such interfaces as `protected`, or giving them package scope (undeclared). When the interfaces stabilize, you may redeclare them as being `public`.
- In C++, consider declaring components with published interfaces `private` or `protected`, and declare as `friends` the clients that are permitted to use them. When the interfaces stabilize, redeclare the components as `public`, and delete the declarations of `friends`.
- In Smalltalk, consider declaring categories of published components. Also consider declaring published message categories to distinguish stable and unstable messages.
- Consider decorating the names of unstable components or interfaces to indicate their "published" status. When the component becomes public, rename it and patch all its clients or deprecate the version with the old name (Deprecate Obsolete Interfaces, Pattern 7.10).

Trade-offs   Pros

- Clients of published interfaces are aware that they are likely to change.

PATTERN 7.9 *continued*

Cons

- Identifying an interface as "published" is purely a matter of convention and discipline.
- Promoting an interface from published to public entails a certain overhead for clients who should upgrade to the new interface.

Difficulties

- Clients can be put in a bind: should they use an unstable published interface, or continue to use the legacy service?

Known Uses
Published Interface is another pattern of the ADAPTOR pattern language [Ocal00].

Rationale
Clients are in a better position to evaluate the risk of using a component if they know its interface is declared to be "published" but not yet public.

Related Patterns
When you Present the Right Interface (Pattern 7.8) to a legacy component, the new interface may not be stable, so be careful to Distinguish Public from Published Interfaces (Pattern 7.9). When the new interface stabilizes, or is substituted by a stable replacement component, the interface may become public.

Upgrading an interface to public may entail a change to the way it is accessed. Be sure to Deprecate Obsolete Interfaces (Pattern 7.10).

PATTERN

7.10 Deprecate Obsolete Interfaces

Also Known As: Deprecation [Stev98]

Intent: Give clients time to react to changes to public interfaces by flagging obsolete interfaces as "deprecated."

Problem
How do you modify an interface without invalidating all the clients?

This problem is difficult because

- Changing a public interface can break many clients.
- Leaving an obsolete interface in place will make future maintenance more difficult.
- Not all changes are for the better.

Yet, solving this problem is feasible because

- The old and the new interfaces can coexist for a period of time.

Solution Flag the old interface as being "deprecated," thereby notifying clients that it will almost certainly be removed in the next upcoming release.

Steps

- You have determined that a public interface should be changed, but you do not want to break all clients. Implement the new interface, but "deprecate" the old one. The deprecation mechanism should inform clients that the interface has changed and that a newer interface is recommended instead.
- Evaluate to what extent the deprecated interface continues to be used, and whether it can be permanently retired. Consider removing it in a future release.
- Java supports deprecation as a language feature: Deprecate a feature by adding the tag `@deprecated` to its javadoc documentation. The tag is not only recognized by the javadoc documentation generator, but the compiler will also generate compile-time warnings if code using deprecated features is compiled with the deprecated option.
- Other approaches are the following:
  - Simply inform users in the documentation which interfaces are deprecated.
  - Move or rename the deprecated interface or component. Clients can continue to use them but must adapt and recompile to continue to use the deprecated form.
  - Replace deprecated components by equivalent ones that generate run-time warnings or output warnings to a log file.
  - Alternatively, consider configuring the programming environment or the deprecated components themselves to generate compile-time or link-time warnings.

PATTERN 7.10 *continued*

Trade-offs   Pros

- Clients do not have to immediately adapt to changes.
- There is time to change your mind.

Cons

- Clients are free to ignore deprecation.

Difficulties

- It may be hard to track down all the clients of a deprecated component.
- It can be hard to decide when to really retire a deprecated component.
- If you want to keep the interface but change the semantics, you may need to introduce a new component and deprecate the old one. This can be the case if certain methods should now return default values instead of throwing exceptions (or vice versa).

Known Uses   Perdita Stevens and Rob Pooley identify Deprecation as a common practice for managing evolving APIs in complex systems [Stev98].

Rationale   Deprecation gives you a window of time to evaluate the impact of a change.

PATTERN
7.11   **Conserve Familiarity**

Intent: Avoid radical changes that may alienate users.

Problem   How do you accomplish a major overhaul of a legacy system without disrupting the way users are used to getting their job done?

This problem is difficult because

- The legacy system requires significant changes.
- The users are not happy with the legacy system, but they understand it well.

Yet, solving this problem is feasible because

- You can migrate incrementally to a new solution.

Solution Introduce only a constant, relatively small number of changes with each new release.

Trade-offs Pros

- Users do not have to change their work habits too much between releases.

Difficulties

- Sometimes radical change is necessary. It can be hard to migrate from a command-line interface to a GUI while conserving familiarity.

Rationale Too much change between releases increases the risk of hidden defects and decreases the chance of user acceptance.

Lehman and Belady's law of conservation of familiarity suggests that the incremental change between releases of a system stays roughly constant over time [Lehm85]. This is a relatively natural phenomenon because to do anything else introduces unnecessary risks.

Related Patterns To Conserve Familiarity you must Migrate Systems Incrementally (Pattern 7.3). Involve the Users (Pattern 7.1) to understand what changes will be acceptable. Prototype the Target Solution (Pattern 7.4) to evaluate the potential impact of changes.

PATTERN

7.12 **Use Profiler before Optimizing**

Intent: Avoid squandering reengineering effort on needless "optimizations" by verifying where the bottlenecks are.

Problem When should you rewrite a clearly inefficient piece of code?

This problem is difficult because

- When you are reengineering software, you are likely to encounter many naive algorithms in the legacy code.

PATTERN 7.12 *continued*

- It can be hard to predict what will impact performance, and you can lose a lot of time on pure supposition.

- Optimized code is often more complex than simple, naive code.

Yet, solving this problem is feasible because

- There are tools to tell you where you may have a performance problem.

Solution   Whenever you are tempted to optimize a "clearly inefficient" part of the system, first use a profiler to determine whether it is actually a bottleneck. Don't optimize anything unless your profiler tells you it will make a difference. If you decide to go ahead, prepare benchmarks that will demonstrate the performance gains.

Trade-offs   Pros

- You do not waste time optimizing something that will not make a difference to overall performance.

Cons

- Naive algorithms will survive longer in the system.

Rationale   The performance improvement that you can gain by optimizing a bit of code depends on how much time the program spends in that code in a typical run. A profiler will tell you how much time that is.

"Do it, then do it right, then do it fast" is a well-known aphorism that has been credited to many different sources. Very likely its origin is outside of the field of computer science. The rationale behind it is that you risk making a system complex and hard to maintain if you become preoccupied with performance issues too early. Instead, it is better to first find a solution that works, then clean it up once you understand it. Finally, if you can identify any important performance bottlenecks, that is the time to optimize just those parts that will make a difference.

As a corollary, it may even be a good idea to replace a bit of complex, "optimized" code by a simpler, "naive" solution, if that won't severely impact performance but will make it easier to make other changes.

See also Davis's discussion of "Use Profiler before Optimizing" [Davi95].

Related Patterns   If you Refactor to Understand (Pattern 5.2), you will have started the second step: "do it right."

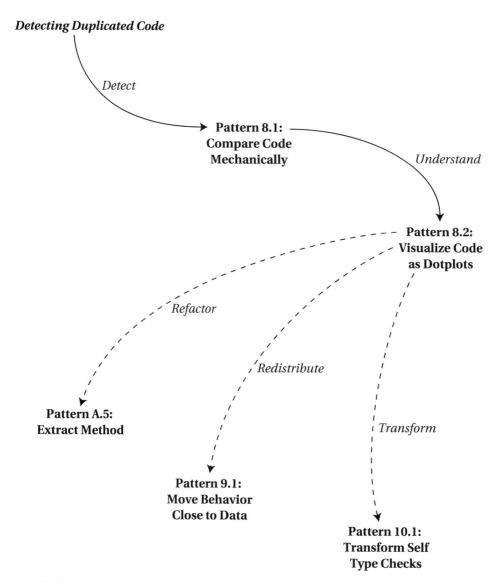

FIGURE **8.1** Two patterns to support Detecting Duplicated Code.

CHAPTER 8

Detecting Duplicated Code

Fowler and Beck have ranked duplicated code as the first of the top 10 code smells indicating the need to refactor a piece of software [Fowl99]. As they like to explain it, whenever you duplicate a piece of code, you are taking out a loan, in the sense that you are getting something now (an almost ready-made piece of software) that you will have to pay for later. There is nothing wrong with taking out a loan, but you have a choice between paying back a small amount now (by taking out the time to refactor your code to eliminate the duplication) or paying back a lot later (in terms of increased complexity and maintenance costs).

Data from empirical studies show that typically between 8% and 12% of industrial software consists of duplicated code [Duca99]. Although this may not seem like much, in fact it is difficult to achieve very high rates of duplication. (Imagine what it would take to have a duplication rate of even 50%!) Duplication rates of 15% to 20% are therefore considered to be severe.

Forces

It is important to identify duplicated code for the following reasons:

- Duplicated code hampers the introduction of changes, since every implemented variant of a piece of functionality will have to be changed. Since it is easy to miss some variants, bugs are likely to pop up in other places.

- Duplicated code replicates and scatters the logic of a system instead of grouping it into identifiable artifacts (classes, methods, packages). It leads to systems that are more difficult to understand and to change. Instead of just having to understand relationships between logical parts, you will first have to identify them and then understand their relationships.

Duplicated code arises for a variety of reasons:

- Whenever a programmer is implementing a piece of functionality that is remotely similar to something that has been done before, it is natural to use the existing code as a model for the new task. If it is a matter of recombining existing procedures, the task will be simple. But if the behavior is more complex, the easiest thing to do is to copy, paste, and modify the old code to achieve the functionality. If both the old and new pieces of code belong to different applications, the harm is minimal. But if they are part of the same system, duplicated code has now been introduced.

- Sometimes code is copied, pasted, and modified between different applications, or different versions of the same application. When multiple versions must be maintained simultaneously, or when different applications or versions must be merged, you immediately have a duplicated code problem.

From a reengineering perspective, usually people know whether or not a system suffers from duplication. First, the development team or the manager will tell you. Second, there are normally some clear signs that duplication has been practiced in a project: for example, two developers cannot develop four million lines of code in less than eight months without copying and pasting existing code. While analyzing the system you will also identify duplicated code by accident. There is a major difference, however, between knowing that a system contains duplicated code and knowing *exactly* which parts have been duplicated.

Overview

Detecting Duplicated Code consists of two patterns: Compare Code Mechanically (Pattern 8.1), which describes how we can detect duplicated code, and Visualize Code as Dotplots (Pattern 8.2), which shows how duplicated code can be better understood by simple matrix visualization (see Figure 8.1 on page 172).

Once you have detected and understood duplication in the system, you may decide on a variety of tactics. Various refactoring patterns, such as Extract Method (Pattern A.5), may help you to eliminate the duplication. Duplication may be a sign of misplaced responsibilities, in which case you may decide to Move Behavior Close to Data (Pattern 9.1).

Complex conditional statements are also a form of duplication and may indicate that multiple clients have to duplicate actions that should belong to the target class. The pattern cluster "Transform Conditionals to Polymorphism" (Chapter 10) can help to resolve these problems.

PATTERN

8.1 Compare Code Mechanically

Intent: Discover duplicated code by comparing all the source code files line by line.

Problem   How do you discover which parts of an application code have been duplicated?

This problem is difficult because

- You may suspect that code has been duplicated but you do not have any a priori evidence where the duplication occurs. For example, you know that two programmers cannot have developed 4 million lines of Cobol in one year without having duplicated some code.
- Browsing the code is not an effective way of discovering duplication; you will only find duplicated code by accident.
- Programmers may have not only copied and pasted code, but also modified variables or changed the shape of the programs.

Yet, solving this problem is feasible because

- Most duplicated code can be detected by mechanical procedures.

Solution   Textually compare each line of the software source code with all the other lines of code.

Steps

- Normalize the lines of code by removing comments, tabs, and blanks.
- Remove lines that contain uninteresting code elements (e.g., just `else` or `}`).
- Compare each line with all the other lines. Reduce search complexity by hashing: (1) preprocessing (compute the hash value for each line), and (2) actual comparison (compare all lines in the same hash bucket).

Variations

This approach may fail to identify some instances of duplicated code due to renaming of variables. By deleting all variable identifiers, or by mapping them to a common symbol, you can detect similar code patterns, while

PATTERN 8.1 *continued*

abstracting from the details of the specific identifiers. This variant, however, requires some syntactic processing of the code.

Trade-offs Pros

- The approach is simple and gives good results while only requiring modest resources.

- It is nearly language independent in the sense that you only have to build a lexical analyzer and not a full parser. That's why a simple perl script can be sufficient, depending on the level of sophistication that you want.

- Simple statistics and percentage rates are easily computed and may help you to gain credibility or more strength in discussions on resource allocation or hiring new people.

Cons

- Code that has been heavily edited after copying may be hard to identify as duplicated code.

- Systems containing a lot of duplicated code will generate a lot of data that can be difficult to analyze effectively.

Example Consider the case of a system written in C++ where you suspect duplicated code. However, you didn't write the code yourself so you don't know where the actual duplication occurs. How can you detect where the duplicated code fragments are? Consistent with Keep It Simple (Pattern 2.7), you do the simplest thing that may possibly work: you write a little script that first normalizes the code to remove all white space from the code and afterward compares each line of code against itself.

The normalization would change the following code:

```
...
// assign same fastid as container
fastid = NULL;
const char* fidptr = getFastid();
if(fidptr != NULL) {
  int l = strlen(fidptr);
  fastid = new char[l+1];
  char *tmp = (char*) fastid;
```

```
  for (int i =0;i<1;i++)
    tmp[i] = fidptr[i];
  tmp[l] = '\0';
}
...
```

into

```
...
fastid=NULL;
constchar*fidptr=getFastid();
if(fidptr!=NULL)
intl=strlen(fidptr);
fastid=newchar[l+1];
char*tmp=(char*)fastid;
for(inti=0;i<l;i++)
tmp[i]=fidptr[i];
tmp[l]='\0';
...
```

Afterward, the line-by-line comparison of the code against itself produces a report telling which sequences of lines are duplicated:

```
Lines:fastid=NULL;;constchar*fidptr=getFastid();;if(fidptr!=NULL);
intl=strlen(fidptr);;fastid=newchar[l+1];;
Locations:
</typesystem/Parser.C>6178/6179/6180/6181/6182
</typesystem/Parser.C>6198/6199/6200/6201/6202
```

Here is a sample of a perl script that will do the trick:

```
#! /usr/bin/env perl -w
# duplocForCPP.pl - detect duplicated lines of code (algorithm only)
# Synopsis: duplocForCPP.pl filename ...
# Takes code (or other) files and collects all line numbers of lines
# equal to each other within these files. The algorithm is linear (in
# space and time) to the number of lines in input.

# Output: Lists of numbers of equal lines.
# Author: Matthias Rieger

$equivalenceClassMinimalSize   = 1;
$slidingWindowSize             = 5;
$removeKeywords                = 0;
```

PATTERN 8.1 *continued*

```
@keywords = qw(if
    then
    else
    for
    {
    }
  );

$keywordsRegExp = join '|', @keywords;

@unwantedlines = qw( else
    return
    return;
    return result;
    }else{
    #else
    #endif
    {
    }
    ;
    };
  );
push @unwantedLines, @keywords;

@unwantedlines{@unwantedlines} = (1) x @unwantedLines;

$totalLines    = 0;
$emptyLines    = 0;
$codeLines     = 0;
@currentLines  = ();
@currentLineNos = ();
%eqLines       = ();
$inComment     = 0;

$start = (times)[0];

while (<>) {
  chomp;
  $totalLines++;
```

```perl
# remove comments of type /* */
my $codeOnly = '';
while(($inComment && m|\*/|) || (!$inComment && m|/\*|)) {
  unless($inComment) { $codeOnly .= $` }
  $inComment = !$inComment;
  $_ = $';
}
$codeOnly .= $_ unless $inComment;
$_ = $codeOnly;

s|//.*$||;                              #remove comments of type //
s/\s+//g;                               #remove white space
s/$keywordsRegExp//og if $removeKeywords;  #remove keywords

# remove empty and unwanted lines
if((!$_ && $emptyLines++)
  || (defined $unwantedLines{$_} && $codeLines++)) { next }

$codeLines++;
push @currentLines, $_;
push @currentLineNos, $.;
if($slidingWindowSize < @currentLines) {
  shift @currentLines;
  shift @currentLineNos;
}

# print STDERR "Line $totalLines >$_<\n";

my $lineToBeCompared = join '', @currentLines;
my $lineNumbersCompared = "<$ARGV>"; # append the name of the file
$lineNumbersCompared .= join '/', @currentLineNos;
# print STDERR "$lineNumbersCompared\n";
if($bucketRef = $eqLines{$lineToBeCompared}) {
  push @$bucketRef, $lineNumbersCompared;
} else {
  $eqLines{$lineToBeCompared} = [ $lineNumbersCompared ];
}

if(eof) { close ARGV } # Reset linenumber-count for next file
}

$end = (times)[0];
$processingTime = $end - $start;
```

PATTERN 8.1 *continued*

```
# print the equivalence classes

$numOfMarkedEquivClasses = 0;
$numOfMarkedElements = 0;
foreach $line (sort { length $a <=> length $b } keys %eqLines) {
  if(scalar @{$eqLines{$line}} > $equivalenceClassMinimalSize) {
    $numOfMarkedEquivClasses++;
    $numOfMarkedElements += scalar @{$eqLines{$line}};
    print "Lines: $line\n";
    print "Locations: @{$eqLines{$line}}\n\n";
  }
}

print "\n\n\n";
print "Number of Lines processed: $totalLines\n";
print "Number of Empty Lines:     $emptyLines\n";
print "Number of Code Lines:      $codeLines\n";
print "Scanning time in seconds:  $processingTime\n";
print "Lines per second:          @{[$totalLines/$processingTime]}\n";
print "-------------------------------------\n";
print "Total Number of equivalence classes: @{[scalar keys %eqLines]}\n";
print "Size of Sliding window:                $slidingWindowSize\n";
print "Lower bound of eqiv-class Size: $equivalenceClassMinimalSize\n";
print "Number of marked equivalence classes: $numOfMarkedEquivClasses\n";
print "Number of marked elements: $numOfMarkedElements\n";
```

Known Uses In the context of software reengineering, the pattern has been applied to detect duplicated code in FAMOOS case studies containing up to 1 million lines of C++. It also has been applied to detect duplicated code in a COBOL system of 4 million lines of code. DATRIX has investigated multiple versions of a large telecommunications system, wading through 89 million lines of code in all [Lagu97].

PATTERN

8.2   Visualize Code as Dotplots

Intent: Gain insight into the nature of the duplication by studying the patterns in the dotplots.

Problem   How can you gain insight into the scope and nature of code duplication in a software system?

This problem is difficult because

- Just knowing where in the system duplicated code exists does not necessarily help you to understand its nature or what should be done about it.

Yet, solving this problem is feasible because

- A picture is worth a thousand words.

Solution   Visualize the code as a matrix in which the two axes represent two source code files (possibly the same file), and dots in the matrix occur where source code lines are duplicated.

Steps

If you want to analyze two files A and B:

- Normalize the contents of the two files to eliminate noise (white space, etc.).
- Let each axis of the matrix represent elements (e.g., the lines of code) of the normalized files.
- Represent a match between two elements as a dot in the matrix.
- Interpret the obtained pictures: a diagonal represents duplicated code between the two files.

To analyze the duplication inside a single file, plot the elements of that file on both axes.

Interpretations

The interpretation of the obtained matrices are illustrated in Figure 8.2. Some interesting configurations formed by the dots in the matrices are the following:

- *Exact copies:* Diagonals of dots indicate copied sequences of source code.
- *Copies with variations:* Sequences that have holes in them indicate that a portion of a copied sequences has been changed.
- *Inserts/deletes:* Broken sequences with parts shifted to the right or left indicate that a portion of code has been inserted or deleted.

PATTERN 8.2 *continued*

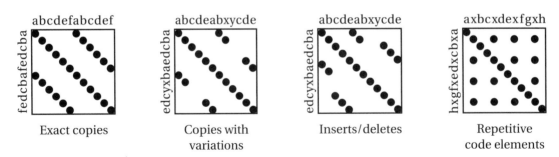

FIGURE **8.2** Possible sequences of dots and their associated interpretations.

- *Repetitive code elements:* Rectangular configurations indicate periodic occurrences of the same code. An example is the break at the end of the individual cases of a C or C ++ switch statement, or recurring preprocessor commands like `#ifdef SOME CONDITION`.

Trade-offs

Pros

- The approach is largely language independent, since only the code normalization depends on the language syntax.
- The approach works well when reverse engineering large amounts of unknown code because the dotplots attract your eye to certain parts of the code to be studied more closely.
- The idea is simple yet works surprisingly well. A simple version of the approach can be implemented by a good programmer using appropriate tools in a couple of days. (One of our better students made a small dotplot browser in Delphi in two days.)

Cons

- Dotplots only present pairwise comparisons. They do not necessarily help you identify all instances of duplicated elements in the entire software system. Although the approach can easily be extended to present multiple files across each axis, the comparisons are still only pairwise.

Difficulties

- A naive implementation of a dotplot visualizer may not scale well to large systems. Tuning and optimizing the approach for large data sets can compromise the simplicity of the approach.

Before   After

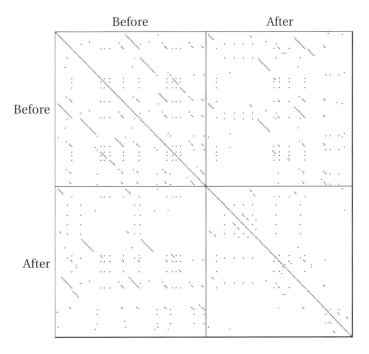

Before

After

FIGURE **8.3**   Code duplication before and after refactoring.

- The interpretation of the data may be more subtle than it appears at first glance. Indeed, while comparing multiple files, the diagonals represent more duplication than is really in the system because we are comparing duplicated fragments with themselves over different files, as shown by Figures 8.3 and 8.4.

- The screen size limits the amount of information that can be visualized. Some success has been achieved with so-called mural visualization approaches [Jerd96]. However, these techniques are significantly more difficult to implement than simple dotplots and are not worth the extra effort.

Example   In Figure 8.3 we see a dotplot of two versions of a piece of software, before and after the duplication has been removed. The first version is compared to itself in the top-left square. The line down the diagonal simply shows us that every line of code is being compared to itself. What is more interesting is that several other diagonal lines occur in the dotplot, which means that code has been duplicated within this file. A second version of the same file is compared to itself in the lower-right square. Here we see no significant duplication aside from the main diagonal, which reflects the fact that all the duplicated code has been successfully refactored.

PATTERN 8.2 *continued*

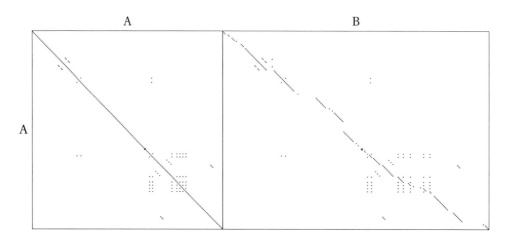

FIGURE **8.4**   Python file A being compared to itself and to a second file B.

The bottom-left and top-right squares are mirror images of each other. They tell us how the before and after files have been reorganized. Since there is no strong diagonal, this tells us that significant reorganization has taken place. The diagonal stripes show us which parts of the old version have survived and where they appear in the new version. From the dotplot alone, we can guess that about half of the code has survived, and another half of the code has been significantly rewritten.

Dotplots are also useful to detect duplication across multiple files. Figure 8.4 shows a dotplot comparing two Python files. The comparison of A versus A shows that there is essentially no internal duplication. Very likely there are some switch statements in the bottom half of the file, indicated by the matrix pattern.

When we compare file A to file B, however, we detect a staggering amount of duplication. It looks very much like file B is just a copy of file A that has been extended in various ways. Closer investigation showed this to be the case. In fact, file A was just an older version of file B that had inadvertently been left in the release.

Dotplots can also be useful to detect other problems. Figure 8.5 presents four clones that represent a switch statement over a type variable that is used to call individual construction code. The duplicated code could perhaps be eliminated by applying "Transform Conditionals to Polymorphism" (Chapter 10).

Known Uses   The pattern has been applied in biological research to detect DNA sequences [Pust82]. The Dotplot tool [Helf95] has been used to detect simi-

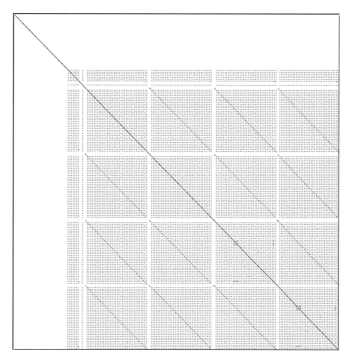

FIGURE **8.5** Dotplots produced by four switch statements.

larities in manual pages, literary texts, and names from file systems. In the FAMOOS project, the pattern has been applied to build Duploc, a tool for identifying duplication in software source code [Duca99]. The Dup tool [Bake92] has been used to investigate the source code of the X-Window system and uses a dotplot matrix graphical representation.

Related Patterns Once you have detected duplicated code, numerous refactoring patterns may apply, in particular Extract Method (Pattern A.5).

Very often duplicated code arises because clients assume too many responsibilities. In that case, Move Behavior Close to Data (Pattern (9.1) will help you to eliminate the duplication.

Dotplots also help to detect large conditional constructs. You should probably Transform "Conditionals to Polymorphism" (Chapter 10) to eliminate these conditionals and thereby achieve a more flexible design.

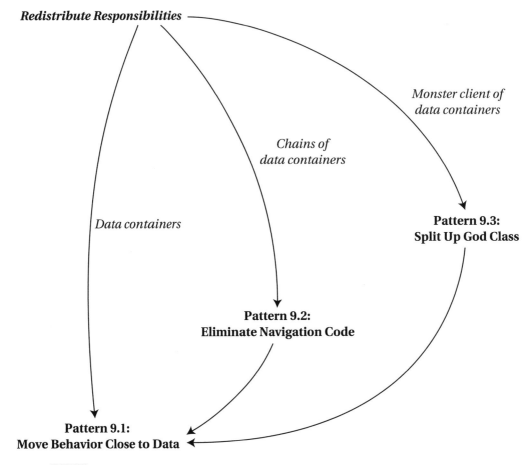

FIGURE **9.1** Data containers are the clearest sign of misplaced responsibilities. These three patterns redistribute responsibilities by moving behavior close to data.

## CHAPTER 9

Redistribute Responsibilities

You are responsible for reengineering the information system that manages all employee records for a large branch of the public administration. Due to recent political upheavals, you know that there will be many changes required in the system to cope with privatization, new laws, and new regulations, but you do not know exactly what they will be. The existing system consists of a nominally object-oriented reimplementation of an older procedural system. The code contains many pseudo-objects: data containers masquerading as objects and big procedural "god classes" that implement most of the logic of individual subsystems. One class, called TaxRevision2000, has a single method consisting essentially of a case statement that is 3000 lines long.

As long as the system was relatively stable, this design posed no particular problems, but now you see that even relatively modest changes to the system require months of planning, testing, and debugging due to weak encapsulation of data. You are convinced that migrating to a more object-oriented design will make the system more robust and easier to adapt to future requirements. But how do you know where the problems lie? Which responsibilities should be redistributed? Which data containers should you redesign, which ones should you wrap, and which ones are better left alone?

Forces

As usual, there is a set of conflicting forces to be resolved.

- Data containers (objects that just provide access to data, but have no behavior of their own) are a simple and convenient way to share information between many subsystems. Among others, data containers are the easiest way to provide access to database entities.

- However, data containers expose the data representation and hence are difficult to change when many application components depend on them. Consequently, a proliferation of data containers leads to fragile navigation code in the implementation of business logic.

- It is hard to teach an old dog new tricks. Many designers received training in functional decomposition and will fall into old habits when doing an object design.

- However, functional decomposition tends to generate god classes—big classes that do all of the work and have a myriad of tiny provider classes around them. God classes are hard to extend, modify, or subclass because such changes affect large numbers of other methods or instance variables.

Overview

This cluster deals with problems of misplaced responsibilities. The two extreme cases are *data containers* (classes that are nothing but glorified data structures and have almost no identifiable responsibilities) and *god classes* (procedural monsters that assume too many responsibilities).

Although there are sometimes borderlines cases where data containers and god classes may be tolerated, particularly if they are buried in a stable part of the system that will not change, generally they are a sign of a fragile design.

Data containers lead to violations of the *law of Demeter* (LOD) [Lieb88]. In a nutshell, the law of Demeter provides a number of design guidelines to reduce coupling between distantly related classes. Although the law of Demeter has various forms, depending on whether one focuses on objects or classes, and depending on which programming language is being used, the law essentially states that methods should only send messages to instance variables, method arguments, self, super, and the receiver class.

Violations of the law of Demeter typically take the form of *navigation code* in which an *indirect client* accesses an *indirect provider* by accessing either an instance variable or an acquaintance of an *intermediate provider*. The indirect client and provider are thereby unnecessarily coupled, making future enhancements more difficult to realize (Figure 9.2). The intermediate provider may take the form of a data container or may open its encapsulation by providing accessor methods. Designs with many data containers present suffer from complex navigation code in which indirect clients may have to navigate through a chain of intermediates to reach the indirect provider.

Whereas data containers have too few responsibilities, god classes assume too many. A god class can be a single class that implements an entire subsystem, consisting of thousands of lines of code and hundreds of

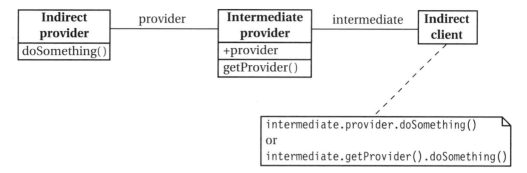

FIGURE **9.2** An indirect client violates the law of Demeter by navigating through an intermediate provider to an indirect provider, unnecessarily coupling the two.

methods and instance variables. Particularly vicious god classes consist of only static instance variables and methods; that is, all data and behavior have class scope, and the god class is never instantiated. Such god classes are purely procedural beasts and are object-oriented in name only.

Occasionally some procedural classes known as *utility classes* are convenient. The best-known examples are object-oriented interfaces to math libraries or collections of algorithms. Real god classes, however, are not libraries but complete applications or subsystems that control the entire application execution.

God classes and data containers often occur together, with the god class assuming all the control of the application and treating other classes as glorified data structures. Since they assume too many responsibilities, god classes are hard to understand and maintain. Incremental modification and extension of a god class through inheritance is next to impossible due to the complexity of its interface and the absence of a clear subclassing contract.

Figure 9.1 on page 186 provides a number of patterns to eliminate data containers and god classes by redistributing responsibilities and thereby improving encapsulation:

- Move Behavior Close to Data (Pattern 9.1) moves behavior defined in indirect clients to an intermediate data container to make it more "objectlike." This pattern not only decouples indirect clients from the contents of the data container, but also typically eliminates duplicated code occurring in multiple clients of the data container.

- Eliminate Navigation Code (Pattern 9.2) is technically very similar to Move Behavior Close to Data (Pattern 9.1) in terms of the reengineering steps, but is rather different in its intent. This pattern focuses on redistributing responsibilities down chains of data containers to eliminate navigation code.

- Split Up God Class (Pattern 9.3) refactors a procedural god class into a number of simple, more cohesive classes by moving all data to external data containers, applying Move Behavior Close to Data (Pattern 9.1)to promote the data containers to objects, and finally removing or deprecating the facade that remains.

PATTERN

9.1 Move Behavior Close to Data

Intent: Strengthen encapsulation by moving behavior from indirect clients to the class containing the data it operates on.

Problem How do you transform a class from being a mere data container into a real service provider?

This problem is difficult because

- Data containers offer only accessor methods or public instance variables, and not real behavior, forcing clients to define the behavior themselves instead of just using it. New clients typically have to reimplement this behavior.

- If the internal representation of a data container changes, many clients have to be updated.

- Data containers cannot be used polymorphically since they define no behavior and their interfaces consist mainly of accessor methods. As a consequence, clients will be responsible for deciding which behavior is called for in any given context.

Yet, solving this problem is feasible because

- You know what operations clients perform with the data.

Solution Move behavior defined by indirect clients to the container of the data on which it operates.

Detection

Look for the following:

- Data containers—classes defining mostly public accessor methods and few behavior methods (e.g., the number of methods is approximately two times larger than the number of attributes).

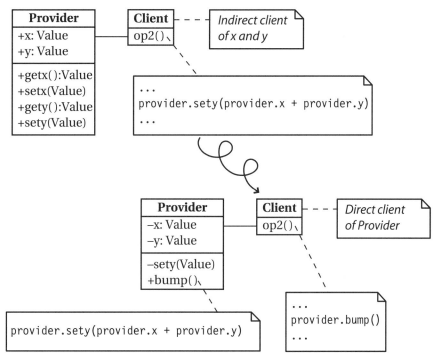

FIGURE **9.3** Classes that were mere data containers are transformed into real service providers.

- Duplicated client code that manipulates data of separate provider classes. If multiple clients implement *different* behavior, consider instead applying Transform Client Type Checks (Pattern 10.2).

- Methods in client classes that invoke a sequence of accessor methods (see Eliminate Navigation Code, Pattern 9.2).

Steps

Move Behavior Close to Data makes use of the refactorings Extract Method (Pattern A.5) and Move Method (Pattern A.6), since the behavior in question will have to be extracted from a client method and then moved to a provider class (see Figure 9.3).

1. *Identify the client behavior that you want to move,* that is, the complete method or a part of a method that accesses provider data.

   - Look for the invocations of the accessor methods of the data container.

   - Look for duplicated code in multiple clients that access the same provider data.

2. *Create the corresponding method in the provider class,* if it does not already exist. Be sure to check that moving the code will not introduce any naming conflicts. Tools like the Refactoring Browser [Robe97] automate these steps:

   - If the extracted functionality is a complete method with arguments, check that the arguments do not conflict with attributes of the provider class. If so, rename the arguments.

   - If the extracted functionality uses temporary variables, check that the local variables do not conflict with attributes or variables in the target scope. If so, rename the temporary variables.

   - Check if the extracted functionality accesses local variables of the client classes (attributes, temporary variables, etc.). If so, add arguments to the method to represent these client variables.

3. *Give an intention-revealing name* to the new method. Among others, intention revealing names do not contain references to the class they belong to because this makes the method less reusable. For instance, instead of defining a method addToSet() on a class Set, it is better to name it simply add(). Similarly, it is not such a good idea to define a method binarySearch() on a class Array because the method name implies a sorted random access collection, while the name search() does not have such implications.

4. In the client, *invoke the new provider method* with the correct parameters.

5. *Clean up the client code.* In the case that the moved functionality was a complete method of the client class:

   - check all the methods that invoke the old, moved method and ensure that they now call the new provider method instead, and

   - remove the old method from the client or deprecate it (Deprecate Obsolete Interfaces, Pattern 7.10).

   It may be the case that the calling methods defined on the same object also have to be moved to the provider. In such a case, repeat the steps for the methods.

6. *Repeat* for multiple clients. Note that duplicated code in multiple clients will be removed in step 2, since there is no need to move code that has already been transferred to the provider. If many similar but not identical methods are introduced to the provider, consider factoring out the duplicated fragments as protected helper methods.

Trade-offs   Pros

- Data containers are converted to service providers with clear responsibilities.
- The service providers become more useful to other clients.
- Clients are no longer responsible for implementing provider behavior.
- Clients are less sensitive to internal changes of the provider.
- Code duplication in the system decreases.

Cons

- If the moved behavior also accesses client data, turning these accesses into parameters will make the interface of the provider more complex and introduce explicit dependencies from the provider to the client.

Difficulties

- It may not be clear whether client code really should be moved to the data provider. Some classes like Stream or Set are really designed as data providers. Consider moving the code to the provider if
  - the functionality represents a *responsibility* of the provider. For example, a class Set should provide mathematical operations like union and intersection. On the other hand, a generic Set should not be responsible for operations on sets of Employees.
  - the functionality accesses the attributes of the provider.
  - the functionality is defined by multiple clients.
- If the provider is really designed as a data container, consider defining a new provider class that wraps an instance of the data provider and holds the associated behavior. For example, an EmployeeSet might wrap a Set instance and provide a more suitable interface.

When the Legacy Solution Is the Solution

Data containers may have been automatically generated from a database schema to provide an object interface to an existing database. It is almost always a bad idea to modify generated classes, since you will lose your changes if the code ever needs to be regenerated. In this case, you may decide to implement wrapper classes to hold the behavior that should be associated with the generated classes. Such a wrapper would function as an Adapter (Pattern A.11) that converts the generated data container to a real service provider.

PATTERN 9.1 *continued*

Sometimes you know that a class defined in a library is missing crucial functionality—for example, an operation `convertToCapitals` is missing for class `String`. In such a case it is typically impossible to add code to the library, so you may have to define it in the client class. In C++, for example, it may be the only way to avoid recompilation or to extend a class when the code is not available [Alpe98, p. 378]. In Smalltalk you have the possibility of extending or modifying the library; however, you should pay particular attention to separate the additional code so you can easily merge it with future releases of the library and quickly detect any conflicts.

The Visitor pattern is one of the few cases where you want to have classes access the data of a separate provider class. Visitor allows you to dynamically add new operations to a set of stable classes without having to change them, as shown by the pattern intent (Pattern A.22):

> Represent an operation to be performed on the elements of an object structure in a class separate from the elements themselves. Visitor lets you define a new operation without changing the classes of the elements on which it operates. [Gamm95]

Configuration classes are classes that represent the configuration of a system (e.g., global parameters, language-dependent representation, policies in place). For example, in a graphic tool the default size of the boxes, edges, and widths of the lines can be stored in such a class, and other classes refer to it when needed.

Mapping classes are classes used to represent mappings between objects and their user interface or database representation. For example, a software metric tool should graphically represent the available metrics in a widget list so that the user can select the metrics to be computed. In such a case the graphical representation of the different metrics will certainly differ from their internal representation. A mapping class keeps track of the association.

Example   One of the recurring complaints of customers is that it takes too much time to change the reports generated by the information system. By talking to the maintainers you learn that they find generating the reports quite boring. "It's always the same code you have to write," says Chris, one of the maintainers. "You fetch a record out of the database, print its fields, and then proceed to the next record."

You strongly suspect a case of data containers, and a closer examination of the code confirms your suspicion. Almost all of the classes interfacing with the database contain accessor methods only, and the programs generating reports are forced to use these accessors. One striking example

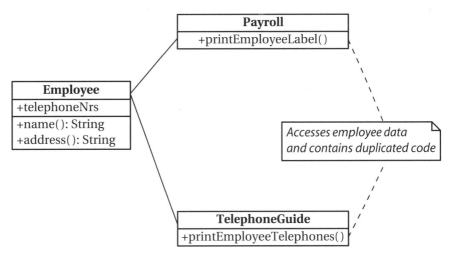

FIGURE **9.4** The `Payroll` and `Telephone` classes access the internal representation of the class `Employee` to print a representation.

is the case of the `Payroll` application, which has lots in common with the `TelephoneGuide` application. You decide to try to move the common functionality to the `Employee` class.

Before

As shown in Figure 9.4, both the `Payroll` and `TelephoneGuide` classes print labels, treating `Employee` instances as data containers. Thus, `Payroll` and `TelephoneGuide` are indirect clients of the attributes of `Employee` and define printing code that should have been provided by the `Employee` class. The following code shows how this would look in Java:

```java
public class Employee {
  public String[] telephoneNumbers = {};
  ...
  public String name() {
    return _name;}

  public String address() {
    return _address;}
}

public class Payroll {

  public static Employee currentEmployee;
```

PATTERN 9.1 *continued*

```
public static void printEmployeeLabel () {
  System.out.println(currentEmployee.name());
  System.out.println(currentEmployee.address());
  for (int i=0; i < currentEmployee.telephoneNumbers.length; i++) {
    System.out.print(currentEmployee.telephoneNumbers[i]);
    System.out.print(" ");}
  System.out.println("");}
...
}

public class TelephoneGuide {

  public static void printEmployeeTelephones (Employee emp) {
    System.out.println(emp.name());
    System.out.println(emp.address());
    for (int i=0; i < emp.telephoneNumbers.length - 1; i++) {
      System.out.print(emp.telephoneNumbers[i]);
      System.out.print("--");}
    System.out.print(emp.telephoneNumbers[
        emp.telephoneNumbers.length - 1]);
    System.out.println("");}
  ...
}
```

Note that although both print methods implement essentially the same functionality, there are some slight differences. Among others, Telephone-Guide.printEmployeeTelephones uses a different separator while printing out the telephone numbers.

Steps

The different separators can easily be dealt with by defining a special parameter representing the separator to be used. Thus TelephoneGuide. printEmployeeTelephones gets rewritten as follows:

```
public static void printEmployeeTelephones
        (Employee emp, String separator) {
  ...
  for (int i=0; ...
    System.out.print(seperator);}
  ...}
...
```

Next, move the printEmployeeTelephones method from TelephoneGuide to Employee. Thus, copy the code and replace all references to the emp parameter with a direct reference to the attributes and methods. Also, ensure that the new method has an intention-revealing name and omit the "Employee" part from the method name, resulting in a method printLabel.

```java
public class Employee {
  ...
  public void printLabel (String separator) {

    System.out.println(_name);
    System.out.println(_address);
    for (int i=0; i < telephoneNumbers.length - 1; i++) {
      System.out.print(telephoneNumbers[i]);
      System.out.print(separator);
    }
    System.out.print(telephoneNumbers[telephoneNumbers.length - 1]);
    System.out.println("");
  }
```

Then replace the method bodies of Payroll.printEmployeeLabel and TelephoneGuide.printEmployeeTelephones with a simple invocation of the Employee.printLabel method:

```java
public class Payroll {
  ...
  public static void printEmployeeLabel () {
    currentEmployee.printLabel(" ");
  ...}

public class TelephoneGuide {
  ...
  public static void printEmployeeTelephones (Employee emp) {
    emp.printLabel("--");}
  ...}
```

Finally, verify which other methods refer to the name(), address(), and telephoneNumbers. If no such methods exist, consider declaring those methods and attributes as private.

After

After applying Move Behavior Close to Data, the class Employee now provides a printLabel method that takes one argument to represent the dif-

PATTERN 9.1 *continued*

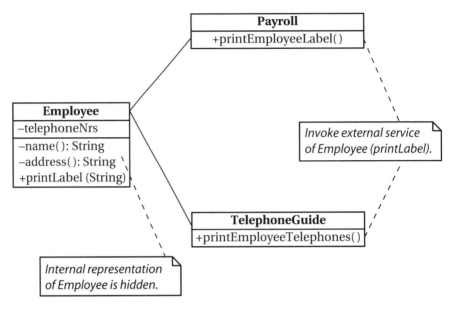

F I G U R E **9.5**   The Payroll class uses the public interface of the class Employee to print a representation of Employee; data accessors became private.

ferent separators (see Figure 9.5). This is a better situation because now
clients do not rely on the internal representation of Employee. Moreover, by
moving the behavior near the data it operates, the class represents a conceptual entity with an emphasis on the services it provides instead of
structure it implements.

Rationale   Keep related data and behavior in one place.

[Riel96], Heuristic 2.9

Data containers impede evolution because they expose structure and force
clients to define their behavior rather than sharing it. By promoting data
containers to service providers, you reduce coupling between classes and
improve cohesion of data and behavior.

Related   Encapsulate Field (Pattern A.4) offers heuristics that help determine where
Patterns   methods should be defined during a design phase. The text offers a rationale for applying Move Behavior Close to Data.

PATTERN

| 9.2 | **Eliminate Navigation Code** |

Also Known As: Law of Demeter [Lieb88]

Intent: Reduce the impact of changes by shifting responsibility down a chain of connected classes.

Problem How do you reduce coupling due to classes that navigate through the object graph?

This problem is difficult because

- Changes in the interfaces of a class will affect not only direct clients, but also all the indirect clients that navigate to reach it.

Yet, solving this problem is feasible because

- Navigation code is typically a sign of misplaced responsibilities and violation of encapsulation.

Solution Iteratively move behavior defined by an indirect client to the container of the data on which it operates.

Note that the actual reengineering steps are basically the same as those of Move Behavior Close to Data (Pattern 9.1), but the manifestation of the problem is rather different, so different detection steps apply.

Detection

Look for *indirect providers:*

- Each time a class changes, for example, by modifying its internal representation or collaborators, not only its direct but also its *indirect* client classes have to be changed.
- Look for classes that contain a lot public attributes, accessor methods, or methods returning as value attributes of the class.
- Big aggregation hierarchies containing mostly data classes often play the role of indirect provider.

Look for *indirect clients* that contain a lot of *navigation code.* Navigation code is of two kinds:

PATTERN 9.2 *continued*

- A *sequence of attribute accesses,* for example, a.b.c.d, where b is an attribute of a, c is an attribute of b, and d an attribute of c. The result of such a sequence can be assigned to a variable, or a method of the last object can be invoked, for example, a.b.c.d.op(). Such a sequence navigation does not occur in Smalltalk, where all the attributes are protected.

- A *sequence of accessor method calls.* In Java and C++ such a sequence has the form object.m1().m2().m3(), where object is an expression returning an object, m1 is a method of the object, m2 a method of the object returned by the invocation of m1, m3 a method of the object returned by the invocation of m2, and so on. In Smalltalk, navigation code has the following form: receiver m1 m2 ... mn The same navigation code sequence is repeated in different methods on the same or different clients.

Navigation code can be detected by simple pattern matching. However, to really detect a method call navigation sequence leading to coupled classes, you should filter out sequences of calls converting one object to another one. For example, the following two Java expressions are not problematic because they deal with object conversion:

```
leftSide().toString()
i.getValue().isShort()
```

To deal with this case you can

- look for more than two calls, or
- eliminate from consideration known object conversion calls, including standard method invocations for converting to and from primitive types.

The use of additional variables can sometimes disguise navigation code, so reading the code is often necessary. For instance, the following Java code does not contain a chain of invocations:

```
Token token;
token = parseTree.token();
if (token.identifier() != null) {
  ...
```

However, it is equivalent to the following code, which does contain a chain of invocations:

```
if (parseTree.token().identifier() != null) {
  ...
```

Smalltalk. Simply searching for sequences of calls in Smalltalk code can create a lot of noise because Smalltalk does not have predefined control structures but uses messages even for implementing control structures. The previous example with the disguised navigation code would read as follows in Smalltalk (note the messages isNil and ifFalse:[...]):

```
| token |
token := parseTree token.
token identifier isNil ifFalse:[...]
```

The equivalent version with navigation code becomes

```
parseTree token identifier isNil ifFalse: [...]
```

The following code segments contain a sequence of invocations but do not pose any problems because the first deals with boolean testing and the second with conversion (abuse of conversion, in fact):

```
(a isNode) & (a isAbstract) ifTrue: [...]
aCol asSet asSortedCollection asOrderedCollection
```

Java. For Java or C++, primitive data types and control structures are not implemented using objects, so simple pattern-matching produces less noise. For example, a simple Unix command like

```
egrep '.*\(\).*\(\).*\(\).' *.java
egrep '.*\..*\..*\..' *.java
```

identifies lines of code like the following ones, which are examples of navigation code coupling between classes, and filters out the conversions mentioned earlier:

```
a.getAbstraction().getIdentifier().traverse(this)
a.abstraction.identifier.traverse(this)
```

More sophisticated matching expressions can reduce the noise produced by the parentheses of casts or other combinations.

AST Matching. If you have a way to express tree matching, you can detect navigation code. For example, the Rewrite Rule Editor that comes with the Refactoring Browser [Robe97] can detect navigation code using the pattern '@object 'mess1 'mess2 'mess3. To narrow the analysis of the results, you should only consider messages that belong to the domain objects and eliminate all the method selectors of libraries objects like (`isNil`, `not`, `class`, etc.).

Steps

The recipe for eliminating navigation code is to recursively Move Behavior Close to Data (Pattern 9.1). Figure 9.6 illustrates the transformation.

1. *Identify* the navigation code to move.
2. *Apply* Move Behavior Close to Data (Pattern 9.1) to remove one level of navigation. (At this point your regression tests should run.)
3. *Repeat* if necessary.

Caution: It is important to note that the refactoring process relies on pushing code *from the clients to the providers*—in the example, from `Car` to `Engine` and from `Engine` to `Carburetor`. A common mistake is to try to eliminate navigation code by defining accessors at the client class level that access the attributes of the provider attribute values, for example, defining an accessor `getCarburetor` in the class `Car`. Instead of reducing coupling between the classes, it just increases the number of public accessors and makes the system more complex.

Trade-offs   Pros

- Chains of dependencies between classes are eliminated, so changes in classes at the lowest level will impact fewer clients.
- Functionality that was implicit in the system is now named and explicitly available to new clients.

Cons

- The systematic application of Eliminate Navigation Code may lead to large interfaces. In particular, if a class defines many instance variables that are collections, then Eliminate Navigation Code would force you to define a large number of additional methods to shield the underlying collections.

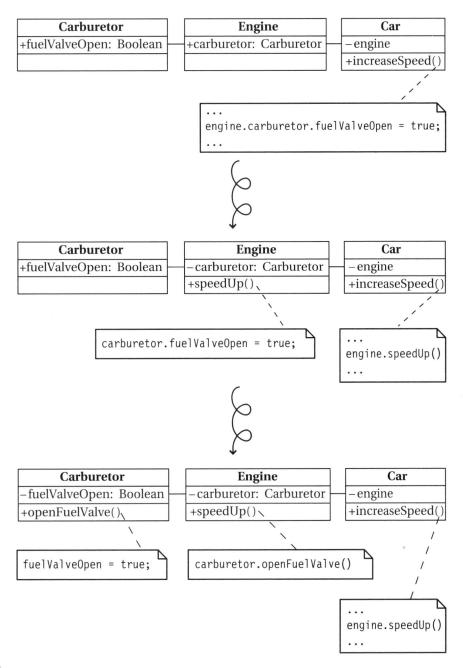

FIGURE **9.6** Chains of data containers can be converted into service providers, thereby eliminating navigation code and reducing coupling between classes.

PATTERN 9.2 *continued*

Difficulties

* Deciding when to apply Eliminate Navigation Code can be difficult. Defining methods that merely delegate requests to class collaborators may not always be the solution. It may happen that giving away internal information can reduce the interface of a class. For example, if a class implements some well-defined behaviors but also serves as a Facade (Pattern A.12) to other collaborators, it may be simpler to give access to the collaborator directly to reduce the interface of the class.

When the Legacy Solution Is the Solution

Navigation code may be the best solution when objects are graphically presented or mapped to a database. In such cases the goal really is to expose and mimic the structural relationships between classes. Eliminating navigation code will be a futile exercise.

It is sometimes necessary for a client to talk with its indirect providers. This is true when direct providers play the role of an object *server* that returns certain objects given certain properties (OOID, keys, etc.). In this situation the client calls the object server (a direct provider) that returns objects (indirect providers) to which the client sends messages.

Example After having modified the Employee, Payroll, and TelephoneGuide classes, you noticed that it took half an hour to rebuild the whole project. The next time you see Chris (one of the maintainers) you ask him why this build took so long. "You probably changed the Employee class" he answers. "We don't dare touch that class anymore since so many classes depend on it."

You decide to examine this Employee class in further detail and find many unnecessary dependencies. For instance (as shown in Figure 9.7), there is a class Reports, implementing one method countHandledFiles, which counts for each Department the number of files that are handled by all of its employees. Unfortunately, there is no direct relationship between Department and File, and consequently the ReportHandledFiles must navigate over a department's employees to enumerate all the files and access the handled() status.

The following Java code shows the situation before and after applying Eliminate Navigation Code. The bold textual elements highlight problems and the solutions in the before and after situations.

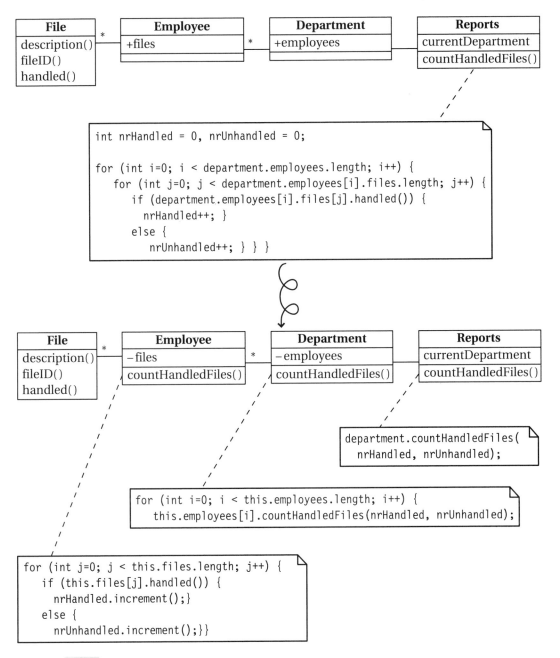

FIGURE **9.7** How to remove the unnecessary dependencies between the Reports class and the File and Employee classes.

PATTERN 9.2 *continued*

Before

```
public class Reports {
...
  public static void countHandledFiles(Department department) {
    int nrHandled = 0, nrUnhandled = 0;

    for (int i=0; i < department.employees.length; i++) {
      for (int j=0; j < department.employees[i].files.length; j++) {
        if (department.employees[i].files[j].handled()) {
          nrHandled++;}
        else {
          nrUnhandled++;}}}
...}
```

The method `countHandledFiles` counts the number of handled files, by asking the current department for its `employees` and for each of these the `files`. The classes `Department` and `Employee` have to declare those attributes public. With this implementation, two problems occur:

1. The `Reports` class must know how to enumerate the associations between `Department`, `Employee`, and `File`, and this information must be accessible in the public interface of each of the classes. If one of these public interfaces changes, then this change will affect all associated classes.
2. The method `countHandledFiles` is implemented by directly accessing the variables `employees` and `files`. This unnecessarily couples the class `Reports` and the classes `Department` and `Employee`. If the class `Department` or `Employee` changes the data structure used to hold the associated objects, then all the methods in class `Reports` will have to be adapted.

Steps

The solution is to extract the nested for loops as separate methods and move them to the appropriate classes. This is actually a two-step process.

First, extract the outer for loop from `Reports.countHandledFiles` as a separate method (name it `countHandledFiles` as well) and move it to the class `Department`:

```
public class Department {
...
```

```
      public void countHandledFiles
          (Counter nrHandled, Counter nrUnhandled) {
      for (int i=0; i < this.employees.length; i++) {
        for (int j=0; j < this.employees[i].files.length; j++) {
          if (this.employees[i].files[j].handled()) {
            nrHandled.increment();}
          else {
            nrUnhandled.increment();}}}}
...}

public class Reports {
...
  private static void countHandledFiles(Department department) {
    Counter nrHandled = new Counter (0), nrUnhandled = new Counter (0);

    department.countHandledFiles(nrHandled, nrUnhandled);
...}
```

Next, extract the inner for loop from Department.countHandledFiles
(also named countHandledFiles) and move it to the class Employee.

```
public class Employee {
...
  public void countHandledFiles
      (Counter nrHandled, Counter nrUnhandled) {
    for (int j=0; j < this.files.length; j++) {
      if (this.files[j].handled()) {
        nrHandled.increment();}
      else {
        nrUnhandled.increment();}}}
...}

public class Department {
...
  public void countHandledFiles
      (Counter nrHandled, Counter nrUnhandled) {
    for (int i=0; i < this.employees.length; i++) {
      this.employees[i].countHandledFiles(nrHandled, nrUnhandled);}}
...}
```

If all direct accesses to the employees and files variables are removed,
these attributes can be declared private.

PATTERN 9.2 *continued*

Rationale   A method "M" of an object "O" should invoke only the methods of the following kinds of objects.

1. itself

2. its parameters

3. any object it creates/instantiates

4. its direct component objects

—Law of Demeter

Navigation code is a well-known symptom of misplaced behavior [Lore94] [Shar97] [Riel96] that violates the law of Demeter [Lieb88]. It leads to unnecessary dependencies between classes, and as a consequence changing the representation of a class requires *all* clients to be adapted.

Related Patterns   Eliminate Navigation Code and Compare Code Mechanically (Pattern 8.1) reinforce each other: navigation code that is spread across different clients spreads duplicated code over the system. Compare Code Mechanically (Pattern 8.1) helps to detect this phenomenon. Eliminate Navigation Code brings the duplicated code together, where it is easier to refactor and eliminate.

PATTERN

9.3   Split Up God Class

Also Known As: The Blob [Brow98], God Class [Riel96]

Intent: Split up a class with too many responsibilities into a number of smaller, cohesive classes.

Problem   How do you maintain a class that assumes too many responsibilities?

This problem is difficult because

- By assuming too many responsibilities, a god class monopolizes control of an application. Evolution of the application is difficult because nearly every change touches this class and affects multiple responsibilities.

- It is difficult to understand the different abstractions that are inter-mixed in a god class. Most of the data of the multiple abstractions is accessed from different places.

- Identifying where to change a feature without impacting the other functionality or other objects in the system is difficult. Moreover, changes in other objects are likely to impact the god class, thus hampering the evolution of the system.

- It is nearly impossible to change a part of the behavior of a god class in a black-box way.

Yet, solving this problem is feasible because

- You don't have to fix the problem in one shot.

- You can use Semantic Wrapper to wrap it and present interfaces.

Solution Incrementally redistribute the responsibilities of the god class either to its collaborating classes or to new classes that are pulled out of the god class. When there is nothing left of the god class but a facade, remove or depre-cate the facade.

Detection

A god class may be recognized in various ways:

- A single huge class treats many other classes as data structures.

- A "root" class or other huge class has a name containing words like "System," "Subsystem," "Manager," "Driver," or "Controller."

- Changes to the system always result in changes to the same class.

- Changes to the class are extremely difficult because you cannot identify which parts of the class they affect.

- Reusing the class is nearly impossible because it covers too many design concerns.

- The class is a domain class holding the majority of attributes and meth-ods of a system or subsystem. (Note that the threshold is not absolute because some UI frameworks produce big classes with lots of methods, and some database interface classes may need a lot of attributes.)

- The class has an unrelated set of methods working on separated in-stance variables. The cohesiveness of the class is usually low.

- The class requires long compile times, even for small modifications.

PATTERN 9.3 *continued*

- The class is difficult to test due to the many responsibilities it assumes.
- The class uses a lot of memory.
- People tell you: "This is the heart of the system."
- When you ask for the responsibility of a god class, you get various, long, and unclear answers.
- God classes are the nightmare of maintainers, so ask what classes are huge and difficult to maintain. Ask what is the class they would not like to work on. (Variant: Ask people to choose which class they want to work on. The one that everybody avoids may be a god class.)

Steps

The solution relies on incrementally moving behavior away from the god class. During this process, data containers will become more objectlike by acquiring the functionality that the god class was performing on their data. Some new classes will also be extracted from the god class.

The following steps describe how this process ideally works. Note, however, that god classes can vary greatly in terms of their internal structure, so different techniques may be used to implement the transformation steps. Furthermore, it should be clear that a god class cannot be cured in one shot, so a safe way to proceed is to first transform a god class into a lightweight god class, then into a Facade (Pattern A.12) that delegates behavior to its acquaintances. Finally, clients are redirected to the refactored data containers and the other new objects, and the Facade can be removed. The process is illustrated in Figure 9.8.

The following steps are applied iteratively. Be sure to apply Regression Test after Every Change (Pattern 7.6):

1. Identify cohesive subsets of instance variables of the god class, and convert them to external data containers. Change the initialization methods of the god class to refer to instances of the new data containers.

2. Identify all classes used as data containers by the god class (including those created in step 1) and apply Move Behavior Close to Data (Pattern 9.1) to promote the data containers into service providers. The original methods of the god class will simply delegate behavior to the moved methods.

3. After iteratively applying steps 1 and 2, there will be nothing left of the god class except a facade with a big initialization method. Shift the responsibility for initialization to a separate class, so only a pure facade is left. Iteratively redirect clients to the objects for which the former god

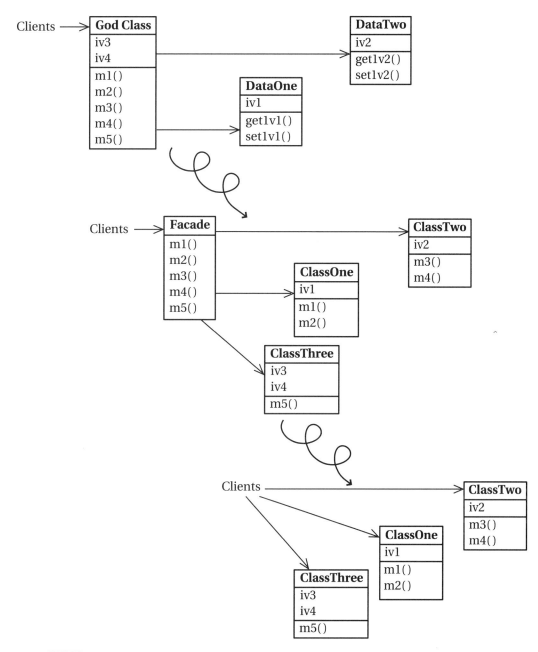

FIGURE **9.8** A god class is refactored in two stages, first by redistributing responsibilities to data containers, or by spawning off new classes, until there is nothing left but a facade, and second by removing the facade.

P A T T E R N 9 . 3 *continued*

class is now a facade, and either deprecate the facade (see Deprecate Obsolete Interfaces, Pattern 7.10) or simply remove it.

Trade-offs Pros

- Application control is no longer centralized in a single monolithic entity but distributed among entities that each assume a well-defined set of responsibilities. The design evolves from a procedural design toward an object-oriented design based on autonomous interacting objects.
- Parts of the original god class are easier to understand and to maintain.
- Parts of the original god class are more stable because they deal with fewer issues.
- Overall compilation time may be reduced due to the simplification of system dependencies.

Cons

- Splitting up a god class is a long, slow, and tedious process.
- Maintainers will no longer be able to go to a single god class to locate behavior to fix.
- The number of classes will increase.

Difficulties

- God class methods may themselves be large, procedural abstractions with too many responsibilities. Such methods may need to be decomposed before cohesive sets of instance variables and methods can be teased out as classes.

When the Legacy Solution Is the Solution

What is riskier? To Split Up God Class or to leave it alone? A real god class is a large, unwieldy beast. Splitting it up into more robust abstractions may introduce considerable cost.

The key issue is whether the god class needs to be *maintained*. If the god class consists of stable legacy code that rarely needs to be extended or modified, then refactoring it is a questionable investment of effort.

Suppose, on the other hand, that it is the *clients* of the god class that are unstable and need to be frequently adapted to changing requirements. Then the clients should be shielded from the god class since it is not presenting a clean interface. Consider instead applying Present the Right Interface (Pattern 7.8), which will introduce a layer of clean object-oriented abstractions between the clients and the god class, and may make it easier to evolve the clients.

Rationale   Do not create god classes/objects in your system.

[Riel96], Heuristic 3.2

God classes impede evolution because they achieve only a low level of procedural abstraction, so changes may affect many parts of the god class, its data containers, and its clients. By splitting a god class up into object-oriented abstractions, changes will tend to be more localized and therefore easier to implement.

Related Patterns   Foote and Yoder in "Big Ball of Mud" [Foot00] note that god classes (and worse) arise naturally in software development.

> People build BIG BALLS OF MUD because they work. In many domains, they are the only things that have been shown to work. Indeed, they work where loftier approaches have yet to demonstrate that they can compete.

> It is not our purpose to condemn BIG BALLS OF MUD. Casual architecture is natural during the early stages of a system's evolution. The reader must surely suspect, however, that our hope is that we can aspire to do better. By recognizing the forces and pressures that lead to architectural malaise, and how and when they might be confronted, we hope to set the stage for the emergence of truly durable artifacts that can put architects in dominant positions for years to come. The key is to ensure that the system, its programmers, and, indeed the entire organization, learn about the domain, and the architectural opportunities looming within it, as the system grows and matures.

Present the Right Interface (Pattern 7.8) is a competing pattern that should be applied when the god class itself rarely needs to be modified or extended.

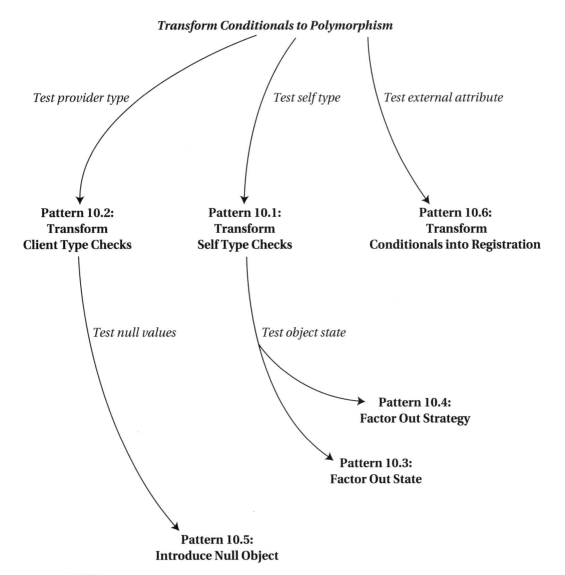

F I G U R E **10.1** Relationships between the patterns constituting Transform Conditionals to Polymorphism.

10

Transform Conditionals to Polymorphism

After duplicated code, data containers, and god classes, one of the most striking signs of misplaced responsibilities in object-oriented software is the occurrence of large methods consisting almost entirely of case statements that test the type of some argument.

Although case statements are not inherently bad, in object-oriented code they are frequently a sign that the object doing the testing is assuming responsibilities that would better be distributed to the objects being tested. Big conditionals arise naturally over time, just as duplicated code does. As the software is adapted to handle new cases, these cases pop up as conditionals in the code. The problem with these big conditionals is that they can make the code much more fragile in the long term.

Forces

The following forces are at play:

- As requirements change over time, classes in a software system will have to be adapted to handle new and special cases.

- Adding new classes or subclasses to a system clutters the namespace.

- The quickest way to adapt a working piece of software to handle a new requirement is often to add a conditional test for the special case at some point in the code.

- Over time a simple design tends to get cluttered with many conditional tests for special cases.

- Case statements group all the variants into a single place instead of spreading the different cases across different classes. However, they lead to design that is less flexible if the case statement appears in more than one place.

- In some programming languages, case statements are a more conventional idiom to implement varying behavior than polymorphism.

Large conditionals are often a sign that behavior implemented by clients should probably be be shifted to the provider classes. Typically a new method will be introduced to the provider hierarchy, and the individual cases of the conditional statement will each move to one of the provider classes.

Although the symptom is readily recognizable, the technical details and the preferred solution may differ considerably. In particular, when the provider hierarchy already exists, and the conditions explicitly check the class of the provider instance, the refactoring is relatively straightforward. But often the provider hierarchy does not exist, and the conditions test attributes that only implicitly model type information. Furthermore, the conditionals may occur not only in external clients, but even in the provider hierarchy itself.

Overview

Transform Conditionals to Polymorphism is a pattern language that describes how to redistribute responsibilities to eliminate these large conditionals, thereby reducing coupling between classes and improving flexibility in the face of future changes.

This pattern language consists of six patterns that address the most common problems that occur when conditionals are used to simulate polymorphism. Transform Self Type Checks (Pattern 10.1) and Transform Client Type Checks (Pattern 10.2) address the most typical cases that arise when explicit type checks are performed. Transform Conditionals into Registration (Pattern 10.6) occurs less frequently. We also include Factor Out State (Pattern 10.3), Factor Out Strategy (Pattern 10.4) and Introduce Null Object (Pattern 10.5), not in order to copy three established design patterns (State, Pattern A.18; Strategy, Pattern A.20; and Null Object, Pattern A.15) but rather to show how these design patterns may apply in a reengineering context to eliminate type-checking conditionals.

Figure 10.1 on page 214 summarizes the relationships and the differences between the patterns:

- Transform Self Type Checks (Pattern 10.1) eliminates conditionals over type information in a provider class by *introducing subclasses* for each type case. The conditional code is replaced by a single polymorphic method call to an instance of one of the new subclasses.
- Transform Client Type Checks (Pattern 10.2) transforms conditionals over type information in a client class by *introducing a new method* to

each of the provider classes. The conditional is replaced by a single polymorphic call to the new method.

- Factor Out State (Pattern 10.3) handles a special case of Transform Self Type Checks (Pattern 10.1) in which the type information that is being tested may change dynamically. *Introduce a State object* (Pattern A.18) in the provider class to model the changing state, and the conditional is replaced by a call to a method of the new State object.

- Factor Out Strategy (Pattern 10.4) is another special case of Transform Self Type Checks (Pattern 10.1) in which the algorithms to handle the various provider cases are factored out by *introducing a new Strategy object* (Pattern A.20). The key difference with Factor Out State is that the algorithm rather than the state may vary dynamically.

- Introduce Null Object (Pattern 10.5) addresses the special case of Transform Client Type Checks (Pattern 10.2) in which the test performed checks whether or not the provider is defined. The conditional is eliminated by *introducing a Null Object* (Pattern A.15) which implements the appropriate default behavior.

- Transform Conditionals into Registration (Pattern 10.6) addresses the situation in which the conditional is responsible for starting up an external tool based on some attribute of an object to be handled. The solution is to *introduce a lookup service* where tools are registered as plug-ins. The conditional is then replaced by a simple lookup for the registered plug-in. The solution is then fully dynamic because new plug-ins can be added or removed without any changes to the tool users.

PATTERN

10.1   Transform Self Type Checks

Intent: Improve the extensibility of a class by replacing a complex conditional statement with a call to a hook method implemented by subclasses.

Problem   A class is hard to modify or extend because it bundles multiple possible behaviors in complex conditional statements that test some attribute representing the current "type" of the object.

This problem is difficult because

- Conceptually simple extensions require many changes to the conditional code.

PATTERN 10.1 *continued*

- Subclassing is next to impossible without duplicating and adapting the methods containing the conditional code.
- Adding a new behavior always results in changes to the same set of methods and always results in adding a new case to the conditional code.

Yet, solving this problem is feasible because

- Self type checks simulate polymorphism. The conditional code tells you what subclasses you should have instead.

Solution   Identify the methods with complex conditional branches. In each case, replace the conditional code with a call to a new hook method. Identify or introduce subclasses corresponding to the cases of the conditional. In each of these subclasses, implement the hook method with the code corresponding to that case in the original case statement.

Detection

Most of the time, the type discrimination will jump in your face while you are working on the code, so this means that you will not really need to detect where the checks are made. However, it can be interesting to have simple techniques to quickly assess if unknown parts of a system suffer from similar practices. This can be a valuable source of information for evaluating the state of a system.

- Look for long methods with complex decision structures on some immutable attribute of the object that models type information. In particular look for attributes that are set in the constructor and never changed.
- Attributes that are used to model type information typically take on values from some enumerated type, or from some finite set of constant values. Look for constant definitions whose names represent entities or concepts that one would usually expect to be associated with classes (like RetiredEmployee or PendingOrder). The conditionals will normally just compare the value of a fixed attribute to one of these constant values.
- Especially look for classes where *multiple* methods switch on the same attribute. This is another common sign that the attribute is being used to simulate a type.
- Since methods containing switch statements tend to be long, it may help to use a tool that sorts methods by lines of code or visualizes classes and methods according to their size. Alternatively, search for classes or methods with a large number of conditional statements.

- For languages like C++ or Java where it is common to store the implementation of a class in a separate file, it is straightforward to search for and count the incidence of conditional keywords (`if`, `else`, `case`, etc.). On a Unix system, for example,

```
grep switch `find . -name "*.cxx" -print`
```

  enumerates all the files in a directory tree with extension `.cxx` that contain a `switch`. Other text processing tools like agrep offer possibilities for posing finer-granularity queries. Text processing languages like perl may be better suited for evaluating some kinds of queries, especially those that span multiple lines.

- *C/C++:* Legacy C code may simulate classes by means of union types. Typically the union type will have one data member that encodes the actual type. Look for conditional statements that switch on such data members to decide which type to cast a union to and which behavior to employ.

  In C++ it is fairly common to find classes with data members that are declared as `void` pointers. Look for conditional statements that cast such pointers to a given type based on the value of some other data member. The type information may be encoded as an `enum` or (more commonly) as a constant integer value.

- *Ada:* Because Ada83 did not support polymorphism (or subprogram access types), discriminated record types are often used to simulate polymorphism. Typically an enumeration type provides the set of variants, and the conversion to polymorphism is straightforward in Ada95.

- *Smalltalk:* Smalltalk provides only a few ways to manipulate types. Look for applications of the methods `isMemberOf:` and `isKindOf:`, which signal explicit type checking. Type checks might also be made with tests like `self class = anotherClass`, or with property tests throughout the hierarchy using methods like `isSymbol`, `isString`, `isSequenceable`, `isInteger`.

Steps

The following steps are illustrated in Figure 10.2:

1. Identify the class to transform and the different conceptual classes that it implements. An enumeration type or set of constants will probably document this well.

2. Introduce a new subclass for each behavior that is implemented. Modify clients to instantiate the new subclasses rather than the original class. Run the tests.

PATTERN 10.1 *continued*

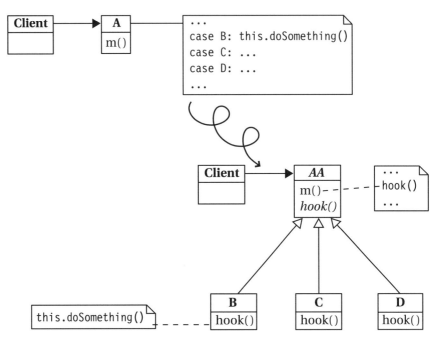

FIGURE **10.2**   Transformation of explicit type check into self polymorphic method calls.

3. Identify all methods of the original class that implement varying behavior by means of conditional statements. If the conditionals are surrounded by other statements, move them to separate, protected hook methods. When each conditional occupies a method of its own, run the tests.

4. Iteratively move the cases of the conditionals down to the corresponding subclasses, periodically running the tests.

5. The methods that contain conditional code should now all be empty. Replace these by abstract methods and run the tests.

6. Alternatively, if there are suitable default behaviors, implement these at the root of the new hierarchy.

7. If the logic required to decide which subclass to instantiate is nontrivial, consider encapsulating this logic as a factory method of the new hierarchy root. Update clients to use the new factory method and run the tests.

Trade-offs Pros

- New behaviors can now be added in an incremental manner, without having to change a set of methods of a single class containing all the behavior. A specific behavior can now be understood independently from the other variations.

- A new behavior represents its data independently from the others, thereby minimizing the possible interference and increasing the understandability of the separated behaviors.

- All behaviors now share a common interface, thereby improving their readability.

Cons

- All the behaviors are now dispersed into multiple but related abstractions, so getting an overview of the behavior may be more difficult. However, the concepts are related and share the interface represented by the abstract class, reducing the problem.

- The larger number of classes makes the design more complex and potentially harder to understand. If the original conditional statements are simple, it may not be worthwhile to perform this transformation.

- Explicit type checks are not always a problem, and we can sometimes tolerate them. Creating new classes increases the number of abstractions in the applications and can clutter namespaces. Hence, explicit type checks may be an alternative to the creation of new classes when

  - the set over which the method selection is fixed and will not evolve in the future, and
  - the type check is only made in a few places.

Difficulties

- Since the requisite subclasses do not yet exist, it can be hard to tell when conditionals are being used to simulate multiple types.

- Wherever instances of the transformed class were originally created, now instances of different subclasses must be created. If the instantiation occurred in client code, that code must now be adapted to instantiate the right class. Factory objects or methods may be needed to hide this complexity from clients.

- If you do not have access to the source code of the clients, it may be difficult or impossible to apply this pattern since you will not be able to change the calls to the constructors.

PATTERN 10.1 *continued*

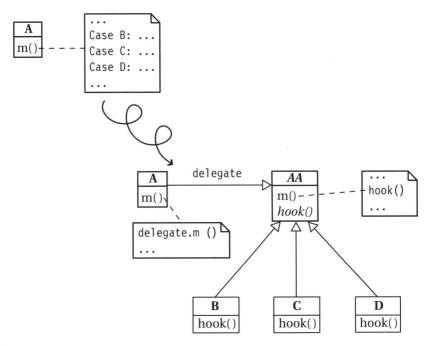

FIGURE **10.3** Combining simple delegation and Transform Self Type Checks when the class cannot be subclassed.

- If the case statements test more than one attribute, it may be necessary to support a more complex hierarchy, possibly requiring multiple inheritance. Consider splitting the class into parts, each with its own hierarchy.

- When the class containing the original conditionals cannot be subclassed, Transform Self Type Checks can be composed with delegation. The idea is to exploit polymorphism on another hierarchy by moving part of the state and behavior of the original class into a separate class to which the method will delegate, as shown in Figure 10.3.

When the Legacy Solution Is the Solution

There are some situations in which explicit type checks may nevertheless be the right solution:

- The conditional code may be generated from a special tool. Lexers and parsers, for example, may be automatically generated to contain the kind of conditional code we are trying to avoid. In these cases, however, the generated classes should never be manually extended, but simply regenerated from the modified specifications.

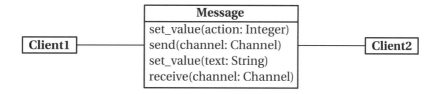

```
class Message {                     Message::send(Channel c) {
public:                                 switch (type_) {
    Message();                          case TEXT:
    set_value(char* text);                  ...
    set_value(int action);              case ACTION:
    void send(Channel c);                   ...
    void receive(Channel c);            }
    ...                             }
private:                            void Client1::doit() { ...
    void* data_;                        Message * myMessage =
    int type_;                              new Message();
    static const int TEXT = 1;          myMessage->set_Value("...");
    static const int ACTION = 2;        ...
    ...                             }
}
```

FIGURE **10.4**   Initial design and source code.

Example   We worked on a complex system that controls large, physical machines by sending them messages. These messages are represented by the class Message and can be of different types.

Before

A message class wraps two different kinds of messages (TEXT and ACTION) that must be serialized to be sent across a network connection, as shown in Figure 10.4. We would like to be able to send a new kind of message (say, VOICE), but this will require changes to several methods of Message.

After

Since Message conceptually implements two different classes, Text_Message and Action_Message, we introduce these as subclasses of Message, as shown in Figure 10.5. We introduce constructors for the new classes, we modify the clients to construct instances of Text_Message and Action_Message rather than Message, and we remove the set_value() methods. Our regression tests should run at this point.

PATTERN 10.1 *continued*

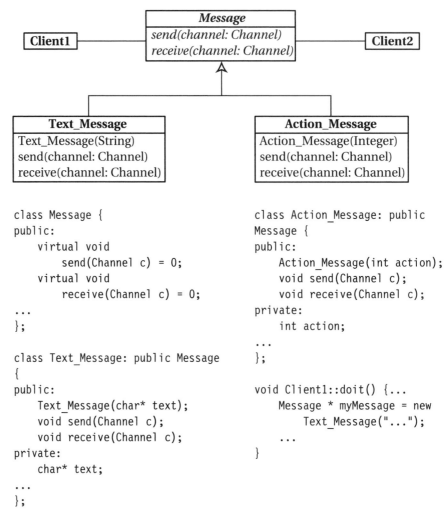

```
class Message {
public:
    virtual void
        send(Channel c) = 0;
    virtual void
        receive(Channel c) = 0;
...
};


class Text_Message: public Message
{
public:
    Text_Message(char* text);
    void send(Channel c);
    void receive(Channel c);
private:
    char* text;
...
};
```

```
class Action_Message: public
Message {
public:
    Action_Message(int action);
    void send(Channel c);
    void receive(Channel c);
private:
    int action;

...
};


void Client1::doit() {...
    Message * myMessage = new
        Text_Message("...");
    ...
}
```

FIGURE **10.5** Resulting hierarchy and source code.

Now we find methods that switch on the type_ variable. In each case, we move the entire switch statement to a separate, protected hook method, unless the switch already occupies the entire method. In the case of send(), this is already the case, so we do not have to introduce a hook method. Again, all our tests should still run.

Now we iteratively move cases of the switch statements from Message to its subclasses. The TEXT case of Message::send() moves to Text_Message::

send() and the ACTION case moves to Action_Message::send(). Every time we move such a case, our tests should still run.

Finally, since the original send() method is now empty, it can be redeclared to be abstract (i.e., virtual void send(Channel) = 0). Again, our tests should run.

Rationale

Classes that masquerade as multiple data types make a design harder to understand and extend. The use of explicit type checks leads to long methods that mix several different behaviors. Introducing new behavior then requires changes to be made to all such methods instead of simply specifying one new class representing the new behavior.

By transforming such classes to hierarchies that explicitly represent the multiple data types, you improve cohesion by bringing together all the code concerning a single data type, you eliminate a certain amount of duplicated code (i.e., the conditional tests), and you make your design more transparent and consequently easier to maintain.

Related Patterns

In Transform Self Type Checks the condition to be transformed tests type information that is represented as an attribute of the class itself.

If the conditional tests the *mutable* state of the host object, consider instead applying Factor Out State (Pattern 10.3), or possibly Factor Out Strategy (Pattern 10.4).

If the conditional occurs in a *client* rather than in the provider class itself, consider applying Transform Client Type Checks (Pattern 10.2).

If the conditional code tests some type attribute of a second object in order to *select some third handler object,* consider instead applying Transform Conditionals into Registration (Pattern 10.6).

PATTERN

10.2   Transform Client Type Checks

Intent: Reduce client/provider coupling by transforming conditional code that tests the type of the provider into a polymorphic call to a new provider method.

Problem

How do you reduce the coupling between clients and providers of services, where the clients explicitly test the type of providers and have the responsibility to compose providers' code?

PATTERN 10.2 *continued*

This problem is difficult because

- Adding a new subclass to the provider hierarchy requires making changes to many clients, especially where the tests occur.

- Clients and providers tend to be strongly coupled, since clients are performing actions that should be the responsibility of the providers.

Yet, solving this problem is feasible because

- The conditionals tell you to which classes you should transfer behavior.

Solution   Introduce a new method into the provider hierarchy. Implement the new method in each subclass of the provider hierarchy by moving the corresponding case of the client's conditional to that class. Replace the entire conditional in the client by a simple call to the new method.

Detection

Apply essentially the same techniques described in Transform Self Type Checks (Pattern 10.1) to detect case statements, but look for conditions that test the type of a separate service provider that *already* implements a hierarchy. You should also look for case statements occurring in different clients of the same provider hierarchy.

- *C++:* Legacy C++ code is not likely to make use of run-time type information (RTTI). Instead, type information will likely be encoded in a data member that takes its value from some enumerated type representing the current class. Look for client code switching on such data members.

- *Ada:* Detecting type tests falls into two cases. If the hierarchy is implemented as a single discriminated record, then you will find case statements over the discriminant. If the hierarchy is implemented with tagged types, then you cannot write a case statement over the types (they are not discrete); instead an if-then-else structure will be used.

- *Smalltalk:* As in Transform Self Type Checks (Pattern 10.1), look for applications of `isMemberOf:` and `isKindOf:`, and tests like `self class = anotherClass`.

- *Java:* Look for applications of the operator `instanceof`, which tests membership of an object in a specific, known class. Although classes in Java are not objects as in Smalltalk, each class that is loaded into the virtual machine is represented by a single instance of `java.lang.Class`. It is therefore possible to determine if two objects, x and y, belong to the same class by performing the test

```
x.getClass() == y.getClass()
```

Alternatively, class membership may be tested by comparing class names:

```
x.getClass().getName().equals(y.getClass().getName())
```

Steps

Figure 10.6 illustrates how the following steps transform type-checking code into polymorphic methods:

1. Identify the clients performing explicit type checks.
2. Add a new, empty method to the root of the provider hierarchy representing the action performed in the conditional code.
3. Iteratively move a case of the conditional to some provider class, replacing it with a call to that method. After each move, the regression tests should run.
4. When all methods have been moved, each case of the conditional consists of a call to the new method, so replace the entire conditional by a single call to the new method.
5. Consider making the method abstract in the provider's root. Alternatively implement suitable default behavior here.

Other Steps to Consider

- It may well be that multiple clients are performing exactly the same test and taking the same actions. In this case, the duplicated code can be replaced by a single method call after one of the clients has been transformed. If clients are performing different tests or taking different actions, then the pattern must be applied once for each conditional.
- If the case statement does not cover all the concrete classes of the provider hierarchy, a new abstract class may need to be introduced as a common superclass of the concerned classes. The new method will then be introduced only for the relevant subtree. Alternatively, if it is not possible to introduce such an abstract class given the existing inheritance hierarchy, consider implementing the method at the root with either an empty default implementation, or one that raises an exception if it is called for an inappropriate class.
- If the conditionals are nested, the pattern may need to be applied recursively.

PATTERN 10.2 *continued*

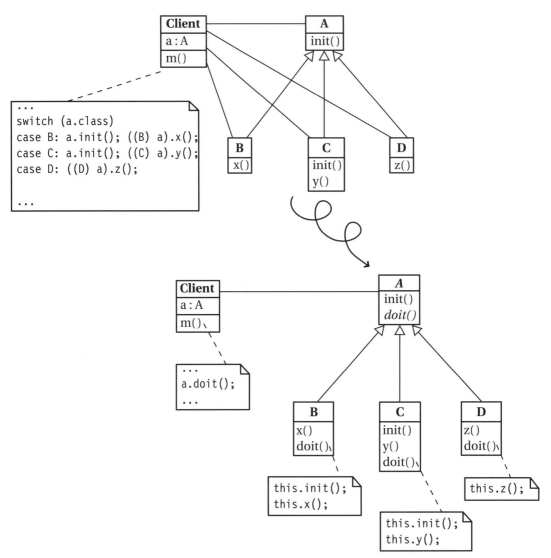

Trade-offs Pros

- The provider hierarchy offers a new, polymorphic service available to other clients as well.

- The code of the clients is now better organized and does not have to deal anymore with concerns that are now under the responsibility of the provider.

- All the code concerning the behavior of a single provider is now together in a single location.
- The fact that the provider hierarchy offers a uniform interface allows providers to be modified without impacting clients.

Cons

- Sometimes it is convenient to see the code handling different cases in a single location. Transform Client Type Checks redistributes the logic to the individual provider classes, with the result that the overview is lost.

Difficulties

- Normally instances of the provider classes should already have been created so we do not have to look for the creation of the instances; however, refactoring the interface will affect all clients of the provider classes and must not be undertaken without considering the full consequences of such an action.

When the Legacy Solution Is the Solution

Client type checks may nevertheless be the right solution when the provider instance does not yet exist or when its class cannot be extended:

- An Abstract Factory (Pattern A.10) object may need to test a type variable in order to know which class to instantiate. For example, a factory may stream objects in from a text file representation, and test some variable that tells it which class the streamed object should belong to.
- Software that interfaces to a non-object-oriented library, such as a legacy GUI library, may force the developer to simulate the dispatch manually. It is questionable whether, in such cases, it is cost-effective to develop an object-oriented facade to the procedural library.
- If the provider hierarchy is frozen (e.g., because the source code is not available), then it will not be possible to transfer behavior to the provider classes. In this case, wrapper classes may be defined to extend the behavior of the provider classes, but the added complexity of defining the wrappers may overwhelm any benefits.

Example Before

The following C++ code illustrates misplaced responsibilities since the client must explicitly type check instances of Telephone to determine what action to perform. The code in bold highlights the difficulties with this approach.

PATTERN 10.2 *continued*

```cpp
class Telephone {
public:
  enum PhoneType { POTSPHONE, ISDNPHONE, OPERATORPHONE };
  Telephone() {}
  PhoneType phoneType() { return myType; }

private:
  PhoneType myType;
protected:
  void setPhoneType(PhoneType newType) { myType = newType; }
};

class POTSPhone : public Telephone {

public:
  POTSPhone() { setPhoneType(POTSPHONE); }
  void tourneManivelle();
  void call();
};
...

class ISDNPhone: public Telephone {
public:
  ISDNPhone() { setPhoneType(ISDNPHONE);}
  void initializeLine();
  void connect();
};
...

class OperatorPhone: public Telephone {
public:
  OperatorPhone() { setPhoneType(OPERATORPHONE); }
  void operatorMode(bool onOffToggle);
  void call();
};

void initiateCalls(Telephone ** phoneArray, int numOfCalls) {
  for(int i = 0; i<numOfCalls ;i++ ) {
    Telephone * p = phoneArray[i];

    switch(p->phoneType()) {
    case Telephone::POTSPHONE: {
```

```
      POTSPhone *potsp = (POTSPhone *) p;
      potsp->tourneManivelle();
      potsp->call();
      break;
    }
  case Telephone::ISDNPHONE: {
      ISDNPhone *isdnp = (ISDNPhone *) p;
      isdnp->initializeLine();
      isdnp->connect();
      break;
    }
  case Telephone::OPERATORPHONE: {
      OperatorPhone *opp = (OperatorPhone *) p;
      opp->operatorMode(true);
      opp->call();
      break;
    }
    default:  cerr << "Unrecognized Phonetype" << endl;
    };
  }
}
```

After

Figure 10.7 summarizes the changes. After applying the pattern the client code will look like the following. We highlight the changes in bold:

```
class Telephone {
public:
  Telephone() {}
  virtual void makeCall() = 0;
};

Class POTSPhone : public Telephone {
  void tourneManivelle();
  void call();
public:
  POTSPhone() {}
  void makeCall();
};
void POTSPhone::makeCall() {
  this->tourneManivelle();
  this->call();
}
```

PATTERN 10.2 *continued*

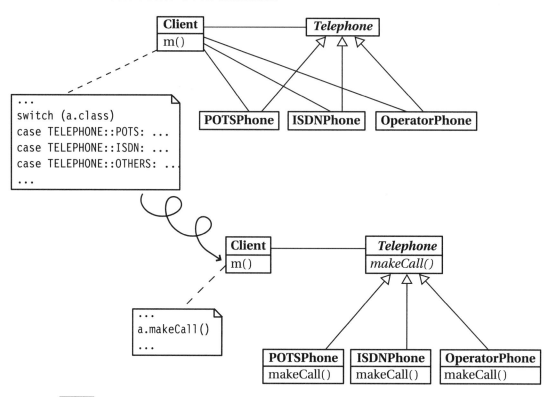

FIGURE **10.7**   Transforming explicit type checks to polymorphic method invocations.

```
class ISDNPhone: public Telephone {
  void initializeLine();
  void connect();

public:
  ISDNPhone() { }
  void makeCall();
};
void ISDNPhone::makeCall() {
  this->initializeLine();
  this->connect();
}

class OperatorPhone: public Telephone {
  void operatorMode(bool onOffToggle);
  void call();
```

```
public:
  OperatorPhone() { }
  void makeCall();
};
void OperatorPhone::makeCall() {
  this->operatorMode(true);
  this->call();
}
void initiateCalls(Telephone ** phoneArray, int numOfCalls) {
  for(int i = 0; i<numOfCalls ;i++ ) {
    phoneArray[i]->makeCall();
  }
}
```

Rationale
Riel states: "Explicit case analysis on the type of an object is usually an error. The designer should use polymorphism in most of these cases" [Riel96]. Indeed, explicit type checks in clients are a sign of misplaced responsibilities since they increase coupling between clients and providers. Shifting these responsibilities to the provider will have the following consequences:

- The client and the provider will be more weakly coupled since the client will only need to explicitly know the root of the provider hierarchy instead of all of its concrete subclasses.

- The provider hierarchy may evolve more gracefully, with less chance of breaking client code.

- The size and complexity of client code is reduced. The collaborations between clients and providers become more abstract.

- Abstractions implicit in the old design (i.e., the actions of the conditional cases) will be made explicit as methods and will be available to other clients.

- Code duplication may be reduced (if the same conditionals occur multiply).

Related Patterns
In Transform Client Type Checks the conditional is made on the type information of a provider class. The same situation occurs in Introduce Null Object (Pattern 10.5), where the conditional tests over null value before invoking the methods. From this point of view, Introduce Null Object is a specialization of Transform Client Type Checks.

Transform Conditionals into Registration (Pattern 10.6) handles the special case in which the client's conditional is used to select a third object (typically an external application or tool) to handle the argument.

P A T T E R N 1 0 . 2 *continued*

Replace Conditional with Polymorphism (Pattern A.9) is the core refactoring of this reengineering pattern, so the reader may refer to the steps described in [Fowl99].

PATTERN

10.3   Factor Out State

Intent: Eliminate complex conditional code over an object's state by applying the State design pattern (Pattern A.18).

Problem   How do you make a class whose behavior depends on a complex evaluation of its current state more *extensible*?

This problem is difficult because

- There are several complex conditional statements spread out over the methods of the object. Adding new behavior may affect these conditionals in subtle ways.

- Whenever new possible states are introduced, all the methods that test state have to be modified.

Yet, solving this problem is feasible because

- The object's instance variables are typically used to model different abstract states, each of which has its own behavior. If you can identify these abstract states, you can factor the state and the behavior out into a set of simpler, related classes.

Solution   Apply the State pattern (Pattern A.18), that is, encapsulate the state-dependent behavior into separate objects, delegate calls to these objects, and keep the state of the object consistent by referring to the right instance of these state objects (see Figure 10.8).

As in Transform Self Type Checks (Pattern 10.1), transform complex conditional code that tests over quantified states into delegated calls to state classes. Apply the State pattern, delegating each conditional case to a separate State object. We invite you to read the State and State Patterns (Pattern A.19) for a deep description of the problem and discussion [Gamm95] [Alpe98] [Dyso97]. Here we only focus on the reengineering aspects of the pattern.

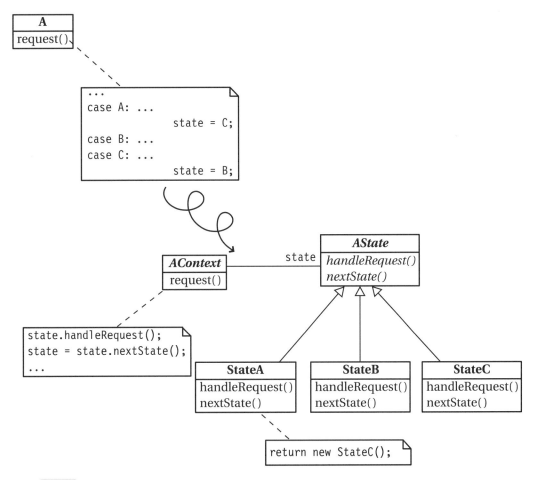

FIGURE **10.8** Transformation to go from a state pattern simulated using an explicit state conditional to a situation where the state pattern has been applied.

Steps

1. Identify the interface of a state and the number of states.

   If you are lucky, each conditional will partition the state space in the same way, and the number of states will equal the number of cases in each conditional. If the conditionals overlap, a finer partitioning will be required.

   The interface of a state depends on how the state information is accessed and updated, and may need to be refined in the subsequent steps.

2. Create a new abstract class, State, representing the interface of the state.

PATTERN 10.3 *continued*

3. Create a new class subclass of State for each state.

4. Define methods of the interface identified in step 1 in each of the State classes by copying the corresponding code of the conditional to the new method. Do not forget to change the state of the instance variable in the Context to refer to the right instance of State class. The State methods have the responsibility to change the Context so that it always refers to the next state instance.

5. Add a new instance variable in the Context class.

6. You may have to include a reference from the State to the Context class to invoke the state transitions from the State classes.

7. Initialize the newly created instance to refer to a default State class instance.

8. Change the methods of the Context class containing the tests to delegate the call to the instance variable.

Step 4 can be performed using the Extract Method operation of the Refactoring Browser. Note that after each step the regression tests should still run. The critical step is the last one, in which behavior is delegated to the new state objects.

Trade-offs   Pros

- The public interface of the original class does not have to change. Since the state instances are accessed by delegation from the original object, the clients are unaffected. In the straightforward case the application of this pattern has a limited impact on the clients.

Cons

- The systematic application of this pattern may lead to an explosion in the number of classes.

- This pattern should not be applied when (1) there are too many possible states or the number of states is not fixed or (2) when it is hard to determine from the code how and when state transitions occur.

When the Legacy Solution Is the Solution

This pattern should not be applied lightly.

- When the states are clearly identified and it is known that they will not be changed, the legacy solution has the advantage of grouping all the state behavior by functionality instead of spreading it over different subclasses.

- In certain domains (such as parsers) table-driven behavior, encoded as conditionals over state, is well understood, and factoring out the state objects may just make the code harder to understand, and hence to maintain.

Known Uses   The Design Patterns Smalltalk Companion presents a step-by-step code transformation [Alpe98].

PATTERN

10.4   Factor Out Strategy

Intent: Eliminate conditional code that selects a suitable algorithm by applying the Strategy design pattern (Pattern A.20).

Problem   How do you make a class whose behavior depends on testing the value of some variable more *extensible*?

This problem is difficult because

- New functionality cannot be added without modifying all the methods containing the conditional code.
- The conditional code may be spread over several classes that make similar decisions about which algorithm to apply.

Yet, solving this problem is feasible because

- The alternative behaviors are essentially interchangeable.

Solution   Apply the Strategy pattern (Pattern A.20), that is, encapsulate the algorithmic dependent behavior into separate objects with polymorphic interfaces and delegate calls to these objects (see Figure 10.9).

Steps

1. Identify the interface of the strategy class.
2. Create a new abstract class, Strategy, representing the interface of the strategies.

PATTERN 10.4 *continued*

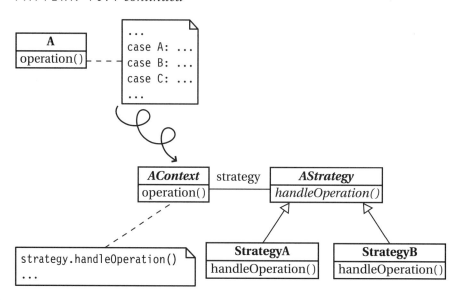

F I G U R E **10.9**   Transformation to go from a state pattern simulated using an explicit state conditional to a situation where the state pattern has been applied.

3. Create a new class subclass of `Strategy` for each identified algorithm.

4. Define methods of the interface identified in step 1 in each of the strategy classes by copying the corresponding code of the test to the method.

5. Add a new instance variable in the `Context` class to refer to the current strategy.

6. You may have to include a reference from the `Strategy` to the `Context` class to provide access to the information maintained by the `Context` (see "Difficulties").

7. Initialize the newly created instance to refer to a default strategy instance.

8. Change the methods of the `Context` class containing the tests by eliminating the tests and delegating the call to the instance variable.

Step 4 can be performed using the Extract Method operation of the Refactoring Browser. Note that after each step the regression tests should still run. The critical step is the last one, in which behavior is delegated to the new `Strategy` objects.

Trade-offs   Pros

- *Limited impact.*   The public interface of the original class does not have to change. Since the `Strategy` instances are accessed by delegation from the original object, the clients are unaffected. In a straightforward case the application of this pattern has a limited impact on the clients. However, the `Context` interface will be reduced because all the previously implemented algorithms are now moved to `Strategy` classes. So you have to check the invocations of these methods and decide on a per-case basis.

- *Improved configurability.*   After applying this pattern, you will be able to plug in new strategies without impacting or modifying the interface of the `Context`. Adding a new strategy does not require recompiling the Context class and its clients.

- *Cleaner interface.*   After applying this pattern, the interface of the `Context` class and the `Strategy` classes will be clearer.

Cons

- *Class explosion.*   The systematic application of this pattern may lead to a class explosion. If you have 20 different algorithms, you may not want to have 20 new classes each with only one method.

- *Object explosion.*   Strategies increase the number of instances in an application.

Difficulties

- There are several ways to share information between the `Context` and the `Strategy` objects, and the trade-offs can be subtle. The information can be passed as argument when the `Strategy` method is invoked, the `Context` object itself can be passed as argument, or the `Strategy` objects can hold a reference to their context. If the relationship between the `Context` and the `Strategy` is highly dynamic, then it may be preferable to pass this information as a method argument. More detailed discussions of this issue exist in the literature on the Strategy pattern (Pattern A.20) [Gamm95] [Alpe98].

Example   The Design Patterns Smalltalk Companion presents a code transformation step by step [Alpe98].

Related Patterns   The symptoms and structure of Factor Out Strategy bear comparison with Factor Out State (Pattern 10.3). The main difference consists in the fact that

PATTERN 10.4 *continued*

Factor Out State identifies behavior with different possible states of objects, whereas Factor Out Strategy is concerned with interchangeable algorithms that are independent of object state. Factor Out Strategy allows you to add new strategies without impacting the existing strategy objects.

PATTERN

10.5   Introduce Null Object

Intent: Eliminate conditional code that tests for null values by applying the Null Object design pattern (Pattern A.15).

Problem How can you ease modification and extension of a class in the presence of repeated tests for null values?

This problem is difficult because

- Client methods are always testing that certain values are not null before actually invoking their methods.
- Adding a new subclass to the client hierarchy requires testing null values before invoking some of the provider methods.

Yet, solving this problem is feasible because

- The client does not need to know that the provider represents a null value.

Solution Apply Null Object (Pattern A.15), that is, encapsulate the null behavior as a separate provider class so that the client class does not have to perform a null test.

Detection

Look for idiomatic null tests.

Null tests may take different forms, depending on the programming language and the kind of entity being tested. In Java, for example, a null object reference has the value null, whereas in C++ a null object pointer has the value 0.

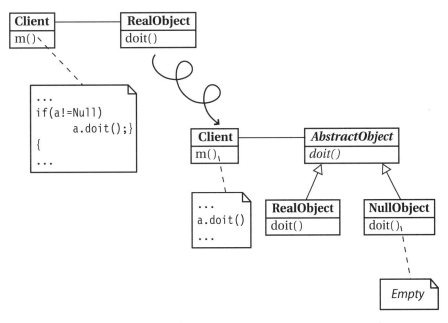

FIGURE **10.10** Transformation from a situation based on an explicit test of null value to a situation where a NullObject is introduced.

Steps

Fowler discusses in detail the necessary refactoring steps illustrated in Figure 10.10 [Fowl99].

1. Identify the interface required for the null behavior. (This will normally be identical to that of the nonnull object.)
2. Create a new abstract superclass as a superclass of the RealObject class.
3. Create a new subclass of the abstract superclass with a name starting with No or Null.
4. Define default methods into the NullObject class.
5. Initialize the instance variable or structure that was checked to now hold at least an instance of the NullObject class.
6. Remove the conditional tests from the client.

If you still want to be able to test for null values in a clean way, you may introduce a query method called isNull in RealObject and NullObject classes, as described by Fowler [Fowl99].

PATTERN 10.5 *continued*

Trade-offs Pros

- The client code is much simpler after applying the pattern.
- The pattern is relatively simple to apply since the interface of the provider does not have to be modified.

Cons

- The provider hierarchy becomes more complex.

Difficulties

- Multiple clients may not agree on the reasonable default behavior of the NullObject. In this case, multiple NullObject classes may need to be defined.

When the Legacy Solution Is the Solution

- If clients do not agree on a common interface.
- When very little code uses the variable directly or when the code that uses the variable is well encapsulated in a single place.

Example The following Smalltalk code is taken from Woolf [Wool98]. Initially the code contains explicit null tests:

```
VisualPart>>objectWantedControl
  ...
  ^ctrl isNil
    ifFalse:
      [ctrl isControlWanted
        ifTrue:[self]
        ifFalse:[nil]]
```

It is then transformed into

```
VisualPart>>objectWantedControl
  ...
  ^ctrl isControlWanted
      ifTrue:[self]
      ifFalse:[nil]
Controller>>isControlWanted
  ^self viewHasCursor
```

```
NoController>>isControlWanted
  ^false
```

Transform Conditionals into Registration

Intent: Improve the modularity of a system by replacing conditionals in clients by a registration mechanism.

Problem How can you reduce the coupling between *tools* providing services and *clients* so that the addition or removal of tools does not lead to changing the code of the clients?

This problem is difficult because

- Having one single place to look for all the kinds of tools makes it easy to understand the system and easy to add new tools.

- However, every time you remove a *tool,* you have to remove one case in some conditional statement, or else certain parts (*tool clients*) would still reflect the presence of the removed tools, leading to fragile systems. Then every time you add a new tool, you have to add a new conditional in all the tool clients.

Yet, solving this problem is feasible because

- Long conditionals make it easy to identify the different type of tools used.

Solution Introduce a *registration mechanism* to which each *tool* is responsible for registering itself, and transform the *tool clients* to query the registration repository instead of performing conditionals.

Steps

The following steps summarize how to transform conditionals in tool users to a registration mechanism (see Figure 10.11):

1. Define a class describing *plug-in* objects—objects encapsulating the information necessary for registering a tool. Although the internal structure of this class depends on the purpose of the registration, a plug-in

P A T T E R N 1 0 . 6 *continued*

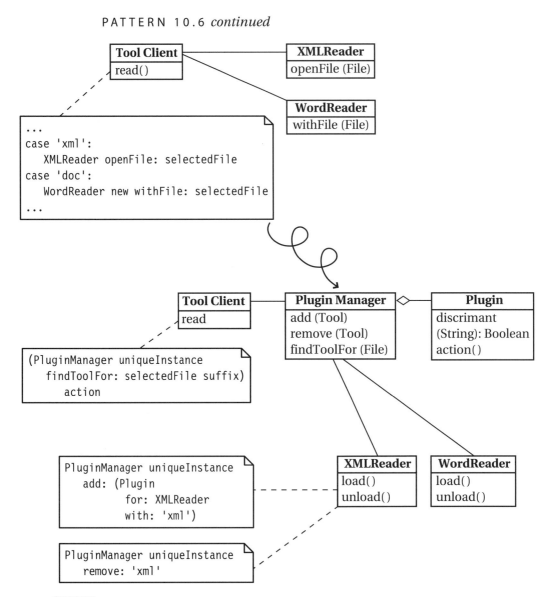

F I G U R E **10.11** Transforming conditionals in tool users by introducing a registration mechanism.

should provide the necessary information so the tool manager can *identify* it, *create* instances of the represented tool, and *invoke* methods. To invoke a tool method, a method or a similar mechanism like a block closure or inner class should be stored in the plug-in object.

2. Define a class representing the *plug-in manager* (i.e., that manages the plug-in objects and that will be queried by the tool clients to check the presence of the tools). This class will certainly be a singleton since the plug-ins representing the tools available should not be lost if a new instance of the plug-in manager is created.

3. For each case of the conditional, define a plug-in *object* associated with the given tool. This plug-in object should be created and registered automatically when the tool it represents is loaded, and it should be unregistered if and when the tool becomes unavailable. Sometimes information from the tool client should be passed to the tool. The current tool client can be passed as argument when the tool is invoked.

4. Transform the entire conditional expression into a query to the tool manager object. This query should return a tool associated with the query and invoke it to access the wished functionality.

5. Remove any tool client actions that directly activate tools. This behavior is now the responsibility of the plug-in manager.

The client or the plug-in object may have the responsibility to invoke a tool. It is better to let the plug-in object have this responsibility (because it already holds the responsibility of representing how to represent the tools) and let the clients just say that they need a tool action.

Example In Squeak [Inga97], the `FileList` is a tool that allows the loading of different kinds of files, such as Smalltalk code, JPEG images, MIDI files, HTML, and so on. Depending on the suffix of the selected file, the `FileList` proposes different actions to the user. We show in the example the loading of the different files depending on their format.

Before

The `FileList` implementation creates different menu items representing the different possible actions depending on the suffix of the files. The dynamic part of the menu is defined in the method `menusForFileEnding:`, which takes a file suffix as its argument and returns a menu item containing the label of the menu item and the name of the corresponding method that should be invoked on the `FileList` object.

```
FileList>>menusForFileEnding: suffix

  (suffix = 'jpg') ifTrue:
    [^MenuItem label:'open image in a window'.
      selector: #openImageInWindow].
```

PATTERN 10.6 *continued*

```
(suffix = 'morph') ifTrue:
  [^MenuItem label: 'load as morph'.
    selector: #openMorphFromFile].
(suffix = 'mid') ifTrue:
  [^MenuItem label: 'play midi file'.
    selector: #playMidiFile].
(suffix = 'st') ifTrue:
  [^MenuItem label: 'fileIn'.
    selector: #fileInSelection].
(suffix = 'swf') ifTrue:
  [^MenuItem label: 'open as Flash'.
    selector: #openAsFlash].
(suffix = '3ds') ifTrue:
  [^MenuItem label: 'Open 3DS file'.
    selector: #open3DSFile].
(suffix = 'wrl') ifTrue:
  [^MenuItem label: 'open in Wonderland'.
    selector: #openVRMLFile].
(suffix = 'html') ifTrue:
  [^MenuItem label: 'open in html browser'.
    selector: #openInBrowser].
(suffix = '*') ifTrue:
  [^MenuItem label: 'generate HTML'.
    selector:#renderFile].
```

The methods whose selectors are associated in the menu are implemented in the FileList class. We give two examples here. First the method checks if the tool it needs is available. If not, it generates a beep; otherwise the corresponding tool is created and then used to handle the selected file.

```
FileList>>openInBrowser
  Smalltalk at: #Scamper ifAbsent: [^ self beep].
  Scamper openOnUrl: (directory url , fileName encodeForHTTP)
```

```
FileList>>openVRMLFile
  | scene |
  Smalltalk at: #Wonderland ifAbsent: [^ self beep].
  scene := Wonderland new.
  scene makeActorFromVRML: self fullName.
```

After

The solution is to give each tool the responsibility to register itself and let the FileList query the registry of available tools to find which tool can be invoked.

Step 1. The solution is to first create the class ToolPlugin representing the registration of a given tool. Here we store the suffix files, the menu label, and the action to be performed when the tools will be invoked.

```
Object subclass: #ToolPlugin
  instanceVariableNames: 'fileSuffix menuLabelName blockToOpen '
```

Step 2. Then the class PluginManager is defined. It defines a structure to hold the registered tools and defines behavior to add, remove, and find registered tools.

```
Object subclass: #PluginManager
  instanceVariableNames: 'plugins '

PluginManager>>initialize
  plugins := OrderedCollection new.

PluginManager>>addPlugin : aPlugin
  plugins add: aRegistree

PluginManager>>removePlugin: aBlock

  (plugins select: aBlock) copy
    do: [:each| plugins remove: each]

PluginManager>>findToolFor: aSuffix
  "return a registree of a tool being able to treat file of format
  aSuffix"

  ^ plugins
     detect: [:each| each suffix = aSuffix]
     ifNone: [nil]
```

Note that the findToolFor: method could take a block to select which of the plug-in objects satisfies it and that it could return a list of plug-ins representing all the tools currently able to treat a given file format.

PATTERN 10.6 *continued*

Step 3. Then the tools should register themselves when they are loaded in memory. Here we present two registrations, showing that a plug-in object is created for each tool. As the tools need some information from the FileList object such as the filename or the directory, the action that has to be performed takes as a parameter the instance of the FileList object that invokes it ([:fileList | in the following code).

In Squeak, when a class specifies a class (static) initialize method, this method is invoked once the class is loaded in memory. We then specialize the class methods initialize on the classes Scamper and Wonderland to invoke the class methods toolRegistration defined below:

```
Scamper class>>toolRegistration

  PluginManager uniqueInstance
    addPlugin:
    (ToolPlugin
        forFileSuffix: 'html'
        openingBlock:
          [:fileList |
          self openOnUrl:
            (fileList directory url ,
              fileList fileName encodeForHTTP)]
        menuLabelName: 'open in html browser')
```

```
Wonderland class>>toolRegistration

  PluginManager uniqueInstance
    addPlugin:
    (ToolPlugin
        forFileSuffix: 'wrl'
        openingBlock:
          [:fileList |
          | scene |
          scene := self new.
          scene makeActorFromVRML: fileList fullName]
        menuLabelName: 'open in Wonderland')
```

In Squeak, when a class is removed from the system, it receives the message removeFromSystem. Here we specialize this method for every tool so that it can unregister itself:

```
Scamper class>>removeFromSystem

  super removeFromSystem.
  PluginManager uniqueInstance
    removePlugin: [:plugin| plugin forFileSuffix = 'html']


Wonderland class>>removeFromSystem

  super removeFromSystem.
  PluginManager uniqueInstance
    removePlugin: [:plugin| plugin forFileSuffix = 'wrl']
```

Step 4. The FileList object now has to use the ToolsManager to identify the right plug-in object depending on the suffix of the selected file. Then if a tool is available for the given suffix, it creates a menu item specifying that the FileList has to be passed as argument of the action block associated with the tool. If there is no tool, a special menu is created whose action is to do nothing.

```
FileList>>itemsForFileEnding: suffix

  | plugin |
  plugin := PluginManager uniqueInstance
            findToolFor: suffix ifAbsent: [nil].
  ^ plugins isNil
      ifFalse: [Menu label: (plugin menuLabelName)
                    actionBlock: (plugin openingBlock)
                    withParameter: self]
      ifTrue: [ErrorMenu new
                 label: 'no tool available for the suffix ', suffix]
```

Trade-offs   Pros

- By applying Transform Conditionals into Registration you obtain a system that is both dynamic and flexible. New tools can be added without impacting tool clients.

- Tool clients no longer have to check whether a given tool is available. The registration mechanism ensures you that the action can be performed.

- The interaction protocol between tools and tool clients is now normalized.

P A T T E R N   1 0 . 6   *continued*

Cons

- You have to define two new classes, one for the object representing tool representation (plug-in) and one for the object managing the registered tools (plug-in manager).

Difficulties

- While transforming a branch of the conditional into a plug-in object, you will have to define an action associated with the tools via the plug-in object. To ensure a clear separation and full dynamic registration, this action should be defined on the tool and not anymore on the tool client. However, as the tool may need some information from the tool client, the tool client should be passed to the tool as a parameter when the action is invoked. This changes the protocol between the tool and the tool client from a single invocation on the tool client to a method invocation to the tool with an extra parameter. This also implies that in some cases the tool client class has to define new public or friend methods to allow the tools to access the tool client's data.

- If each single conditional branch is associated only with a single tool, only one plug-in object is needed. However, if the same tool can be called in different ways, we will have to create multiple plug-in objects.

When the Legacy Solution Is the Solution

- If there is only a single tool client class, if all the tools are always available, and if you will never add or remove a tool at run time, a conditional is simpler.

Related Patterns   Both Transform Conditionals into Registration and Transform Client Type Checks (Pattern 10.2) eliminate conditional expressions that decide which method should be invoked on which object. The key difference between the two patterns is that Transform Client Type Checks moves behavior from the client to the service provider, whereas Transform Conditionals into Registration deals with behavior that cannot be moved because it is implemented by an external tool.

Script: Identifying Simulated Switches in C++

This perl script searches the methods in C++ files and lists the occurrences of statements used to simulate switch statements with if-then-else, that is, matching the following expression: elseXif where *X* can be replaced by {, // ... or some white space including carriage return.

```perl
#!/opt/local/bin/perl
$/ = '::';
# new record delim.,
$elseIfPattern = 'else[\s\n]*{?[\s\n]*if';
$linecount = 1;
while (<>) {
  s/(//.*)//g; # remove C++ style comments
  $lc = (split /\n/) - 1; # count lines

  if(/$elseIfPattern/) {
  # count # of lines until first
  # occurrence of "else if"
  $temp = join(","$',$&);
  $l = $linecount + split(/\n/,$temp) - 1;
  # count the occurrences of else-if pairs,
  # flag the positions for an eventual printout
  $swc = s/(else)([\s\n]*{?[\s\n]*if)
                    /$1\n     * HERE *$2/g;
  printf "\n%s: Statement with
          %2d else-if's, first at: %d",
          $ARGV, $swc, $l;
 }
 $linecount += $lc;
 if(eof) {
  close ARGV;
  $linecount = 0;
  print "\n";
 }
}
```

Thumbnail Patterns

There are many patterns that are not specifically concerned with reengineering, but are still relevant to the reengineering process. In this appendix we have listed only those patterns that are specifically referred to at some point in this book. We have grouped them into the following three categories:

- *Testing patterns.* These patterns help you to focus your testing efforts. Our principal source is a pattern language by DeLano and Rising [DeLa98], although of course a vast literature is available on the subject. Binder, for example, devotes an entire book to the subject [Bind99].

- *Refactoring patterns.* These patterns focus on individual refactoring steps that you might apply during a reengineering project, or that you might just as well apply during any forward engineering project. Our principal sources are Fowler et al. [Fowl99], and Roberts's Ph.D. thesis [Robe99].

- *Design patterns.* Very frequently the result of a reengineering operation is to put a particular design pattern into place. Here we remind you of some of the most common design patterns that pop up in a reengineering context. Our main source is, of course, the *Design Patterns* book [Gamm95].

Testing Patterns

PATTERN **A.1** **Retest Persistent Problems**

Problem: How do you know what areas of the system should receive concentrated testing, irrespective of the features being implemented?

Solution: Keep a list of persistent problem areas and test cases to verify them, not just for resolving the current problems but also for use in subsequent testing. Test these areas thoroughly, even if there are no new features going into them. Retest regularly, even one last time before the release goes out the door.

Source: [DeLa98]

Referenced from: Regression Test after Every Change (Pattern 7.6)

PATTERN **A.2** **Test Fuzzy Features**

Problem: How can possible problem areas of the system be pinpointed so that the most problems can be found in the least amount of time?

Solution: Study the documentation available on the system. Look for areas that seems ambiguous or ill defined. Write test plans that cover these areas more thoroughly and concentrate testing in these areas. If designers can tell you all about a feature, it probably works. It's what they can't tell you that needs attention during testing.

Source: [DeLa98]

Referenced from: Grow Your Test Base Incrementally (Pattern 6.2)

PATTERN **A.3** **Test Old Bugs**

Problem: What areas of the system should be targeted for testing so that the most problems can be found in the least amount of time?

Solution: Examine problem reports from previous releases to help select test cases. Since it would be inefficient to test for all old problems, look at problems reported after the last valid snapshot of the system. Categorize problem reports to see if a trend is determined that could be used for additional testing.

Source: [DeLa98]

Referenced from: Grow Your Test Base Incrementally (Pattern 6.2)

Refactorings

PATTERN **A.4** **Encapsulate Field**

Also Known As: Abstract Instance Variable [Robe99]

Intent: There is a public field. Make it private and provide accessors.

Source: [Fowl99]

Referenced from: Eliminate Navigation Code (Pattern 9.2)

PATTERN **A.5**   **Extract Method**

Intent: You have a code fragment that stands on its own. Turn the fragment into a method whose name explains the purpose of the method.

Source: [Fowl99]

Referenced from: Refactor to Understand (Pattern 5.2), Visualize Code as Dotplots (Pattern 8.2), Move Behavior Close to Data (Pattern 9.1)

PATTERN **A.6**   **Move Method**

Intent: A method is, or will be, using or used by more features of another class than the class on which it is defined. Create a new method with a similar body in the class it uses most. Either turn the old method into a simple delegation, or remove it altogether.

Source: [Fowl99]

Referenced from: Refactor to Understand (Pattern 5.2), Move Behavior Close to Data (Pattern 9.1)

PATTERN **A.7**   **Rename Attribute**

Intent: Rename an instance variable and update all references to it.

Source: [Robe99]

Referenced from: Refactor to Understand (Pattern 5.2)

PATTERN **A.8**   **Rename Method**

Intent: The name of a method does not reveal its purpose. Change the name of the method.

Source: [Fowl99]

Referenced from: Refactor to Understand (Pattern 5.2)

PATTERN **A.9**   **Replace Conditional with Polymorphism**

Intent: You have a conditional that chooses different behavior depending on the type of an object. Move each leg of the conditional to an overriding method in a subclass. Make the original method abstract.

Source: [Fowl99]

Referenced from: Transform Client Type Checks (Pattern 10.2)

Design Patterns

PATTERN **A.10 Abstract Factory**

Intent: Provide an interface for creating families of related or dependent objects without specifying their concrete classes.

Source: [Gamm95]

Referenced from: Look for the Contracts (Pattern 5.4), Transform Client Type Checks (Pattern 10.2)

PATTERN **A.11 Adapter**

Intent: Convert the interface of a class into another interface clients expect. Adapter lets classes work together that couldn't otherwise because of incompatible interfaces.

Source: [Gamm95]

Referenced from: Present the Right Interface (Pattern 7.8), Move Behavior Close to Data (Pattern 9.1)

PATTERN **A.12 Facade**

Intent: Provide a unified interface to a set of interfaces in a subsystem. Facade defines a higher-level interface that makes the subsystem easier to use.

Source: [Gamm95]

Referenced from: Eliminate Navigation Code (Pattern 9.2), Split Up God Class (Pattern 9.3)

PATTERN **A.13 Factory Method**

Intent: Define an interface for creating an object, but let subclasses decide which class to instantiate. Factory Method lets a class defer instantiation to subclasses.

Source: [Gamm95]

Referenced from: Look for the Contracts (Pattern 5.4)

PATTERN **A.14 Flyweight**

Intent: Use sharing to support large numbers of fine-grained objects efficiently.

Source: [Gamm95]

Referenced from: Speculate about Design (Pattern 4.2)

PATTERN **A.15 Null Object**

Intent: A Null Object provides a surrogate for another object that shares the same interface but does nothing. Thus, the Null Object encapsulates the implementation decisions of how to do nothing and hides those details from its collaborators.

Source: [Wool98]

Referenced from: Introduce Null Object (Pattern 10.5)

PATTERN **A.16 Quantity**

Problem: Representing a value such as 6 feet or $5.

Solution: Use a quantity type that includes both the amount and the unit. Currencies are a kind of unit.

Source: [Fowl97]

Referenced from: Analyze the Persistent Data (Pattern 4.1)

PATTERN **A.17 Singleton**

Intent: Ensure a class has only one instance, and provide a global point of access to it.

Source: [Gamm95]

Referenced from: Read All the Code in One Hour (Pattern 3.2)

PATTERN **A.18 State**

Intent: Allow an object to alter its behavior when its internal state changes. The object will appear to change its class.

Source: [Gamm95]

Referenced from: Factor Out State (Pattern 10.3)

PATTERN **A.19 State Patterns**

Intent: The State Patterns pattern language refines and clarifies the State Pattern.

Source: [Dyso97]

Referenced from: Factor Out State (Pattern 10.3)

PATTERN **A.20 Strategy**

Intent: Define a family of algorithms, encapsulate each one in a separate class, and define each class with the same interface so they can be interchangeable. Strategy lets the algorithm vary independently from clients that use it.

Source: [Gamm95]

Referenced from: Factor Out Strategy (Pattern 10.4)

PATTERN **A.21 Template Method**

Intent: Define the skeleton of an algorithm in an operation, deferring some steps to subclasses. Template Method lets subclasses redefine certain steps of an algorithm without changing the algorithm's structure.

Source: [Gamm95]

Referenced from: Look for the Contracts (Pattern 5.4)

PATTERN **A.22 Visitor**

Intent: Represent an operation to be performed on the elements of an object structure. Visitor lets you define a new operation without changing the classes of the elements on which it operates.

Source: [Gamm95]

Referenced from: Move Behavior Close to Data (Pattern 9.1)

References

[Alpe98]   Alpert, Sherman R., Kyle Brown, and Bobby Woolf, *The Design Patterns Smalltalk Companion*, Addison-Wesley, 1998.

[Arno92]   Arnold, Robert S., *Software Reengineering*, IEEE, 1992.

[Bake92]   Baker, Brenda S., "A Program for Identifying Duplicated Code," *Computing Science and Statistics*, vol. 24, 1992, pp. 49–57.

[Ball96]   Ball, T., and S. Eick, "Software Visualization in the Large," *IEEE Computer*, 1996, pp. 33–43.

[Barn94]   Barnard, Jack, and Art Price, "Managing Code Inspection Information," *IEEE Software*, vol. 11, no. 2, March 1994, pp. 59–69.

[Bass98]   Bass, Len, Paul Clements, and Rick Kazman, *Software Architecture in Practice*, Addison-Wesley, 1998.

[Beck97]   Beck, Kent, *Smalltalk Best Practice Patterns*, Prentice Hall, 1997.

[Beck98]   Beck, Kent, and Erich Gamma, "Test Infected: Programmers Love Writing Tests," JUnit documentation, 1998.

[Beck99]   Beck, Kent, *Kent Beck's Guide to Better Smalltalk*, Sigs Books, 1999.

[Beck00]   Beck, Kent, *Extreme Programming Explained: Embrace Change*, Addison-Wesley, 2000.

[Beck01]   Beck, Kent, and Martin Fowler, *Planning Extreme Programming*, Addison-Wesley, 2001.

[Beed00]   Beedle, Mike, Martine Devos, Yonat Sharon, Ken Schwaber, and Jeff Sutherland, "SCRUM: A Pattern Language for Hyperproductive Software Development," *Pattern Languages of Program Design 4*, Neil Harrison, Brian Foote, and Hans Rohnert (Eds.), pp. 637–652, Addison-Wesley, 2000.

[Bell97]   Bellin, David, and Susan Suchman Simone, *The CRC Card Book*, Addison-Wesley, 1997.

[Benn99]   Bennett, Simon, Steve McRobb, and Ray Farmer, *Object-Oriented System Analysis and Design Using UML*, McGraw Hill, 1999.

[Bigg89]   Biggerstaff, T. J., "Design Recovery for Maintenance and Reuse," *IEEE Computer*, October 1989, pp. 36–49.

[Bigg93]   Biggerstaff, Ted J., Bharat G. Mittbander, and Dallas Webster, "The Concept Assignment Problem in Program Understanding," *Proceedings of the 15th International Conference on Software Engineering (ICSE 1993),* IEEE, 1993.

[Bigg94]   Biggerstaff, Ted J., Bharat G. Mittbander, and Dallas E. Webster, "Program Understanding and the Concept Assignment Problem," *Communications of the ACM,* vol. 37, no. 5, May 1994, pp. 72–82.

[Bind99]   Binder, Robert V., *Testing Object-Oriented Systems: Models, Patterns, and Tools,* Addison-Wesley, Object Technology Series, 1999.

[Blah98]   Blaha, M., D. LaPlant, and E. Marvak, "Requirements for Repository Software," *Proceedings of WCRE'98,* IEEE, 1998, pp. 164–173.

[Boeh88]   Boehm, Barry W., "A Spiral Model of Software Development and Enhancement," *IEEE Computer,* vol. 21, no. 5, 1988, pp. 61–72.

[Booc94]   Booch, Grady, *Object Oriented Analysis and Design with Applications* (2nd edition), Benjamin Cummings, 1994.

[Bray95]   Bray, Olin, and Michael M. Hess, "Reengineering a Configuration Management System," *IEEE Software,* vol. 12, no. 1, January 1995, pp. 55–63.

[Brod95]   Brodie, Michael L., and Michael Stonebraker, *Migrating Legacy Systems,* Morgan Kaufmann, 1995.

[Broo75]   Brooks, Frederick P., *The Mythical Man-Month,* Addison-Wesley, 1975.

[Broo87]   Brooks, Frederick P., "No Silver Bullet," *IEEE Computer,* vol. 20, no. 4, April 1987, pp. 10–19.

[Brow96a]   Brown, Kyle, "Design Reverse-Engineering and Automated Design Pattern Detection in Smalltalk," Ph.D. thesis, North Carolina State University, 1996.

[Brow96b]   Brown, Kyle, and Bruce G. Whitenack, "Crossing Chasms: A Pattern Language for Object-RDBMS Integration," *Pattern Languages of Program Design 2,* John M. Vlissides, James O. Coplien, and Norman L. Kerth (Eds.), pp. 227–238, Addison-Wesley, 1996.

[Brow98]   Brown, William J., Raphael C. Malveau, Hays W. McCormick, III, and Thomas J. Mowbray, "AntiPatterns," John Wiley, 1998.

[Busc96]   Buschmann, Frank, Regine Meunier, Hans Rohnert, Peter Sommerlad, and Michael Stad, *Pattern-Oriented Software Architecture—A System of Patterns,* John Wiley, 1996.

[Came96]   Cameron, Debra, Bill Rosenblatt, and Eric Raymond, *Learning GNU Emacs* (2nd edition), O'Reilly, 1996.

[Chik92]   Chikofsky, Elliot J., and James H. Cross, II, "Reverse Engineering and Design Recovery: A Taxonomy," *Software Reengineering,* Robert S. Arnold (Ed.), pp. 54–58, IEEE, 1992.

[Cock93]   Cockburn, Alistair, "The Impact of Object-Orientation on Application Development," *IBM Systems Journal,* vol. 32, no. 3, March 1993, pp. 420–444.

[Conw68]   Conway, Melvin E., "How Do Committees Invent?," *Datamation,* vol. 14, no. 4, April 1968, pp. 28–31.

[Cook01] Cook, Stephen, Rachel Harrison, and Brian Ritchie, "Assessing the Evolution of Financial Management Information Systems," *ECOOP 2001 Workshop Reader,* LNCS 30, Springer-Verlag, 2001.

[Copl92] Coplien, James O., *Advanced C++: Programming Styles and Idioms,* Addison-Wesley, 1992.

[Copl95] Coplien, James O., "A Development Process Generative Pattern Language," *Pattern Languages of Program Design,* James O. Coplien, and Douglas Schmidt (Eds.), pp. 183–237, Addison-Wesley, 1995.

[Corb89] Corbi, T. A., "Program Understanding: Challenge for the 1990's," *IBM Systems Journal,* vol. 28, no. 2, 1989, pp. 294–306, republished in [Arno92].

[Davi95] Davis, Alan Mark, *201 Principles of Software Development,* McGraw-Hill, 1995.

[DeLa98] DeLano, David E., and Linda Rising, "Patterns for System Testing," *Pattern Languages of Program Design 3,* Robert Martin, Dirk Riehle, and Frank Buschmann (Eds.), Addison-Welsey, 1998, pp. 503–527.

[DeMa82] DeMarco, Tom, *Controlling Software Projects,* Yourdon Press, 1982.

[DeMa99] DeMarco, Tom, and Timothy Lister, *Peopleware, Productive Projects and Teams* (2nd edition), Dorset House, 1999.

[Deme97] Demeyer, Serge, and Harald Gall (Eds.), *Proceedings of the ESEC/FSE Workshop on Object-Oriented Re-engineering,* Technical University of Vienna, Information Systems Institute, Distributed Systems Group, TUV-1841-97-10, September 1997.

[Deme99a] Demeyer, Serge, and Stéphane Ducasse, "Metrics, Do They Really Help?," *Proceedings LMO'99 (Languages et Modèles à Objets),* Jacques Malenfant (Ed.), HERMES Science Publications, Paris, 1999, pp. 69–82.

[Deme99b] Demeyer, Serge, Stéphane Ducasse, and Michele Lanza, "A Hybrid Reverse Engineering Platform Combining Metrics and Program Visualization," *Proceedings WCRE'99 (6th Working Conference on Reverse Engineering),* Francoise Balmas, Mike Blaha, and Spencer Rugaber (Eds.), IEEE, October 1999.

[Deme00] Demeyer, Serge, Stéphane Ducasse, and Oscar Nierstrasz, "Finding Refactorings via Change Metrics," *Proceedings of OOPSLA'2000, ACM SIGPLAN Notices,* 2000, pp. 166–178.

[Duca99] Ducasse, Stéphane, Matthias Rieger, and Serge Demeyer, "A Language Independent Approach for Detecting Duplicated Code," *Proceedings ICSM'99 (International Conference on Software Maintenance),* Hongji Yang, and Lee White (Eds.), IEEE, September 1999, pp. 109–118.

[Duca00] Ducasse, Stéphane, Michele Lanza, and Sander Tichelaar, "Moose: An Extensible Language-Independent Environment for Reengineering Object-Oriented Systems," *Proceedings of the Second International Symposium on Constructing Software Engineering Tools (CoSET 2000),* June 2000.

[Dyso97]   Dyson, Paul, and Bruse Anderson, "State Patterns," *Pattern Languages of Program Design 3,* Robert Martin, Dirk Riehle, and Frank Buschmann (Eds.), Addison-Wesley, 1997.

[Fent96]   Fenton, Norman, and Shari Lawrence Pfleeger, *Software Metrics: A Rigorous and Practical Approach* (2nd edition), International Thomson Computer Press, London, UK, 1996.

[Fjel79]   Fjeldstad, R. K., and W. T. Hamlen, "Application Program Maintenance Study: Report to Our Respondents," *Proceedings of GUIDE 48,* The Guide Corporation, 1979.

[Flor97]   Florijn, Gert, Marco Meijers, and Pieter van Winsen, "Tool Support for Object-Oriented Patterns," *Proceedings ECOOP'97,* Mehmet Aksit, and Satoshi Matsuoka (Eds.), LNCS 1241, Springer-Verlag, Jyvaskyla, Finland, June 1997, pp. 472–495.

[Foot00]   Foote, Brian, and Joseph W. Yoder, "Big Ball of Mud," *Pattern Languages of Program Design,* N. Harrison, B. Foote, and H. Rohnert (Eds.), pp. 654–692, Addison-Wesley, 2000.

[Fowl97]   Fowler, Martin, *Analysis Patterns: Reusable Objects Models,* Addison-Wesley, 1997.

[Fowl99]   Fowler, Martin, Kent Beck, John Brant, William Opdyke, and Don Roberts, *Refactoring: Improving the Design of Existing Code,* Addison-Wesley, 1999.

[Fros94]   Frost, Stuart, "Modelling for the RDBMS Legacy," *Object Magazine,* September 1994, pp. 43–51.

[Gall98]   Gall, Harald, Karin Hajek, and Mehdi Jazayeri, "Detection of Logical Coupling Based on Product Release History," *Proceedings of the International Conference on Software Maintenance 1998 (ICSM'98),* 1998, pp. 190–198.

[Gall99]   Gall, Harald, and Johannes Weidl, "Object-Model Driven Abstraction-to-Code Mapping," *Proceedings of the 2nd Workshop on Object-Oriented Reengineering (WOOR 1999),* Technical University of Vienna, Technical Report TUV-1841-99-13, 1999.

[Gamm95]   Gamma, Erich, Richard Helm, Ralph Johnson, and John Vlissides, *Design Patterns,* Addison-Wesley, 1995.

[Gilb93]   Gilb, Tom, and Dorothy Graham, *Software Inspection,* Addison-Wesley, 1993.

[Glass97]   Glass, Robert L., *Building Quality Software,* Prentice Hall, 1997.

[Gold95]   Goldberg, Adele, and Kenneth S. Rubin, *Succeeding with Objects: Decision Frameworks for Project Management,* Addison-Wesley, 1995.

[Hain96]   Hainaut, J.-L., V. Englebert, J. Henrard, J.-M. Hick, and D. Roland, "Database Reverse Engineering: From Requirements to CARE Tools," *Automated Software Engineering,* vol. 3, no. 1–2, June 1996.

[Harri96]   Harrison, Neil B., "Organizational Patterns for Teams," *Pattern Languages of Program Design 2,* John M. Vlissides, James O. Coplien, and Norman L. Kerth (Eds.), pp. 345–352, Addison-Wesley, 1996.

[Helf95]   Helfman, Jonathan, "Dotplot Patterns: A Literal Look at Pattern Languages," *TAPOS*, vol. 2, no. 1, 1995, pp. 31–41.

[Inga97]   Ingalls, Daniel, Ted Kaehler, John Maloney, Scott Wallace, and Alan Kay, "Back to the Future: The Story of Squeak, A Practical Smalltalk Written in Itself," *Proceedings OOPSLA '97, ACM SIGPLAN Notices,* vol. 21, no. 11, November 1997.

[Jack00]   Jackson, Daniel, and John Chapin, "Redesigning Air Traffic Control: An Exercise in Software Design," *IEEE Software,* vol. 17, no. 3, May 2000, pp. 63–70.

[Jaco92]   Jacobson, Ivar, Magnus Christerson, Patrik Jonsson, and Gunnar Overgaard, *Object-Oriented Software Engineering—A Use Case Driven Approach,* Addison-Wesley/ACM Press, 1992.

[Jaco97]   Jacobson, Ivar, Martin Griss, and Patrik Jonsson, *Software Reuse,* Addison-Wesley/ACM Press, 1997.

[Jahn97]   Jahnke, Jens H., Wilhelm Schäfer, and Albert Zündorf, "Generic Fuzzy Reasoning Nets as a Basis of Reverse Engineering Relational Database Applications," *Proceedings of ESEC/FSE'97*, LNCS, 1301, 1997, pp. 193–210.

[Jaza99]   Jazayeri, Mehdi, Harald Gall, and Claudio Riva, "Visualizing Software Release Histories: The Use of Color and Third Dimension," *ICSM'99 Proceedings (International Conference on Software Maintenance),* IEEE, 1999.

[Jeff01]   Jeffries, Ron, Ann Anderson, and Chet Hendrickson, *Extreme Programming Installed,* Addison-Wesley, 2001.

[Jerd96]   Jerding, Dean F., and John T. Stasko, "The Information Mural: Increasing Information Bandwidth in Visualizations," Technical Report GIT-GVU-96-25, Georgia Institute of Technology, October 1996.

[Kazm98]   Kazman, Rick, and S. Jeromy Carriere, "View Extraction and View Fusion in Architectural Understanding," *Proceedings of the 5th International Conference on Software Reuse,* Victoria, B.C., 1998.

[Kazm99]   Kazman, Rick, and S. J. Carriere, "Playing Detective: Reconstructing Software Architecture from Available Evidence," *Automated Software Engineering,* April 1999.

[Kell98]   Keller, Wolfgang, and Jens Coldewey, "Accessing Relational Databases: A Pattern Language," *Pattern Languages of Program Design 3,* Robert Martin, Dirk Riehle, and Frank Bushmann (Eds.), pp. 313–343, Addison-Wesley, 1998.

[Kell00]   Keller, Wolfgang, "The Bridge to the New Town—A Legacy System Migration Pattern," *Proceedings of Europlop 2000,* 2000.

[Knut92]   Knuth, Donald E., *Literate Programming,* Center for the Study of Language and Information, 1992.

[Lagu97]   Laguë, Bruno, Daniel Proulx, Ettore M. Merlo, Jean Mayrand, and John Hudepohl, "Assessing the Benefits of Incorporating Function Clone Detection in a Development Process," *Proceedings of ICSM (International Conference on Software Maintenance),* IEEE, 1997.

[Lanz99]   Lanza, Michele, "Combining Metrics and Graphs for Object Oriented Reverse Engineering," Master's thesis, University of Bern, October 1999.

[Lea96]   Lea, Doug, *Concurrent Programming in Java, Design Principles and Patterns,* Addison-Wesley, The Java Series, 1996.

[Lehm85]   Lehman, M. M., and L. Belady, *Program Evolution—Processes of Software Change,* London Academic Press, 1985.

[Lieb88]   Lieberherr, Karl J., Ian M. Holland, and Arthur Riel, "Object-Oriented Programming: An Objective Sense of Style," *Proceedings OOPSLA '88, ACM SIGPLAN Notices,* vol. 23, no. 11, November 1988, pp. 323–334.

[Lore94]   Lorenz, Mark, and Jeff Kidd, *Object-Oriented Software Metrics: A Practical Guide,* Prentice-Hall, 1994.

[Love93]   Love, Tom, *Object Lessons—Lessons Learned in Object-Oriented Development Projects,* SIGS Books, 1993.

[Mayr96]   Mayrand, J., C. Leblanc, and E. Merlo, "Experiment on the Automatic Detection of Function Clones in a Software System Using Metrics," *International Conference on Software Systems Using Metrics,* 1996, pp. 244–253.

[Meye96]   Meyers, Scott, *More Effective C++,* Addison-Wesley, 1996.

[Meye98]   Meyers, Scott, *Effective C++* (2nd edition), Addison-Wesley, 1998.

[Mull00]   Müller, Hausi A., Jens H. Janhke, Dennis B. Smith, Margaret-Anne Storey, Scott R. Tilley, and Kenny Wong, "Reverse Engineering: A Roadmap," *The Future of Software Engineering 2000,* A. Finkelstein (Ed.), ACM Press, 2000.

[Murp97]   Murphy, Gail C., and David Notkin, "Reengineering with Reflexion Models: A Case Study," *IEEE Computer,* vol. 8, 1997, pp. 29–36.

[Nesi98]   Nesi, Paolo, "Managing OO Project Better," *IEEE Software,* July 1988.

[Niel93]   Nielsen, Jakob, *Usability Engineering,* Morgan Kaufmann, 1999.

[Ocal99]   O'Callaghan, Alan, Ping Dai, and Ray Farmer, "Patterns for Change—Sample Patterns from the ADAPTOR Pattern Language," *Proceedings of Europlop 1999,* 1999.

[Ocal00]   O'Callaghan, Alan, "Patterns for Architectural Praxis," *Proceedings of Europlop 2000,* 2000.

[Opdy92]   Opdyke, William F., "Refactoring Object-Oriented Frameworks," Ph.D. thesis, University of Illinois, 1992.

[Pelr01]   Pelrine, Joseph, and Alan Knight, *Mastering ENVY/Developer,* Cambridge University Press, 2001.

[Pree94]   Pree, Wolfgang, "Meta Patterns—A Means for Capturing the Essentials of Reusable Object-Oriented Design," *Proceedings ECOOP'94,* M. Tokoro and R. Pareschi (Eds.), LNCS 821, Springer-Verlag, Bologna, Italy, July 1994, pp. 150–162.

[Prem94]   Premerlani, William J., and Michael R. Blaha, "An Approach for Reverse Engineering of Relational Databases," *Communications of the ACM,* vol. 37, no. 5, May 1994, pp. 42–49.

[Pres94] Pressman, Roger S., *Software Engineering: A Practitioner's Approach,* McGraw-Hill, 1994.

[Pust82] Pustell, J., and F. Kafatos, "A High Speed, High Capacity Homology Matrix: Zooming through sv40 and Polyoma," *Nucleid Acids Research,* vol. 10, no. 15, 1982, pp. 4765–4782.

[Reen89] Reenskaug, Trygve, and Anna Lise Skaar, "An Environment for Literate Smalltalk Programming," *Proceedings OOPSLA '89, ACM SIGPLAN Notices,* vol. 24, no. 10, October 1989, pp. 337–346.

[Reen96] Reenskaug, Trygve, *Working with Objects: The OOram Software Engineering Method,* Manning Publications, 1996.

[Rich99] Richner, Tamar, and Stéphane Ducasse, "Recovering High-Level Views of Object-Oriented Applications from Static and Dynamic Information," *Proceedings ICSM'99 (International Conference on Software Maintenance),* Hongji Yang and Lee White (Eds.), IEEE, September 1999, pp. 13–22.

[Rieh98] Riehle, Dirk, and Thomas Gross, "Role Model Based Framework Design and Integration," *Proceedings OOPSLA '98 ACM SIGPLAN Notices,* October 1998, pp. 117–133.

[Riel96] Riel, Arthur J., *Object-Oriented Design Heuristics,* Addison-Wesley, 1996.

[Risi00] Rising, Linda, "Customer Interaction Patterns," *Pattern Languages of Program Design 4,* Neil Harrison, Brian Foote, and Hans Rohnert (Eds.), pp. 585–609, Addison-Wesley, 2000.

[Robe97] Roberts, Don, John Brant, and Ralph E. Johnson, "A Refactoring Tool for Smalltalk," *Theory and Practice of Object Systems (TAPOS),* vol. 3, no. 4, 1997, pp. 253–263.

[Robe99] Roberts, Donald Bradley, "Practical Analysis for Refactoring," Ph.D. thesis, University of Illinois, 1999.

[Robs91] Robson, D. J., K. H. Bennet, B. J. Cornelius, and M. Munro, "Approaches to Program Comprehension," *Journal of Systems and Software,* vol. 14, February 1991, pp. 79–84, republished in [Arno92].

[Ruga98] Rugaber, Spencer, and Jim White, "Restoring a Legacy: Lessons Learned," *IEEE Software,* vol. 15, no. 4, July 1998, pp. 28–33.

[Scha99] Schauer, Reinhard, Sébastian Robitaille, Francois Martel, and Rudolf Keller, "Hot Spot Recovery in Object-Oriented Software with Inheritance and Composition Template Methods," *Proceedings of the International Conference on Software Maintenance (ICSM'99),* IEEE, 1999.

[Schm00] Schmidt, Douglas C., Michael Stal, Hans Rohnert, and Frank Buschmann, *Pattern-Oriented Software Architecture Volume 2—Networked and Concurrent Objects,* John Wiley and Sons, 2000.

[Schn98] Schneider, Geri, and Jason P. Winters, *Applying Use Cases,* Addison-Wesley, 1998.

[Shar97] Sharp, Alec, *Smalltalk by Example,* McGraw-Hill, 1997.

[Shaw96]   Shaw, Mary, and David Garlan, *Software Architecture: Perspectives on an Emerging Discipline,* Prentice-Hall, 1996.

[Snee99]   Sneed, Harry M., "Risks Involved in Reengineering Projects," *Proceedings of the 6th Working Conference on Reverse Engineering (WCRE),* IEEE, 1999.

[Somm96]   Sommerville, Ian, *Software Engineering* (5th edition), Addison-Wesley, 1996.

[Stev98]   Stevens, Perdita, and Rob Pooley, "System Reengineering Patterns," *Proceedings of FSE-6,* ACM-SIGSOFT.

[Stey96]   Steyaert, Patrick, Carine Lucas, Kim Mens, and Theo D'Hondt, "Reuse Contracts: Managing the Evolution of Reusable Assets," *Proceedings of OOPSLA '96 Conference,* ACM Press, 1996, pp. 268–285.

[Tayl00]   Taylor, Paul, "Capable, Productive, and Satisfied: Some Organizational Patterns for Protecting Productive People," *Pattern Languages of Program Design,* N. Harrison, B. Foote, and H. Rohnert (Eds.), pp. 611–636, Addison-Wesley, 2000.

[Thom98]   Thomsett, Rob, "The Year 2000 Bug: A Forgotten Lesson," *IEEE Software,* vol. 15, no. 4, July 1998, pp. 91–93,95.

[Weid98]   Weidl, Johannes, and Harald Gall, "Binding Object Models to Source Code: An Approach to Object-Oriented Rearchitecting," *Proceedings of the 22nd Computer Software and Application Conference (COMPSAC 1998),* IEEE, 1998.

[Wirf90]   Wirfs-Brock, Rebecca, Brian Wilkerson, and Lauren Wiener, *Designing Object-Oriented Software,* Prentice Hall, 1990.

[Wong95]   Wong, Kenny, Scott R. Tilley, Hausi A. Müller, and Margaret-Anne D. Storey, "Structural Redocumentation: A Case Study," *IEEE Software,* vol. 12, no. 1, Jan 1995, pp. 46–54.

[Wool98]   Woolf, Bobby, "Null Object," *Pattern Languages of Program Design 3,* Robert Martin, Dirk Riehle, and Frank Buschmann (Eds.), pp. 5–18, Addison-Wesley, 1998.

[Wuyt98]   Wuyts, Roel, "Declarative Reasoning about the Structure Object-Oriented Systems," *Proceedings of the TOOLS USA '98 Conference,* IEEE, 1998, pp. 112–124.

[Your97]   Yourdon, Edward, *Death March,* Prentice Hall, 1997.

Index

A

Abstract Factory (Pattern A.10), 111, 256
activities in project plan, 31
Ada
   detecting client type checks in, 226
   detecting self type checks in, 219
Adapter (Pattern A.11), 164, 193, 256
Agree on Maxims (Pattern 2.1), 18–19
Alexander, Christopher, 9–10
algorithms, white-box testing for, 139
Allen, Woody, 42
Always Have a Running Version (Pattern 7.5)
   Build Confidence (Pattern 7.2) helped by, 158
   intent, 157
   main discussion, 157–159
   Migrate Systems Incrementally (Pattern 7.3) and, 148
   problem, 157–158
   rationale, 159
   Regression Test after Every Change (Pattern 7.6) with, 159
   related patterns, 159
   solution, 158
   steps, 158
   tests as precondition to, 123, 127
   trade-offs, 158
   Write Tests to Enable Evolution (Pattern 6.1) as prerequisite, 127
Analyze the Persistent Data (Pattern 4.1)
   as bottom-up method, 67, 75
   class diagram derivation, steps for, 69–73
   documentation by, 67–68
   example, 74–75
   incorporating associations, 70–72
   incorporating inheritance, 70
   incorporating operations, 72–73
   intent, 68
   known uses, 76
   limited scope of, 73
   main discussion, 68–76
   preparing an initial model, 69–70
   problem, 68–69
   rationale, 75–76
   Read All the Code in One Hour (Pattern 3.2) as preparation for, 44
   refining the class diagram, 76
   repeated application of, 67
   Skim the Documentation (Pattern 3.3) as preparation for, 50
   solution, 69–73
   time required for, 67
   trade-offs, 73–74
   verifying the classes, 72
   what next, 76
annotating code
   comment-based annotations, 98–99, 101
   conventions for, 99
   eliminating annotations, 101
   granularity for, 100
   hints, 99–100
   method-based annotations, 99, 102–103
   motivating programmers, 101
   at point where comment applies, 96
   risks of error introduction, 99, 105
   updating annotations with answers, 100
Appoint a Navigator (Pattern 2.2), 19, 155
architectural vision, maintaining, 19
architecture, Speculate about Architecture variation (Pattern 4.2), 79
"Arranging the furniture" pattern, 106
associations
   classes, 71
   complementary, merging, 71
   incorporating in class diagram, 70–72
   multiplicities for, 72
   qualified, identifying, 72
AST matching, 201–202
attributes
   access sequences in navigation code, 200
   multiple methods switching on, 218
   Rename Attribute (Pattern A.7), 104, 255
   renaming to convey roles, 104
   self type checks and, 218
automation, as property of well-designed tests, 124, 126, 127

B

Ball, T., 116
Beck, Kent, 4, 20, 43, 136, 173
behavior. *See* Move Behavior Close to Data (Pattern 9.1)
Belady, L., 169
"Big Ball of Mud," 213
Binder, Robert V., 253
Black-Box Testing pattern. *See* Test the Interface, Not the Implementation (Pattern 6.4)
Blob pattern. *See* Split Up God Class (Pattern 9.3)
Boehm, Barry, 6
bottlenecks, Split Up God Class (Pattern 9.3) and, 23
bottom-up approach
   to design extraction, 83

bottom-up approach (*continued*)
to study of source code, 67
white noise from, 83
Brant, John, 106
breakpoints for Step through the
Execution (Pattern 5.3), 108
"Bridge to the New Town, The,"
162. *See also* Make a Bridge
to the New Town (Pattern 7.7)
Brodie, Michael L., 162
Brooks, Frederick P., 95, 157
Brown, Kyle, 112–113
bugs
Chat with the Maintainers
(Pattern 3.1) about, 32–33
reengineering needed for, 3
Build Confidence (Pattern 7.2)
Always Have a Running Version
(Pattern 7.5) and, 158
intent, 151
Involve the Users (Pattern 7.1)
and, 148, 151, 153
as key motivation, 148
main discussion, 151–153
Make a Bridge to the New Town
(Pattern 7.7) and, 153, 162
Migrate Systems Incrementally
(Pattern 7.3) and, 148
Most Valuable First pattern
and, 22
for overcoming skepticism,
148, 151
problem, 151–152
Prototype the Target Solution
(Pattern 7.4) and, 153
rationale, 153
Regression Test after Every
Change (Pattern 7.6) and, 159
related patterns, 153
risk minimized by, 148
solution, 152
trade-offs, 152
building the system, Do a Mock
Installation (Pattern 3.5) to
ensure ability, 58–63
business model
need for agreement on, 19
understanding customer's, 21
business objects, Speculate about
Business Objects variation
(Pattern 4.2), 78
business rules. *See* Record Business
Rules as Tests (Pattern 6.5)

C

C++
detecting client type checks in,
226
detecting self type checks in, 219
perl script for identifying simulated switches in, 251

candidate keys, determining, 69
case statements
flexibility lost by, 215
programming languages and,
216
responsibilities assumed by, 215
See also Transform Conditionals
to Polymorphism
change logs/change requests
concentration of software
defects and, 22
for determining valuable artifacts, 21
fixing unstable design and, 117
Chat with the Maintainers (Pattern
3.1)
after Do a Mock Installation
(Pattern 3.5), 62
after Interview during Demo
(Pattern 3.4), 57, 58
after Skim the Documentation
(Pattern 3.3), 50
for determining causes of
instability, 117
example, 34–35
intent, 31
known uses, 36–37
main discussion, 31–37
as maintainer-oriented meeting,
36
problem, 31–32
questions to ask, 32–33
rationale, 35–36
Read All the Code in One Hour
(Pattern 3.2) and, 40, 43
related patterns, 37
solution, 32–33
trade-offs, 33–34
verifying information gained, 37
what next, 37
checkers graph for class size overview, 88–89
Chicken Little pattern. *See* Migrate
Systems Incrementally (Pattern 7.3)
Chikofsky, Elliot J., 5, 9
class diagram
adapting based on mismatches,
78
encapsulation of data and,
75–76
incorporating associations,
70–72
incorporating inheritance, 70
incorporating operations, 72–73
initial model for, 69–70
maintaining consistency in, 79
refining, 76
steps for deriving, 69–73
steps for refining, 77–78
trade-offs, 73–74

verifying the classes, 72
See also Analyze the Persistent
Data (Pattern 4.1); Speculate
about Design (Pattern 4.2)
classes
analyzing inheritance, 89–90
association classes, 71
configuration classes, 194
data providers, 193
describing plug-in manager,
245
describing plug-in objects,
243–244
god classes, 188–189, 208–213
improving extensibility of,
217–225, 234–243
Look for the Contracts (Pattern
5.4), 73, 76, 97, 109–113, 117
mapping classes, 194
measuring size of, 88–89
Read All the Code in One Hour
(Pattern 3.2) and, 39
renaming to convey purpose, 105
Split Up God Class (Pattern 9.3),
23, 189, 208–213
static structure vs. dynamic
behavior, 96
super calls and assumptions
about subclasses and, 112
utility classes, 189
client. *See* customer
client type checks. *See* Transform
Client Type Checks (Pattern
10.2)
coarse-grained architectural problems, 8
code
annotating, 96, 98–100
Chat with the Maintainers
(Pattern 3.1) about, 33
Compare Code Mechanically
(Pattern 8.1), 175–180, 208
duplicated, 3–4, 105, 172–185
ownership and refactoring, 106
Read All the Code in One Hour
(Pattern 3.2), 30, 37, 38–44,
50, 53, 58
Refactor to Understand (Pattern
5.2), 96–97, 103–107, 144, 170
Tie Code and Questions (Pattern
5.1), 96, 98–103, 106, 107, 108,
144
top-down vs. bottom-up study
of, 67
Use Profiler before Optimizing
(Pattern 7.12), 169–170
Visualize Code as Dotplots
(Pattern 8.2), 180–185
Write Tests to Understand
(Pattern 6.6), 97, 106, 109,
122–123, 130, 142–144

See also Detecting Duplicated Code
code review. *See* Read All the Code in One Hour (Pattern 3.2)
code smells
   If It Ain't Broke, Don't Fix It (Pattern 2.6) and, 24
   recognizing, 38
   reengineering needed for, 3–4
   reporting, 38
CodeCrawler tool, 88, 93
coding idioms, Read All the Code in One Hour (Pattern 3.2) and, 39
coding styles, Read All the Code in One Hour (Pattern 3.2) and, 39
comments
   annotations based on, 96, 98–99
   misleading, 39, 40, 50
   motivating programmers to write, 101
   Read All the Code in One Hour (Pattern 3.2) and, 39, 40
communication
   capturing database schema and improvement in, 73
   design structure and, 35
   effective, 66–67
   as force to be aware of, 17, 66–67
   language for, 66–67
   Tie Code and Questions (Pattern 5.1) for improving, 100
Compare Code Mechanically (Pattern 8.1)
   Eliminate Navigation Code (Pattern 9.2) and, 208
   example, 176–180
   intent, 175
   known uses, 180
   main discussion, 175–180
   perl script for, 177–180
   problem, 175
   solution, 175–176
   steps, 175
   trade-offs, 176
   variations, 175–176
comparing versions or releases. *See* Learn from the Past (Pattern 5.5)
complementary associations, merging, 71
complexity
   flexibility vs., 25
   Keep It Simple (Pattern 2.7), 24–25
   of legacy systems, 28
   Migrate Systems Incrementally (Pattern 7.3) for avoiding, 153
   Most Valuable First (Pattern 2.4) and, 22

Step through the Execution (Pattern 5.3) and, 108
concept assignment problem, 84
conditionals. *See* Transform Conditionals to Polymorphism
confidence
   Always Have a Running Version (Pattern 7.5) for, 157, 158
   Build Confidence (Pattern 7.2), 22, 148, 151–153, 158, 159, 162
   built by testing, 123, 124, 126–127
   Regression Test after Every Change (Pattern 7.6) for, 159
configuration classes, 194
Conserve Familiarity (Pattern 7.11), 149, 168–169
constructor calls, contracts and, 111
Continuous Integration pattern, 159
contracts
   defined, 110
   as implicit, 110
   Look for the Contracts (Pattern 5.4), 109–113
   reuse contracts, 113
   validating, 113
Conway's law, 35
Cook, Stephen, 37
credibility
   Do a Mock Installation (Pattern 3.5) and, 60
   Interview during Demo (Pattern 3.4) and, 53
critical path, Most Valuable First (Pattern 2.4) and, 19, 23
Cross, James H., 5, 9
culture of continuous reengineering, need for, 5, 9
customer
   changing perceptions of, 22
   determining what is valuable to, 21–22
   expectations as forces, 122
   initial tasks most valuable to, 20–21
   measurable goal of, 21
   selling tests to, 124
   stakeholders vs., 21
   test writing by, 140
"Customer Interaction Patterns," 57

D
data
   Analyze the Persistent Data (Pattern 4.1), 44, 50, 67, 68–76
   as deceptive, 66
   encapsulation of, 75–76
   interpreting, 88

junk, 68, 73
migrating to new system, 160–162
Move Behavior Close to Data (Pattern 9.1), 174, 185, 189, 190–198, 199, 202, 210
samples for verifying classes, 72
data bridge, 161, 162
data containers
   defined, 187, 188
   detecting, 190
   forces, 187–188
   generated from database schema, 193
   god classes with, 189
   law of Demeter (LOD) violations and, 188
   polymorphism and, 190
   responsibilities lacking in, 188, 190
   as sign of misplaced responsibilities, 186
   wrapping, 193
   See also Move Behavior Close to Data (Pattern 9.1)
database schema
   data containers generated from, 193
   improved communication and, 73
   polluted, 74
   See also class diagram
Davis, Alan Mark, 160, 170
debuggers, Step through the Execution (Pattern 5.3) requirements, 109
DeLano, David E., 253
demo. *See* Interview during Demo (Pattern 3.4)
Demonstrate to Yourself variation (Pattern 3.4), 52
Deprecate Obsolete Interfaces (Pattern 7.10), 149, 166–168
DESEL (Designing for Ease of System Evolution) project, 37
design
   evolution of, 96
   implicit aspects of, 95–96, 97
   thumbnail patterns, 253, 256–258
design concept recovery. *See* Speculate about Design (Pattern 4.2)
design exposure. *See* Detailed Model Capture
design extraction tools, 111
Design Patterns, 253
Design Patterns Smalltalk Companion, 237, 239
design problem identification. *See* Study the Exceptional Entities (Pattern 4.3)

DESIRE tool, 84
Detailed Model Capture
    forces, 95–96
    Learn from the Past (Pattern
        5.5), 113–117
    Look for the Contracts (Pattern
        5.4), 109–113
    map of patterns, 94
    overview, 96–97
    Record Business Rules as Tests
        (Pattern 6.5) and, 97
    Refactor to Understand (Pattern
        5.2), 103–107
    Step through the Execution
        (Pattern 5.3), 107–109
    Test the Interface, Not the
        Implementation (Pattern 6.4)
        and, 97
    Tie Code and Questions (Pattern
        5.1), 98–103
    what next, 97
    See also specific patterns
details, importance of, 95
Detecting Duplicated Code
    Compare Code Mechanically
        (Pattern 8.1), 175–180
    Extract Method (Pattern A.5)
        and, 174
    forces, 173–174
    map of patterns, 172
    Move Behavior Close to Data
        (Pattern 9.1) and, 174
    overview, 174
    Transform Conditionals to Poly-
        morphism and, 174, 184, 185
    Visualize Code as Dotplots (Pat-
        tern 8.2), 180–185
    See also specific patterns
developers
    Chat with the Maintainers
        (Pattern 3.1) about, 33
    departure of, need for
        reengineering and, 3
    as documentation audience, 44,
        46, 49
    duplicated code known by, 174
    team organization and design
        structure, 35
    test writing by, 140
    testing resisted by, 125
    user information from, 52
    vocabulary of, 40
Distinguish Public from Published
    Interfaces (Pattern 7.9), 149,
    164–166
Do a Mock Installation (Pattern
    3.5)
    after Read All the Code in One
        Hour (Pattern 3.2), 43
    example, 60–62

intent, 58
Interview during Demo (Pattern
    3.4) and, 53, 63
known uses, 62
main discussion, 58–63
patterns complementing, 53
problem, 58–59
report for, 59
solution, 59
time required for, 59, 60
trade-offs, 59–60
verifying maintainers' input, 37
what next, 62–63
"Do it, then do it right, then do it
    fast" aphorism, 170
documentation
    by Analyze the Persistent Data
        (Pattern 4.1), 67–68
    audience for, 44, 46
    Chat with the Maintainers (Pat-
        tern 3.1) about, 33
    class diagram, 69–74, 75–76
    historical and political context
        missing from, 31
    of Initial Understanding, 65–66
    insufficient, 48–49
    of interfaces for stable design
        parts, 117
    language for, 66–67
    misleading, 50
    need for reengineering and, 2
    Record Business Rules as Tests
        (Pattern 6.5), 58, 97, 108, 130,
        139–142
    reverse engineering and
        redocumentation, 7–8
    Skim the Documentation (Pat-
        tern 3.3), 30, 37, 40, 43, 44–50,
        53, 58
    by Speculate about Design (Pat-
        tern 4.2), 67–68
    tests as system description, 124,
        142
    See also reports; Skim the Docu-
        mentation (Pattern 3.3)
Dotplot tool, 184–185
dotplots. See Visualize Code as
    Dotplots (Pattern 8.2)
Dup tool, 185
duplicated code
    Compare Code Mechanically
        (Pattern 8.1), 175–180, 208
    Extract Method (Pattern A.5) for,
        174
    forces, 173–174
    importance of identifying, 173
    manipulating data of separate
        provider classes, 191
    Move Behavior Close to Data
        (Pattern 9.1) for, 174

origins of, 174
perl script for detecting, 177–180
reengineering needed for, 3–4
removing during Refactor to
    Understand (Pattern 5.2),
    105
signs of, 174
subclassing and, 218
Transform Conditionals to Poly-
    morphism and, 174, 184, 185
Visualize Code as Dotplots (Pat-
    tern 8.2), 180–185
See also Detecting Duplicated
    Code
dynamic behavior, static structure
    vs., 96

E

Eick, S., 116
Eliminate Navigation Code
    (Pattern 9.2)
    Compare Code Mechanically
        (Pattern 8.1) and, 208
    detection, 199–202
    example, 204–207
    intent, 199
    main discussion, 199–208
    Move Behavior Close to Data
        (Pattern 9.1) and, 199, 202
    overview, 189
    problem, 199
    rationale, 208
    related patterns, 208
    solution, 199–202, 203
    steps, 202
    trade-offs, 202, 204
    when the legacy solution is the
        solution, 204
Encapsulate Field (Pattern A.4),
    198, 254
encapsulation of data, 75–76
end users. See users
Engage Customers pattern. See
    Involve the Users (Pattern 7.1)
entities, exceptional. See Study the
    Exceptional Entities (Pattern
    4.3)
evolution
    of design, 96
    of requirements, 5
evolutionary prototypes
    exploratory prototypes vs., 156
    Make a Bridge to the New Town
        (Pattern 7.7) with, 157
exceptional values, studying. See
    Study the Exceptional Entities
    (Pattern 4.3)
execution, stepping through. See
    Step through the Execution
    (Pattern 5.3)

expectations
   Chat with the Maintainers
      (Pattern 3.1) about, 33, 34
   Involve the Users (Pattern 7.1)
      and, 151
   risks of raising, 22
explicit type checks. *See* Transform
   Client Type Checks (Pattern
   10.2); Transform Self Type
   Checks (Pattern 10.1)
exploratory prototypes, evolutionary prototypes vs., 156
exposing the design. *See* Detailed
   Model Capture
Extract Method of Refactoring
   Browser, 236, 238
Extract Method (Pattern A.5)
   for eliminating duplicated code,
      174
   Move Behavior Close to Data
      (Pattern 9.1) and, 191
   overview, 255
   Refactor to Understand (Pattern
      5.2) and, 104
   tools for, 105–106
   Visualize Code as Dotplots
      (Pattern 8.2) and, 185
extracting system design
   as reason for reengineering, 2
   tools, 111
Extreme Programming, 127, 160

F

Facade (Pattern A.12), 210, 256
Factor Out State (Pattern 10.3)
   in Design Patterns Smalltalk
      Companion, 237
   Extract Method of Refactoring
      Browser and, 236
   Factor Out Strategy (Pattern
      10.4) vs., 239–240
   intent, 234
   known uses, 237
   main discussion, 234–237
   overview, 217
   problem, 234
   solution, 234–236
   State (Pattern A.18) and, 216, 234
   State Patterns (Pattern A.19)
      and, 234
   steps, 235–236
   trade-offs, 236–237
   Transform Self Type Checks
      (Pattern 10.1) and, 225
   when the legacy solution is the
      solution, 236–237
Factor Out Strategy (Pattern 10.4)
   in Design Patterns Smalltalk
      Companion, 239
   example, 239

Extract Method of Refactoring
   Browser and, 238
   Factor Out State (Pattern 10.3)
      vs., 239–240
   intent, 237
   main discussion, 237–240
   overview, 217
   problem, 237
   related patterns, 239–240
   solution, 237–238
   steps, 237–238
   Strategy (Pattern A.20) and, 216,
      237
   trade-offs, 239
   Transform Self Type Checks
      (Pattern 10.1) and, 225
Factory Method (Pattern A.13),
   111, 256
faithful colleagues, 29
familiarity. *See* Conserve Familiarity (Pattern 7.11)
FAMOOS project
   CodeCrawler tool in, 93
   Compare Code Mechanically
      (Pattern 8.1) in, 180
   Demonstrate to Yourself pattern
      in, 57
   insufficient documentation in, 49
   misleading comments in, 50
   mock installation in, 62
   Read All the Code in One Hour
      (Pattern 3.2) and, 43
   Refactor to Understand (Pattern
      5.2) in, 106
   Visualize Code as Dotplots (Pat-
      tern 8.2) in, 185
feasibility, assessing during First
   Contact, 26
feedback. *See* user feedback
fence-sitting colleagues, 29
figures, Skim the Documentation
   (Pattern 3.3) and, 45
FileList tool in Squeak, 245–249
fine-grained design problems, 8
First Contact
   assessing feasibility during, 26
   Chat with the Maintainers
      (Pattern 3.1), 31–37
   Do a Mock Installation (Pattern
      3.5), 58–63
   forces, 27–29
   Interview during Demo (Pattern
      3.4), 50–58
   map of patterns, 26
   overview, 29–30
   Read All the Code in One Hour
      (Pattern 3.2), 38–44
   Skim the Documentation
      (Pattern 3.3), 44–50
   what next, 30–31

See also specific patterns
first impressions
   danger of, 29
   Read All the Code in One Hour
      (Pattern 3.2), 38–44
Fix Problems, Not Symptoms
   (Pattern 2.5), 19, 23
Fjeldstadt, R. K., 49
flexibility
   case statements and loss of, 215
   complexity vs., 25
   Keep It Simple (Pattern 2.7) and,
      24–25
Florijn, Gert, 112–113
Flyweight (Pattern A.14), 256–257
Foote, Brian, 157, 213
forces
   Detailed Model Capture, 95–96
   Detecting Duplicated Code,
      173–174
   First Contact, 27–29
   Initial Understanding, 65–67
   Migration Strategies, 147
   Redistribute Responsibilities,
      187–188
   Setting Direction, 17–18
   Tests: Your Life Insurance!,
      121–122
   Transform Conditionals to Poly-
      morphism, 215–216
foreign key relationships
   collecting, 69–70
   resolving targets, 71–72
   SQL statements for identifying,
      72
formal specifications, Skim the
   Documentation (Pattern 3.3)
   and, 45
forward engineering
   defined, 6
   illustrated, 7
   reverse engineering vs., 6, 56–57
Fowler, Martin, 20, 173, 241, 253
framework for testing. *See* Use a
   Testing Framework (Pattern
   6.3)
functionality, Interview during
   Demo (Pattern 3.4) for understanding, 50

G

Gamma, Erich, 136
generality, Keep It Simple (Pattern
   2.7) and, 24–25
goals
   assessing code quality and, 38
   identifying helpful documenta-
      tion and, 44
   measurable, 21
   primary, 21

goals (*continued*)
  reconsidering after Study the
    Exceptional Entities (Pattern
    4.3), 93
  of reengineering, 1
  See also expectations
God Class pattern. *See* Split Up
    God Class (Pattern 9.3)
god classes
  data containers with, 189
  defined, 188
  detecting, 209–210
  generation of, 188
  maintenance and, 212
  responsibilities assumed by,
    188–189
  Split Up God Class (Pattern 9.3),
    23, 189, 208–213
  utility classes vs., 189
Goldberg, Adele, 19
go/no-go decision
  in project plan, 31
  Read All the Code in One Hour
    (Pattern 3.2) and, 43
  Skim the Documentation
    (Pattern 3.3) and, 50
granularity
  coarse-grained architectural
    problems, 8
  of code annotations, 100
  fine-grained design problems, 8
  of testing, 130
Grow Your Test Base Incrementally
    (Pattern 6.2)
  as basis for Write Tests to Enable
    Evolution (Pattern 6.1), 122
  example, 129–130
  hints, 128–129
  intent, 128
  main discussion, 128–130
  Migrate Systems Incrementally
    (Pattern 7.3) with, 155
  problem, 130
  rationale, 130
  Record Business Rules as Tests
    (Pattern 6.5) and, 130, 142
  Regression Test after Every
    Change (Pattern 7.6) and, 160
  related patterns, 130
  solution, 128–129
  Test the Interface, Not the
    Implementation (Pattern 6.4)
    and, 130
  trade-offs, 129
  Use a Testing Framework
    (Pattern 6.3) and, 130
  Write Tests to Enable Evolution
    (Pattern 6.1) and, 122, 127
  Write Tests to Understand
    (Pattern 6.6) and, 130

guidelines
  Agree on Maxims (Pattern 2.1),
    18–19
  to set and maintain direction, 16

H
Hamlen, W. T., 49
hashing, for comparing code, 175
help desk personnel, user informa-
    tion from, 52
historical context. *See* Chat with
    the Maintainers (Pattern 3.1)
hook methods
  detecting semiautomatically,
    113
  specializing classes and, 112
human dependencies, as reason
    for reengineering, 2

I
If It Ain't Broke, Don't Fix It (Pat-
    tern 2.6), 23, 24
implementation. *See* Do a Mock
    Installation (Pattern 3.5); Test
    the Interface, Not the Imple-
    mentation (Pattern 6.4)
implicit aspects of design, 95–96,
    97
incremental testing strategy. *See*
    Grow Your Test Base Incre-
    mentally (Pattern 6.2)
independence, as property of well-
    designed tests, 124, 126
index, Skim the Documentation
    (Pattern 3.3) and, 45
indirect clients, 199–200
indirect providers, 199
inheritance relationships
  bottom-up design extraction
    approach and, 83
  class inheritance, 89–90
  hierarchy, studying, 89–90
  incorporating in class diagram,
    70
  legacy databases and, 68
  method inheritance, 90, 91
  one to one, 70
  rolled down, 70
  rolled up, 70
Initial Understanding
  Analyze the Persistent Data (Pat-
    tern 4.1), 68–76
  documentation of, 65–67
  forces, 65–67
  map of patterns, 64
  overview, 67
  Speculate about Design (Pattern
    4.2), 76–84
  Study the Exceptional Entities
    (Pattern 4.3), 84–93

time required for, 67
  top-down vs. bottom-up study
    of source code, 67
  what next, 67–68
  See also specific patterns
inside knowledge, need for
    reengineering and, 3
installation, mock. *See* Do a Mock
    Installation (Pattern 3.5)
instantiated objects, Step through
    the Execution (Pattern 5.3) for
    discovering, 107–109
integration, continuous. *See*
    Always Have a Running Ver-
    sion (Pattern 7.5)
interests
  coping with conflicting, 18–19
  as force to be aware of, 17
interfaces. *See* public interfaces;
    user interface
Interview during Demo (Pattern
    3.4)
  after Skim the Documentation
    (Pattern 3.3), 50
  Chat with the Maintainers
    (Pattern 3.1) after, 57, 58
  choosing users for, 51–52, 53
  Demonstrate to Yourself varia-
    tion, 52
  for determining causes of insta-
    bility, 117
  Do a Mock Installation (Pattern
    3.5) and, 53, 63
  example, 54–56
  intent, 50
  interviewing skills needed for,
    53, 56
  known uses, 57
  main discussion, 50–58
  order for applying, 30
  patterns complementing, 40, 43,
    53
  as preparation for Record Busi-
    ness Rules as Tests (Pattern
    6.5), 58
  as preparation for Speculate
    about Design (Pattern 4.2), 58
  problem, 50–51
  rationale, 56–57
  Read All the Code in One Hour
    (Pattern 3.2) and, 40, 43, 53,
    58
  real-time software and, 54
  related patterns, 57
  repeating with various users,
    51–52, 53, 57–58
  report for, 51
  Skim the Documentation
    (Pattern 3.3) and, 53, 58
  solution, 51–52

Step through the Execution (Pattern 5.3) scenarios from, 109
trade-offs, 53–54
usage scenarios from, 50–51
verifying maintainers' input, 37
what next, 57–58
interviewing maintainers. *See* Chat with the Maintainers (Pattern 3.1)
Introduce Null Object (Pattern 10.5)
    detection, 240
    example, 242–243
    intent, 240
    main discussion, 240–243
    Null Object (Pattern A.15) and, 216, 240
    overview, 217
    problem, 240
    solution, 240–241
    steps, 241
    trade-offs, 242
    Transform Client Type Checks (Pattern 10.2) and, 233
Involve the Users (Pattern 7.1)
    Build Confidence (Pattern 7.2) and, 148, 151, 153
    Conserve Familiarity (Pattern 7.11) and, 169
    for increasing chances of user acceptance, 148
    intent, 149
    Keep It Simple (Pattern 2.7) and, 25
    as key motivation, 148
    main discussion, 149–151
    Migrate Systems Incrementally (Pattern 7.3) and, 148, 150, 151
    Most Valuable First pattern and, 22
    Planning Game for, 151
    problem, 149–150
    rationale, 151
    related patterns, 151
    risk minimized by, 148
    solution, 150
    steps, 150
    trade-offs, 150–151

J

Java
    detecting client type checks in, 226–227
    detecting navigation code in, 201
    detecting self type checks in, 219
Jazayeri, Mehdi, 116
JUnit
    assertion methods, 132–133

runBare() template method, 132
runTest() method, 132
setup() method, 132, 134
suite() mthoed, 135
tearDown() method, 132
test runner classes, 135
test subclasses, 132, 133–134
TestCase class, 132–133
    as testing framework, 131, 132–136
TestResult class, 132
    unit test example, 126
junk data in relational databases, 73

K

Keep It Simple (Pattern 2.7), 24–25
Keep the Data—Toss the Code pattern. *See* Make a Bridge to the New Town (Pattern 7.7)
Keller, Wolfgang, 162
knowledge, sharing, 66

L

language
    for code annotations, 99
    for documentation, 66–67
    testing frameworks, 136
large structures, Read All the Code in One Hour (Pattern 3.2) and, 39
large systems. *See* scale
law of Demeter (LOD)
    data containers and violations of, 188
    defined, 208
    navigation code as violation of, 188, 208
    See also Eliminate Navigation Code (Pattern 9.2)
Learn from the Past (Pattern 5.5)
    contract evolution and, 113
    hints, 114–115
    intent, 113
    known uses, 116–117
    main discussion, 113–117
    overview, 97
    problem, 113–114
    rationale, 116
    solution, 114–115
    trade-offs, 115–116
    what next, 117
legacy systems
    assessing via Read All the Code in One Hour (Pattern 3.2), 38–44
    complexity and size of, 28
    concentration of software defects in, 22
    distributed and hidden knowledge of, 20

focus on object-oriented systems, 4–5
forces to be aware of, 17–18
goal of reengineering, 1
inheritance relationships and, 68
migrating data from, 160–162
political context as problematical, 31
reasons for reengineering, 1–2
splitting into manageable pieces, 28
symptoms of need for reengineering, 2–4
value of, 1
when the legacy solution is the solution, 193–194, 204, 212–213, 222, 229, 236–237
Lehman, M. M., 169
libraries, 194
LOD. *See* law of Demeter (LOD)
Look for the Contracts (Pattern 5.4)
    for documenting the class interface, 117
    hints, 110–112
    incorporating operations for classes and, 73
    intent, 109
    known uses, 112–113
    Learn from the Past (Pattern 5.5) with, 113
    main discussion, 109–113
    overview, 97
    problem, 109–110
    Refactor to Understand (Pattern 5.2) before, 113
    refining class diagram using, 76
    solution, 110–112
    Step through the Execution (Pattern 5.3) for validation, 113
    trade-offs, 112
    what next, 113
Love, Tom, 157

M

maintenance
    Chat with the Maintainers (Pattern 3.1), 31–37, 40, 43, 50, 57, 58, 62, 117
    defined, 9
    god classes and, 212
    as reason for reengineering, 2–4
    reengineering vs., 9
    as second-class work, 35, 36
    turnover in maintenance teams, 34
    user information from maintainers, 52
    See also Chat with the Maintainers (Pattern 3.1)

Make a Bridge to the New Town
(Pattern 7.7)
Build Confidence (Pattern 7.2)
helped by, 153, 162
intent, 160
known uses, 162
large numbers of defects and, 23
main discussion, 160–162
Migrate Systems Incrementally
(Pattern 7.3) helped by, 149,
155, 162
problem, 161
Prototype the Target Solution
(Pattern 7.4) with, 157
rationale, 162
related patterns, 162
solution, 161–162
steps, 161–162
trade-offs, 162
managers
duplicated code known by, 174
user information from, 52
mapping classes, 194
maxims
agreeing on, 18–19
defined, 19
Setting Direction patterns as, 19
meaningful names, 103, 104
meetings
Chat with the Maintainers (Pattern 3.1), 31–37, 40, 43, 50, 57,
58, 62, 117
Interview during Demo (Pattern
3.4), 30, 37, 40, 43, 50–58, 63,
109, 117
minutes of, 20
sharing knowledge via, 66
Speak to the Round Table (Pattern 2.3), 20, 66
Stand Up, 20
methods
analyzing inheritance, 90, 91
annotations based on, 99
defining bodies with same level
of abstraction, 105
Extract Method (Pattern A.5), 104,
105–106, 174, 185, 191, 255
Factory Method (Pattern A.13),
111, 256
intention-revealing names for,
92
issues for invoking, 110
key methods, finding, 111
measuring size of, 90–92
Move Behavior Close to Data
(Pattern 9.1) and, 192
Move Method (Pattern A.6), 25,
191
multiple, switching on same
attribute, 218

Rename Method (Pattern A.8),
104, 255
renaming to convey intent, 104
replacing condition branches by,
105
restarting to verify scenario, 108
self type checks and, 218
Template Method (Pattern A.21),
112, 258
template/hook methods, 112
metrics
for Learn from the Past (Pattern
5.5), 114, 115
for Study the Exceptional
Entities (Pattern 4.3), 86
Migrate Systems Incrementally
(Pattern 7.3)
Always Have a Running Version
(Pattern 7.5) needed for, 148,
155
Appoint a Navigator (Pattern
2.2) and, 155
Build Confidence (Pattern 7.2)
helped by, 148
as central message of Migration
Strategies, 148
Conserve Familiarity (Pattern
7.11) and, 169
Deprecate Obsolete Interfaces
(Pattern 7.10) and, 149
Distinguish Public from Pub-
lished Interfaces (Pattern 7.9)
and, 149
Grow Your Test Base Increment-
ally (Pattern 6.2) and, 155
intent, 153
Involve the Users (Pattern 7.1)
helped by, 148, 150, 151
known uses, 154–155
main discussion, 153–155
Make a Bridge to the New Town
(Pattern 7.7) and, 149, 155, 162
Most Valuable First (Pattern 2.4)
and, 155
Present the Right Interface (Pattern 7.8) and, 149, 155
problem, 153
Prototype the Target Solution
(Pattern 7.4) needed for, 148
rationale, 154
Regression Test after Every
Change (Pattern 7.6) needed
for, 148, 155
related patterns, 155
risk minimized by, 148
solution, 153–154
steps, 154
Test the Interface, Not the
Implementation (Pattern 6.4)
and, 155

tests enabling, 123, 127
trade-offs, 154
user feedback and, 22
Write Tests to Enable Evolution
(Pattern 6.1) and, 127, 155
Migrating Legacy Systems, 162
Migration Strategies
Always Have a Running Version
(Pattern 7.5), 157–159
Build Confidence (Pattern 7.2),
151–153
Conserve Familiarity (Pattern
7.11), 168–169
Deprecate Obsolete Interfaces
(Pattern 7.10), 166–168
Distinguish Public from Pub-
lished Interfaces (Pattern 7.9),
164–166
forces, 147
Involve the Users (Pattern 7.1),
149–151
Make a Bridge to the New Town
(Pattern 7.7), 160–162
map of patterns, 146
Migrate Systems Incrementally
(Pattern 7.3), 153–155
overview, 147–149
Present the Right Interface (Pat-
tern 7.8), 163–164
Prototype the Target Solution
(Pattern 7.4), 155–157
Regression Test after Every
Change (Pattern 7.6), 159–160
Tests: Your Life Insurance! as
support for, 123
Use Profiler before Optimizing
(Pattern 7.12), 169–170
See also specific patterns
minutes, for round table meetings,
20
mock installation. *See* Do a Mock
Installation (Pattern 3.5)
Most Valuable First (Pattern 2.4)
critical path and, 19, 23
determining what is valuable, 21
Fix Problems, Not Symptoms
(Pattern 2.5) and, 23
if most valuable part is rat's nest,
22
main discussion, 20–22
Migrate Systems Incrementally
(Pattern 7.3) and, 155
patterns to employ after, 22
problem, 20
risk of raising expectations, 22
solution, 20
Move Behavior Close to Data (Pattern 9.1)
Adapter (Pattern A.11) and, 193
detection, 190–191

for duplicated code, 174, 185
Eliminate Navigation Code (Pattern 9.2) and, 199, 202
Encapsulate Field (Pattern A.4) and, 198
example, 194–198
Extract Method (Pattern A.5) and, 191
intent, 190
main discussion, 190–198
Move Method (Pattern A.6) and, 191
overview, 189
problem, 190
rationale, 198
related patterns, 198
solution, 190–192
Split Up God Class (Pattern 9.3) and, 210
steps, 191–192
trade-offs, 193–194
Transform Client Type Checks (Pattern 10.2) vs., 191
Visitor (Pattern A.22) and, 194
Visualize Code as Dotplots (Pattern 8.2) and, 185
when the legacy solution is the solution, 193–194
Move Method (Pattern A.6), 191, 255
multiplicities for associations, 72
Mythical Man-Month, The, 157

N

names
    enumerating for class diagram, 77
    enumerating for tables, 69
    intention-revealing, for methods, 192
    of key methods, 111
    meaningful, 103, 104
    naming conventions and Read All the Code in One Hour (Pattern 3.2), 39
    for published interfaces, 165
    for reengineering patterns, 10, 11
    tracking in source code, 78
    See also renaming
navigation code
    accessor method calls in, 200
    attribute access sequences in, 200
    defined, 188
    detection, 199–202
    Eliminate Navigation Code (Pattern 9.2), 189, 199–208
    indirect clients and, 199–200
    indirect providers and, 199

as violation of law of Demeter (LOD), 188, 208
Navigator, appointing, 19, 155
Null Object (Pattern A.15), 216, 240, 257

O

object-oriented design, mapping onto procedural implementation, 84
object-oriented systems
    focus of this book on, 4–5
    reuse costs in, 4–5
    transparency needed for, 4
objects
    changing internal state of, 108
    difficulties finding, 4
    instantiated at run time, discovering, 107–109
    plug-in, 145, 150, 243–244
    static structure vs. dynamic behavior, 96
O'Callaghan, Alan, 19, 164
one-to-one inheritance, 70
operations, incorporating in class diagram, 72–73
opportunities
    from Initial Understanding, 67–87
    in project plan, 30
optimizing. *See* Use Profiler before Optimizing (Pattern 7.12)
overengineering, temptation of, 18

P

parameters linking methods to classes, 111
part-whole relationships, 111
Pattern 2.1. *See* Agree on Maxims (Pattern 2.1)
Pattern 2.2. *See* Appoint a Navigator (Pattern 2.2)
Pattern 2.3. *See* Speak to the Round Table (Pattern 2.3)
Pattern 2.4. *See* Most Valuable First (Pattern 2.4)
Pattern 2.5. *See* Fix Problems, Not Symptoms (Pattern 2.5)
Pattern 2.6. *See* If It Ain't Broke, Don't Fix It (Pattern 2.6)
Pattern 2.7. *See* Keep It Simple (Pattern 2.7)
Pattern 3.1. *See* Chat with the Maintainers (Pattern 3.1)
Pattern 3.2. *See* Read All the Code in One Hour (Pattern 3.2)
Pattern 3.3. *See* Skim the Documentation (Pattern 3.3)
Pattern 3.4. *See* Interview during Demo (Pattern 3.4)

Pattern 3.5. *See* Do a Mock Installation (Pattern 3.5)
Pattern 4.1. *See* Analyze the Persistent Data (Pattern 4.1)
Pattern 4.2. *See* Speculate about Design (Pattern 4.2)
Pattern 4.3. *See* Study the Exceptional Entities (Pattern 4.3)
Pattern 5.1. *See* Tie Code and Questions (Pattern 5.1)
Pattern 5.2. *See* Refactor to Understand (Pattern 5.2)
Pattern 5.3. *See* Step through the Execution (Pattern 5.3)
Pattern 5.4. *See* Look for the Contracts (Pattern 5.4)
Pattern 5.5. *See* Learn from the Past (Pattern 5.5)
Pattern 6.1. *See* Write Tests to Enable Evolution (Pattern 6.1)
Pattern 6.2. *See* Grow Your Test Base Incrementally (Pattern 6.2)
Pattern 6.3. *See* Use a Testing Framework (Pattern 6.3)
Pattern 6.4. *See* Test the Interface, Not the Implementation (Pattern 6.4)
Pattern 6.5. *See* Record Business Rules as Tests (Pattern 6.5)
Pattern 6.6. *See* Write Tests to Understand (Pattern 6.6)
Pattern 7.1. *See* Involve the Users (Pattern 7.1)
Pattern 7.2. *See* Build Confidence (Pattern 7.2)
Pattern 7.3. *See* Migrate Systems Incrementally (Pattern 7.3)
Pattern 7.4. *See* Prototype the Target Solution (Pattern 7.4)
Pattern 7.5. *See* Always Have a Running Version (Pattern 7.5)
Pattern 7.6. *See* Regression Test after Every Change (Pattern 7.6)
Pattern 7.7. *See* Make a Bridge to the New Town (Pattern 7.7)
Pattern 7.8. *See* Present the Right Interface (Pattern 7.8)
Pattern 7.9. *See* Distinguish Public from Published Interfaces (Pattern 7.9)
Pattern 7.10. *See* Deprecate Obsolete Interfaces (Pattern 7.10)
Pattern 7.11. *See* Conserve Familiarity (Pattern 7.11)
Pattern 7.12. *See* Use Profiler before Optimizing (Pattern 7.12)
Pattern 8.1. *See* Compare Code Mechanically (Pattern 8.1)

Pattern 8.2. *See* Visualize Code as Dotplots (Pattern 8.2)

Pattern 9.1. *See* Move Behavior Close to Data (Pattern 9.1)

Pattern 9.2. *See* Eliminate Navigation Code (Pattern 9.2)

Pattern 9.3. *See* Split Up God Class (Pattern 9.3)

Pattern 10.1. *See* Transform Self Type Checks (Pattern 10.1)

Pattern 10.2. *See* Transform Client Type Checks (Pattern 10.2)

Pattern 10.3. *See* Factor Out State (Pattern 10.3)

Pattern 10.4. *See* Factor Out Strategy (Pattern 10.4)

Pattern 10.5. *See* Introduce Null Object (Pattern 10.5)

Pattern 10.6. *See* Transform Conditionals into Registration (Pattern 10.6)

Pattern A.1. *See* Retest Persistent Problems (Pattern A.1)

Pattern A.2. *See* Test Fuzzy Features (Pattern A.2)

Pattern A.3. *See* Test Old Bugs (Pattern A.3)

Pattern A.4. *See* Encapsulate Field (Pattern A.4)

Pattern A.5. *See* Extract Method (Pattern A.5)

Pattern A.6. *See* Move Method (Pattern A.6)

Pattern A.7. *See* Rename Attribute (Pattern A.7)

Pattern A.8. *See* Rename Method (Pattern A.8)

Pattern A.9. *See* Replace Conditional with Polymorphism (Pattern A.9)

Pattern A.10. *See* Abstract Factory (Pattern A.10)

Pattern A.11. *See* Adapter (Pattern A.11)

Pattern A.12. *See* Facade (Pattern A.12)

Pattern A.13. *See* Factory Method (Pattern A.13)

Pattern A.14. *See* Flyweight (Pattern A.14)

Pattern A.15. *See* Null Object (Pattern A.15)

Pattern A.16. *See* Quantity (Pattern A.16)

Pattern A.17. *See* Singleton (Pattern A.17)

Pattern A.18. *See* State (Pattern A.18)

Pattern A.19. *See* State Patterns (Pattern A.19)

Pattern A.20. *See* Strategy (Pattern A.20)

Pattern A.21. *See* Template Method (Pattern A.21)

Pattern A.22. *See* Visitor (Pattern A.22)

Pattern Language, A, 9–10

patterns
    application of, 10
    design patterns vs. reengineering patterns, 10–11
    introduction of, 9–10
    Speculate about Patterns variation (Pattern 4.2), 78
    See also reengineering patterns; *specific patterns by name*

performance, as reason for reengineering, 1–2

perl scripts
    for detecting duplicated code, 177–180
    for identifying simulated switches in C++, 251

persistence, as property of well-designed tests, 124, 126

Planning Game, 21, 151

plug-in manager, 245

plug-in objects, 145, 150, 243–244

political context. *See* Chat with the Maintainers (Pattern 3.1)

polymorphism. *See* Transform Conditionals to Polymorphism

Pooley, Rob, 168

porting a system, as reason for reengineering, 2

Present the Right Interface (Pattern 7.8)
    Adapter (Pattern A.11) vs., 164
    Deprecate Obsolete Interfaces (Pattern 7.10) and, 164
    Distinguish Public from Published Interfaces (Pattern 7.9) and, 164, 166
    Fix Problems, Not Symptoms (Pattern 2.5) and, 23
    hints, 163
    intent, 163
    known uses, 164
    main discussion, 163–164
    Migrate Systems Incrementally (Pattern 7.3) helped by, 149, 155
    problem, 163
    rationale, 164
    related patterns, 164
    solution, 163
    Split Up God Class (Pattern 9.3) and, 212–213

trade-offs, 163–164

principles
    Agree on Maxims (Pattern 2.1), 18–19
    to set and maintain direction, 16

priorities
    asking users about, 150
    difficulties setting, 17
    establishing, 18–19
    Most Valuable First (Pattern 2.4) for setting, 20–22, 23
    Planning Game for, 21

products, need for reengineering and, 3

profiler. *See* Use Profiler before Optimizing (Pattern 7.12)

programmers
    motivating to write comments, 101
    testing resisted by, 122

project plan, items to include, 30–31

project scope, in project plan, 30

Prototype the Target Solution (Pattern 7.4)
    Build Confidence (Pattern 7.2) helped by, 153
    Conserve Familiarity (Pattern 7.11) and, 169
    exploratory vs. evolutionary prototypes, 156
    intent, 155
    main discussion, 155–157
    Make a Bridge to the New Town (Pattern 7.7) with, 157
    Migrate Systems Incrementally (Pattern 7.3) and, 148
    problem, 155
    rationale, 157
    related patterns, 157
    solution, 156
    steps, 156
    trade-offs, 156–157

public interfaces
    Deprecate Obsolete Interfaces (Pattern 7.10), 149, 166–168
    Distinguish Public from Published Interfaces (Pattern 7.9), 149, 164–166
    Present the Right Interface (Pattern 7.8), 23, 149, 155, 163–164, 212–213
    Test the Interface, Not the Implementation (Pattern 6.4), 97, 117, 127, 130, 136–139, 155

Published Interface pattern, 166. *See also* Distinguish Public from Published Interfaces (Pattern 7.9)

Q

qualified associations, identifying, 72
Quantity (Pattern A.16), 257

R

Read All the Code in One Hour (Pattern 3.2)
after Skim the Documentation (Pattern 3.3), 50
Chat with the Maintainers (Pattern 3.1) and, 40, 43
checklist for, 39, 42
Do a Mock Installation (Pattern 3.5) after, 43
example, 41–42
intent, 38
Interview during Demo (Pattern 3.4) and, 40, 43, 53, 58
known uses, 43
lines read per hour, 40, 42
main discussion, 38–44
order for applying, 30
patterns complementing, 40, 43, 53, 58
problem, 38
rationale, 42
report for, 38, 42
Skim the Documentation (Pattern 3.3) and, 40, 43
solution, 38–39
time allotted for, 40, 42
trade-offs, 39–40
traditional code reviews vs., 42
verifying maintainers' input, 37
what next, 43–44
real-time software, Interview during Demo (Pattern 3.4) and, 54
rebuilding the system, Do a Mock Installation (Pattern 3.5) to ensure ability, 58–63
Record Business Rules as Tests (Pattern 6.5)
described, 130
Detailed Model Capture information and, 97
examples, 141–142
Grow Your Test Base Incrementally (Pattern 6.2) and, 130
hints, 140
intent, 139
Interview during Demo (Pattern 3.4) as preparation for, 58
main discussion, 139–142
problem, 139–140
rationale, 142
related patterns, 142

solution, 140
Step through the Execution (Pattern 5.3) and, 108
Test the Interface, Not the Implementation (Pattern 6.4) vs., 139
trade-offs, 140–141
Write Tests to Understand (Pattern 6.6) with, 142
Redistribute Responsibilities
Eliminate Navigation Code (Pattern 9.2), 199–208
forces, 187–188
map of patterns, 186
Move Behavior Close to Data (Pattern 9.1), 190–198
overview, 188–190
Split Up God Class (Pattern 9.3), 208–213
See also Transform Conditionals to Polymorphism; specific patterns
reengineering
big-bang, avoiding risk of, 153
coarse-grained architectural problems, 8
continuous, 5, 9
defined, 5
fine-grained design problems, 8
forces inherent to, 121
forces to be aware of, 17–18
goal of, 1
illustrated, 7
maintenance vs., 9
reasons for, 1–2
in reengineering life cycle, 8–9
refactoring, 9
restructuring, 9
reverse engineering vs., 5–6
risks in, 121, 123
symptoms of need for, 2–4
as transformation at all levels, 6
See also Detecting Duplicated Code; Migration Strategies; Redistribute Responsibilities; Tests: Your Life Insurance!; Transform Conditionals to Polymorphism
reengineering life cycle
reengineering, 8–9
reverse engineering, 6–8
terminology, 5–6
"waterfall," 13
reengineering patterns
criteria for good patterns, 11
defined, 10
design patterns vs., 10–11
form of, 11, 12
irrelevant or inapplicable, 30

map of pattern clusters, 11, 13
names for, 10, 11
order for applying, 29–30
overview, 10–11
See also specific patterns by name
Refactor to Understand (Pattern 5.2)
backing up code first, 104
before Look for the Contracts (Pattern 5.4), 113
before Write Tests to Understand (Pattern 6.6), 144
guidelines, 104–105
intent, 103
known uses, 106
main discussion, 103–107
overview, 96–97
problem, 103
refactorings typical for, 104
related patterns, 106
solution, 103–105
Tie Code and Questions (Pattern 5.1) with, 103, 106, 107
trade-offs, 105–106
Use Profiler before Optimizing (Pattern 7.12) and, 170
what next, 106–107
Write Tests to Understand (Pattern 6.6) during, 97, 106
refactoring
code ownership and, 106
defined, 9
Eliminate Navigation Code (Pattern 9.2), 189, 199–208
Encapsulate Field (Pattern A.4), 198, 254
Extract Method (Pattern A.5), 104, 105–106, 174, 185, 191, 255
Learn from the Past (Pattern 5.5) and, 114
Move Method (Pattern A.6), 25, 191
pinpointing problems and, 23
Refactor to Understand (Pattern 5.2), 96–97, 103–107, 144, 170
regression tests after, 103
Rename Attribute (Pattern A.7), 104, 255
Rename Method (Pattern A.8), 104, 255
Replace Conditional with Polymorphism (Pattern A.9), 234, 255
Split Up God Class (Pattern 9.3), 23, 189, 208–213
thumbnail patterns, 253, 254–255
tools for, 105–106
See also specific patterns

Refactoring Browser, 105–106, 201–202, 236, 238
Reflection Model, 83–84
Regression Test after Every Change (Pattern 7.6)
 after Split Up God Class (Pattern 9.3), 210
 Always Have a Running Version (Pattern 7.5) with, 159
 Build Confidence (Pattern 7.2) helped by, 159
 confidence built by, 123
 Grow Your Test Base Incrementally (Pattern 6.2) and, 160
 intent, 159
 main discussion, 159–160
 Migrate Systems Incrementally (Pattern 7.3) and, 148, 155
 problem, 159
 rationale, 160
 related patterns, 160
 Retest Persistent Problems (Pattern A.1) and, 160
 solution, 159
 trade-offs, 159–160
 Write Tests to Enable Evolution (Pattern 6.1) and, 160
relational databases
 class diagram derivation, 69–73
 incorporating associations, 70–72
 incorporating inheritance, 70
 incorporating operations, 72–73
 initial model for, 69–70
 junk data in, 68, 73
 migrating to another database, 76
 verifying the classes, 72
releases, comparing. *See* Learn from the Past (Pattern 5.5)
remodeling, source code/design mismatch and, 78
Rename Attribute (Pattern A.7), 104, 255
Rename Method (Pattern A.8), 104, 255
renaming
 attributes to convey roles, 104
 classes to convey purpose, 104
 to correct class diagram mismatches, 78
 Learn from the Past (Pattern 5.5) sensitivity to, 116
 with meaningful names, 103, 104
 methods to convey intent, 104
 Rename Attribute (Pattern A.7), 104, 255
 Rename Method (Pattern A.8), 104, 255

Renovate the Worst First strategy, 22
repeatability, as property of well-designed tests, 124, 126
Replace Conditional with Polymorphism (Pattern A.9), 234, 255
reports
 for Do a Mock Installation (Pattern 3.5), 59
 for Interview during Demo (Pattern 3.4), 51
 JUnit error reports, 132
 for Read All the Code in One Hour (Pattern 3.2), 38, 42
 samples in documentation, 45
 for Skim the Documentation (Pattern 3.3), 44–45
requirements
 continuous validation of, 150
 evolution of, 5
resources
 applicability of patterns and, 30
 scale of legacy systems and, 28
 Speculate about Design (Pattern 4.2) and, 79
 time as most precious resource, 28–29
responsibilities
 agreeing on, 19
 case statements' assumption of, 215
 data containers' lack of, 188, 190
 god classes' assumption of, 188–189
 See also Redistribute Responsibilities; Transform Conditionals to Polymorphism
restructuring, defined, 9
Retest Persistent Problems (Pattern A.1), 123, 160, 253–254
reuse
 costs of, 4–5
 Keep It Simple (Pattern 2.7) and, 25
 of stable parts of design, 117
 of tests, 136–139
reuse contracts, 113
reverse engineering
 defined, 5
 forward engineering vs., 6, 56–57
 illustrated, 7
 problem identification during, 7–8
 redocumentation during, 7–8
 in reengineering life cycle, 6–8
 reengineering vs., 5–6
 See also Detailed Model Capture; First Contact; Initial Understanding; Setting Direction

reverse engineers, Demonstrate to Yourself pattern for, 52
Rewrite Rule Editor, 201–202
rewriting components, 23
Riel, Arthur J., 233
Rising, Linda, 253
risks
 of big-bang reengineering, 153
 of error introduction during Refactor to Understand (Pattern 5.2), 99, 105
 identifying technical risks, 156
 Migration Strategies for minimizing, 148
 in project plan, 30
 in reengineering, 121, 123
 Study the Exceptional Entities (Pattern 4.3) and, 68
 Write Tests to Enable Evolution (Pattern 6.1) for minimizing, 123–127
Roberts, Don, 106, 253
Robson, D. J., 43
rolled-down inheritance, 70
rolled-up inheritance, 70
round table meetings, 20
round-trip engineering tools, 111
Rubin, Kenneth S., 19

S

sales department personnel, user information from, 52
scale
 build times for large systems, 158
 identifying design problems in large systems, 85
 of legacy systems, 28
 Read All the Code in One Hour (Pattern 3.2) and, 40, 41
 Speculate about Design (Pattern 4.2) and, 79
 Study the Exceptional Entities (Pattern 4.3) and, 87
scenarios for Step through the Execution (Pattern 5.3), 107, 108, 109
Schauer, Reinhard, 113
scope of Analyze the Persistent Data (Pattern 4.1), 73
screen dumps, Skim the Documentation (Pattern 3.3) and, 45
self-test, Do a Mock Installation (Pattern 3.5) and, 59
self type checks. *See* Transform Self Type Checks (Pattern 10.1)
"Semantic Wrapper," 164. *See also* Present the Right Interface (Pattern 7.8)

Setting Direction
  Agree on Maxims (Pattern 2.1),
    18–19
  Appoint a Navigator (Pattern
    2.2), 19
  Fix Problems, Not Symptoms
    (Pattern 2.5), 23
  forces to be aware of, 17–18
  If It Ain't Broke, Don't Fix It
    (Pattern 2.6), 24
  Keep It Simple (Pattern 2.7),
    24–25
  map of patterns, 16
  Most Valuable First (Pattern 2.4),
    20–22
  overview, 18
  principles and guidelines, 16
  Speak to the Round Table
    (Pattern 2.3), 20
  See also specific patterns
simplicity. *See* Keep It Simple
    (Pattern 2.7)
simulated switches, perl script for
    identifying in C++, 251
Singleton (Pattern A.17), 39, 257
skepticism
  Build Confidence (Pattern 7.2)
    for overcoming, 148, 151
  skeptical colleagues, 29
Skim the Documentation (Pattern
    3.3)
  example, 47–48
  intent, 44
  Interview during Demo (Pattern
    3.4) and, 53, 58
  items to look for, 45
  known uses, 49–50
  main discussion, 44–50
  order for applying, 30
  patterns complementing, 40, 43,
    53, 58
  problem, 44
  rationale, 48–49
  Read All the Code in One Hour
    (Pattern 3.2) and, 40, 43
  report for, 44–45
  solution, 44–45
  trade-offs, 46
  verifying maintainers' input, 37
  what next, 50
Smalltalk
  detecting client type checks in,
    226
  detecting navigation code in,
    201
  detecting self type checks in, 219
  extending libraries in, 194
Sneed, Harry, 106
sociological issues, technological
    issues vs., 35

source code browser
  polymorphic method invoca-
    tions and, 114, 115
  for querying method invocation,
    114
Speak to the Round Table (Pattern
    2.3), 20, 66
Speculate about Architecture vari-
    ation (Pattern 4.2), 79
Speculate about Business Objects
    variation (Pattern 4.2), 78
Speculate about Design (Pattern
    4.2)
  documentation by, 67–68
  example, 80–82
  incorporating operations for
    classes and, 73
  intent, 76
  Interview during Demo (Pattern
    3.4) as preparation for, 58
  known uses, 83–84
  main discussion, 76–84
  patterns acting as preparation
    for, 50, 58
  problem, 76–77
  rationale, 83
  refining class diagram using, 76
  repeated application of, 67
  solution, 77–79
  Speculate about Architecture
    variation, 79
  Speculate about Business Ob-
    jects variation, 78
  Speculate about Patterns varia-
    tion, 78
  time required for, 67
  as top-down method, 67
  trade-offs, 79
  what next, 84
Speculate about Patterns variation
    (Pattern 4.2), 78
spiral model of software develop-
    ment, 6
Split Up God Class (Pattern 9.3)
  bottleneck components and, 23
  detection, 209–210
  Facade (Pattern A.12) and, 210
  intent, 208
  main discussion, 208–213
  Move Behavior Close to Data
    (Pattern 9.1) and, 210
  overview, 189
  Present the Right Interface (Pat-
    tern 7.8) and, 212–213
  problem, 208–209
  rationale, 213
  Regression Test after Every
    Change (Pattern 7.6) after, 210
  related patterns, 213
  solution, 209–212

  steps, 210–212
  trade-offs, 212–213
  when the legacy solution is the
    solution, 212–213
SQL statement samples for verify-
    ing classes, 72
Squeak `FileList` tool, 245–249
stable design
  reusing, 117
  signs of, 115
stakeholders
  conflicting interests of, 17, 18–19
  customer vs., 21
  differing agendas of, 29
  getting acquainted with, 29
  limited view of, 23
Stand Up Meetings, 20
State (Pattern A.18), 216, 234, 257
State Patterns (Pattern A.19), 234,
    257
static structure, dynamic behavior
    vs., 96
Step through the Execution
    (Pattern 5.3)
  debugger needed for, 109
  intent, 107
  main discussion, 107–109
  problem, 107
  Record Business Rules as Tests
    (Pattern 6.5) and, 108
  scenarios for, 107, 108, 109
  solution, 108
  Tie Code and Questions (Pattern
    5.1) with, 108
  trade-offs, 108–109
  validating contracts using, 113
  what next, 109
  Write Tests to Understand (Pat-
    tern 6.6) during, 109
Stevens, Perdita, 168
Steyaert, Patrick, 113
Stonebraker, Michael, 162
stored tests, 124, 126
Strategy (Pattern A.20), 216, 237,
    258
Study the Exceptional Entities
    (Pattern 4.3)
  after Speculate about Design
    (Pattern 4.2), 84
  as bottom-up method, 67
  choosing metrics for, 86
  choosing tools for, 85–86
  code browsing for confirmation,
    87
  example, 88–92
  identifying anomalies, 87
  identifying design problems, 85
  intent, 84
  interpreting results, 86–87
  known uses, 93

Study the Exceptional Entities
(Pattern 4.3) (*continued*)
main discussion, 84–93
normal entities and, 87
problem, 85
rationale, 92–93
Read All the Code in One Hour
(Pattern 3.2) as preparation
for, 44
repeated application of, 67
risks revealed by, 68
solution, 85–87
threshold application and, 86
time required for, 67
trade-offs, 87–88
what next, 93
success
initial tasks and, 22
small, frequent iterations for, 22
verifying for mock installation, 59
SUnit, 125, 131
super calls, class assumptions
about subclasses and, 112
Sweeping It under the Rug pattern.
See Present the Right Interface
(Pattern 7.8)
switches
perl script for identifying simulated switches in C++, 251
self type checks and, 218
symptoms
fixing problems instead, 23
of need for reengineering, 2–4
synchronizing business rules, documentation, and implemen-
tation. *See* Record Business
Rules as Tests (Pattern 6.5)
synchronizing code with questions
and answers. *See* Tie Code and
Questions (Pattern 5.1)
system administrators, user information from, 52
system development forces,
121–122
systematic testing, 127, 130–131

T
table of contents for documentation, overview of structure
from, 45
teams
common sense of purpose for, 18
differing agendas of members, 29
effective communication for,
66–67
keeping synchronized, 20
knowing capabilities of members, 36
manageable pieces of legacy
systems for, 28

sharing knowledge with, 66
technological issues, sociological
issues vs., 35
technology, as reason for reengineering, 2
Template Method (Pattern A.21),
112, 258
template/hook methods, specializing classes and, 112
Test Fuzzy Features (Pattern A.2),
123, 254
Test Old Bugs (Pattern A.3), 123, 254
Test the Interface, Not the Implementation (Pattern 6.4)
Detailed Model Capture information and, 97
example, 138–139
granularity of testing and, 130
Grow Your Test Base Incrementally (Pattern 6.2) and, 130
intent, 136
known uses, 139
main discussion, 136–139
Migrate Systems Incrementally
(Pattern 7.3) and, 155
problem, 137
rationale, 137
Record Business Rules as Tests
(Pattern 6.5) vs., 139
related patterns, 139
reusing stable parts of design
and, 117
solution, 137
trade-offs, 137–138
Write Tests to Enable Evolution
(Pattern 6.1) and, 127
testing framework. *See* Use a Testing Framework (Pattern 6.3)
tests
caveat, 121
in code review checklist, 39
customer expectations and, 122
developers' resistance to, 125
as documentation, 124
Grow Your Test Base Incrementally (Pattern 6.2), 122,
127, 128–130, 142, 155, 160
introducing incrementally,
128–130
migration and, 76, 84
missing, need for reengineering
and, 2
programmers' low priority for, 122
Record Business Rules as Tests
(Pattern 6.5), 58, 97, 108, 130,
139–142
reengineering and, 84
Regression Test after Every
Change (Pattern 7.6), 123, 148,
155, 159–160, 210

regression tests after refactoring,
103
Retest Persistent Problems (Pattern A.1), 123, 160, 253–254
reusable, 136–139
reusing stable parts of design
and, 117
selling to client, 124, 125
Step through the Execution
(Pattern 5.3) scenarios as, 109
system development and, 121
systematic testing, 127, 130–131
Test Fuzzy Features (Pattern
A.2), 123, 254
Test Old Bugs (Pattern A.3), 123,
254
Test the Interface, Not the Implementation (Pattern 6.4),
97, 117, 127, 130, 136–139, 155
thumbnail patterns, 253–254
Use a Testing Framework
(Pattern 6.3), 122, 130–136
well-designed, properties of, 124
white-box testing for algorithms,
139
Write Tests to Enable Evolution
(Pattern 6.1), 122, 123–127, 160
Write Tests to Understand
(Pattern 6.6), 97, 106, 109,
122–123, 130, 142–144
writing before implementing
functionality, 160
Tests: Your Life Insurance!
caveat, 121
forces, 121–122
Grow Your Test Base Incrementally (Pattern 6.2), 128–130
map of patterns, 120
Migration Strategies supported
by, 123
overview, 122–123
Record Business Rules as Tests
(Pattern 6.5), 139–142
Test the Interface, Not the
Implementation (Pattern 6.4),
136–139
Use a Testing Framework
(Pattern 6.3), 130–136
Write Tests to Enable Evolution
(Pattern 6.1), 123–127
Write Tests to Understand
(Pattern 6.6), 142–144
See also specific patterns
thumbnail patterns
design patterns, 253, 256–258
refactorings, 253, 254–255
testing patterns, 253–254
Tie Code and Questions (Pattern 5.1)
as fundamental, 96
intent, 98

known uses, 101–103
main discussion, 98–103
problem, 98
rationale, 101
Refactor to Understand (Pattern 5.2) with, 103, 106, 107
related patterns, 103
solution, 98–100
Step through the Execution (Pattern 5.3) with, 108
trade-offs, 100–101
Write Tests to Understand (Pattern 6.6) and, 144
time
comments out of date, 40, 50
deferring time-consuming activities, 28–29
documentation out of date, 45, 46, 48–49
introducing tests incrementally, 128–130
as most precious resource, 28–29
wasting early in a project, 28, 29
time requirements
Do a Mock Installation (Pattern 3.5), 59, 60
for Initial Understanding, 67
Interview during Demo (Pattern 3.4) and, 53
Keep It Simple (Pattern 2.7) and, 25
need for reengineering and, 3
for Read All the Code in One Hour (Pattern 3.2), 40, 42
for Speculate about Design (Pattern 4.2), 79
tools
choosing for Study the Exceptional Entities (Pattern 4.3), 85–86
for class relationship overview, 111
for Learn from the Past (Pattern 5.5), 114, 115
for refactoring, 105–106
testing frameworks, 131, 132–136
for unit testing, 125
top-down study of source code, bottom-up study vs., 67
Transform Client Type Checks (Pattern 10.2)
detection, 226–227
example, 229–233
intent, 225
Introduce Null Object (Pattern 10.5) and, 233
main discussion, 225–234
Move Behavior Close to Data (Pattern 9.1) vs., 191

overview, 216–217
problem, 225–226
rationale, 233
related patterns, 233–234
Replace Conditional with Polymorphism (Pattern A.9) and, 234
solution, 226–228
steps, 227–228
trade-offs, 228–229
Transform Conditionals into Registration (Pattern 10.6) and, 233, 250
Transform Self Type Checks (Pattern 10.1) and, 225
when the legacy solution is the solution, 229
Transform Conditionals into Registration (Pattern 10.6)
example, 245–249
intent, 243
main discussion, 243–251
overview, 217
perl script for identifying simulated switches in C++, 251
problem, 243
related patterns, 250
solution, 243–245
trade-offs, 249–250
Transform Client Type Checks (Pattern 10.2) and, 233, 250
Transform Self Type Checks (Pattern 10.1) and, 225
Transform Conditionals to Polymorphism
duplicated code and, 174, 184, 185
Factor Out State (Pattern 10.3), 234–237
Factor Out Strategy (Pattern 10.4), 237–240
forces, 215–216
Introduce Null Object (Pattern 10.5), 240–243
map of patterns, 214
overview, 216–217
Replace Conditional with Polymorphism (Pattern A.9), 255
Transform Client Type Checks (Pattern 10.2), 225–234
Transform Conditionals into Registration (Pattern 10.6), 243–251
Transform Self Type Checks (Pattern 10.1), 217–225
See also specific patterns
Transform Self Type Checks (Pattern 10.1)
detection, 218–219
example, 223–225

Factor Out State (Pattern 10.3) and, 225
Factor Out Strategy (Pattern 10.4) and, 225
intent, 217
main discussion, 217–225
overview, 216
problem, 217–218
rationale, 225
related patterns, 225
solution, 218–220
steps, 219–220
trade-offs, 221–223
Transform Client Type Checks (Pattern 10.2) and, 225
Transform Conditionals into Registration (Pattern 10.6) and, 225
when the legacy solution is the solution, 222
type checks. *See* Transform Client Type Checks (Pattern 10.2); Transform Self Type Checks (Pattern 10.1)

U

unbundling monolithic systems, as reason for reengineering, 1
understanding, iteration implied by, 66
unit testing
JUnit example, 126
as property of well-designed tests, 124
tools for, 125, 131
Unix, detecting self type checks in, 219
unstable design
detecting, 115
dismissing or fixing, 117
usage scenarios, Interview during Demo (Pattern 3.4) for, 50–51, 58
Use a Testing Framework (Pattern 6.3)
example, 132–136
Grow Your Test Base Incrementally (Pattern 6.2) and, 130
intent, 130
known uses, 136
main discussion, 130–136
organizing tests, 130
overview, 122
problem, 130–131
rationale, 136
solution, 131
steps, 131
trade-offs, 131
Use Profiler before Optimizing (Pattern 7.12), 149, 169–170

user feedback
 Involve the Users (Pattern 7.1) and, 151
 Keep It Simple (Pattern 2.7) and, 25
 Migrate Systems Incrementally (Pattern 7.3) and, 22, 154
user interface, Interview during Demo (Pattern 3.4) for evaluating, 57
users
 choosing for Interview during Demo (Pattern 3.4), 51–52, 53
 departure of, need for reengineering and, 3
 as documentation audience, 44, 46, 49
 ensuring user acceptance, 149–151
 Involve the Users (Pattern 7.1), 22, 25, 148, 149–151, 153, 169
 test writing by, 140
 See also Interview during Demo (Pattern 3.4); public interfaces
utility classes, 189

V

value
 complexity and, 22
 determining valuable data, 68–73
 determining what is valuable, 21–22
 of legacy systems, 1
 Most Valuable First (Pattern 2.4), 19, 20–22, 23, 155
variables, comparing code and, 175–176
verification
 of class diagram, 72
 of maintainers' input, 37
 of mock installation findings, 62–63
 of mock installation success, 59
 tests as, 126
 of users' input, 58
version numbers, documentation currency and, 45
versioning tests, 126

versions, comparing. *See* Learn from the Past (Pattern 5.5)
Visitor (Pattern A.22), 194, 258
Visualize Code as Dotplots (Pattern 8.2)
 example, 183–184
 Extract Method (Pattern A.5) and, 185
 intent, 180
 interpretations, 181–182
 known uses, 184–185
 main discussion, 180–185
 Move Behavior Close to Data (Pattern 9.1) and, 185
 problem, 181
 related patterns, 185
 solution, 181–182
 steps, 181
 trade-offs, 182–183
 Transform Conditionals to Polymorphism and, 184, 185
vocabulary of developers, Read All the Code in One Hour (Pattern 3.2) and, 40

W, X

white-box testing, for algorithms, 139
Woolf, Bobby, 242
wrapping
 Adapter (Pattern A.11) for, 193
 data containers, 193
 data provider instances, 193
 Fix Problems, Not Symptoms (Pattern 2.5) and, 23
 If It Ain't Broke, Don't Fix It (Pattern 2.6) and, 24
 pinpointing problems and, 23
 Present the Right Interface (Pattern 7.8), 12, 149, 155, 163–164, 212–213
Write Tests to Enable Evolution (Pattern 6.1)
 as Always Have a Running Version (Pattern 7.5) prerequisite, 127
 example, 126
 Grow Your Test Base Incrementally (Pattern 6.2) and, 122, 127

importance of, 122
 intent, 123
 main discussion, 123–127
 Migrate Systems Incrementally (Pattern 7.3) with, 127, 155
 problem, 123
 properties of well-designed tests, 124
 rationale, 126–127
 Regression Test after Every Change (Pattern 7.6) and, 160
 related patterns, 127
 solution, 124
 Test the Interface, Not the Implementation (Pattern 6.4) and, 127
 trade-offs, 124–125
Write Tests to Understand (Pattern 6.6)
 during Refactor to Understand (Pattern 5.2), 97, 106
 during Step through the Execution (Pattern 5.3), 109
 Grow Your Test Base Incrementally (Pattern 6.2) and, 130
 intent, 142
 main discussion, 142–144
 overview, 122–123
 priming a test base, 130
 problem, 142–143
 rationale, 144
 Record Business Rules as Tests (Pattern 6.5) with, 142
 Refactor to Understand (Pattern 5.2) before, 144
 related patterns, 144
 Retest Persistent Problems (Pattern A.1), 123
 solution, 143
 Test Fuzzy Features (Pattern A.2), 123
 Test Old Bugs (Pattern A.3), 123
 Tie Code and Questions (Pattern 5.1) and, 144
 trade-offs, 143

Y, Z

Yoder, Joseph W., 157, 213